DevOps Paradox

The truth about DevOps by the people
on the front line

Viktor Farcic

BIRMINGHAM - MUMBAI

DevOps Paradox

Acquisition Editors: Dominic Shakeshaft, Jonathan Malysiak
Project Editor: Kishor Rit
Development Editor: Alex Sorrentino
Technical Editor: Saby D'silva
Copy Editor: Safis Editing
Proofreader: Safis Editing
Indexer: Pratik Shirodkar
Production Coordinator: Sandip Tadge

First published: August 2019

Production reference: 1290819

Published by Packt Publishing Ltd.
Livery Place
35 Livery Street
Birmingham B3 2PB, UK.

ISBN 978-1-78913-363-9

www.packt.com

Contents

Introduction – what is the DevOps paradox?

I love sharing with others. That's my main motivation when I write a book. There's a hard-to-explain joy in knowing that our work as authors might be helping others. But strangely, that's not the case with *DevOps Paradox*.

This time, my motivation was much more self-serving. I wrote this book because I personally wanted to understand what DevOps is. Now if you know anything about me, or have read any of my multi-book *DevOps Toolkit* series (`https://www.devopstoolkitseries.com`), then you're surely thinking that I should already know what DevOps is, especially if I'm trying to spread my knowledge of it through these books.

The thing is, if there's anything that my years of working in the field have taught me, it's that DevOps is not a well-defined process. There is no set of rules that must be followed. As I discovered in my journey, and as you'll read in these pages, it's even questionable whether there is such a thing as a "DevOps department" or a "DevOps engineer." This ambiguity is exactly why DevOps is so fascinating to me, and I hope to you, the reader, as well.

I love going to conferences, but not for the obvious reasons. I rarely listen to talks. Instead, I tend to roam the corridors of conference centers and convention halls looking for the next victim who will allow me to pick his or her brain. The best thing about conferences is networking. The most interesting conversations are not taking place at scheduled talks, but rather in corridors and at the after-parties.

I consider myself lucky for being able to dedicate an important portion of my time attending conferences since I know that I benefit greatly from those "corridor-talks." I wanted to do something similar with this book.

This book is called *DevOps Paradox*. For those of you who may be wondering what it means, the Oxford English Dictionary defines the word "paradox" as:

> *A seemingly contradictory statement or proposition which when investigated may prove to be well founded or true.*

Over the course of these interviews, my objective is to look at these often-contradictory views of what DevOps is, which, as we will investigate, may prove to be well founded.

What we have right now is an idea that people should work more closely together and that we should remove the barriers that slow them down.

As such, anything can be DevOps.

Almost every software company is marketing its products as "DevOps," and "DevOps engineer" is the most sought-after role in job listings. That's not to mention the fact that "DevOps departments" are popping up like mushrooms after the rain.

Yet despite this, almost every person I spoke to in this book gave me a different answer to the fundamental question of "What is DevOps?"

DevOps brings sanity into a very chaotic world created by a misunderstanding that software development is similar to factory production. DevOps continues where Agile left off, and urges us to remove the obstacles that we were often not even aware existed.

The idea of DevOps builds empathy between team members that ultimately results in greater cooperation. It's about culture, but it's also about the processes and the tools. At least, that's what I originally thought, even though I received very opposing definitions from the teams I worked with.

To answer the questions I had about DevOps, I asked a number of DevOps practitioners what they thought DevOps was. Some of them are industry veterans, while others are up-and-coming stars. Some are my friends, while others are people I have admired from afar.

Many of these conversations were recorded via remote sessions, while others took place in pubs or in conference corridors. Whenever I could, I did my best to speak with someone face-to-face.

I wanted the interviews to be casual. I did not want people to answer predefined questions. Instead, my goal was to bring to a wider audience the types of conversations I normally have with experts I meet in conferences and in companies I work with as a consultant. I do believe that some of the best breakthroughs come from corridor-talks. That's the spirit I wanted to maintain in the interviews.

Each conversation starts with the question "What is DevOps?" or some variation thereof. It is only meant to be a conversation-starter and to facilitate something that is an unstructured, unprepared, and very casual conversation. Think of each interview as a conversation with a friend or an acquaintance that I've met in a pub. As a matter of fact, a few of them were actually recorded in a bar over a few beers!

In this book, I wanted to share casual conversations with people who practice and often shape DevOps. My hope is that we'll get insights into what drives those people and come away with a better understanding of what makes DevOps so powerful.

The only thing the people I interviewed have in common is an interest in DevOps itself. You'll see, however, that some of them have very opposing views of what DevOps actually is (or is not), and even whether it's a worthwhile pursuit. You may often feel that what is described by one person contradicts what others have said. This is intentional and, in my opinion, reflects the chaos DevOps is trying to tame. It also serves as a reminder that we are still in the very early stages of adopting DevOps to our workplace cultures, while trying to navigate the complexities of the software industry and finding different solutions to the same problems.

With all that said, I urge you, the reader, to be open-minded. You've almost certainly heard about DevOps, and many of you are likely implementing some form of DevOps in your organizations right now. I just ask that you leave what you know aside. The interviews in this book are likely to turn everything that you think you know upside-down. They will definitely challenge your assumptions and your experience. What this book won't do, however, is tell you on which side of the DevOps debate to pitch your tent. There is no right or wrong answer here. This book also won't tell you how to "do" DevOps, though you may glean some ideas for implementation from the experiences related in these interviews. My goal with this book is solely to present both sides of the DevOps paradox and leave the door open for you to make up your own mind.

Introduction

How ironic that something designed to break down silos within organizations and foster cross-departmental collaboration is the subject of so much debate within the IT community! But that's the crux of the DevOps paradox, isn't it? And that's why it's such a fascinating topic of conversation. You may not agree with everything you read in these interviews, but at the very least they should provoke thought and maybe even debate within your organizations as you and your teams embark upon your own DevOps journeys.

Lastly, before we get started, I'd like to thank those who gave their time to be interviewed, I couldn't be more grateful for all the great contributions you made. Thank you! This book wouldn't be what it is without you!

I do my best to be approachable and help people improve their skills. Feel free to contact me on Twitter (@vfarcic), to send me an email (viktor@farcic.com), or to join Slack workspace DevOps20 (http://slack.devops20toolkit.com/).

Viktor Farcic is a Principal Software Delivery Strategist and Developer Advocate at CloudBees, a member of the Google Developer Experts and Docker Captains groups, and published author.

His big passions are DevOps, microservices, continuous integration, delivery and deployment (CI/CD) and test-driven development (TDD).

He often speaks at community gatherings and conferences.

He published *The DevOps Toolkit Series* (`https://www.devopstoolkitseries.com`) and *Test-Driven Java Development* (`http://www.amazon.com/dp/B00YSIM3SC`).

His random thoughts and tutorials can be found in his blog *TechnologyConversations* (`https://technologyconversations.com/`).

1

Jeff Sussna

Founder and CEO,
Sussna Associates

Introducing Jeff Sussna

In 2011, Jeff Sussna founded Sussna Associates, a company specializing in corporate workshops, coaching, and strategic design that enables clients to integrate DevOps. The author of *Designing Delivery: Rethinking IT in the Digital Service Economy*, Jeff has more than 30 years of IT experience, from software development to IT integration. You can follow him on Twitter at @jeffsussna.

Viktor Farcic: Hi, Jeff. Before we start talking about DevOps, could you introduce yourself?

Jeff Sussna: I'm an independent consultant focused on Agile, DevOps, and coaching design thinking. Through my company, Sussna Associates, I've been in the IT industry for 30 years and during that time, I've built systems and led organizations across the entire development QA (quality assurance) and operation spectrum.

I was introduced to design thinking and, in particular, service design and cloud computing in 2008, which was somewhat of an epiphany for me because I realized that in the 21st century, service is really at the core of cloud computing and IT. Whether it's infrastructure as a service or software as a service or microservices, you're talking about service that needs to be user-centered at every level of the organization.

I've really built that into the heart of my consulting practice, helping IT teams, whether they're enterprises or start-ups, to get them to really think in terms of whether it's their users, customers, database team, network team, application team, or whatever you may have. Because of that, I was responsible for introducing the idea of empathy into DevOps.

In my opinion, at the heart of what I'm doing is learning about how development and operations can think in terms of each other's needs. I brought all of those ideas together in a book I wrote called *Designing Delivery: Rethinking IT in the Digital Service Economy*.

What is DevOps?

Viktor Farcic: In your view, what's the meaning of the word "DevOps"? It's as if nobody has a clear idea of what it is, or at least everybody's idea is different. Some say it's about new tools, some claim it's a change in culture, while others associate it with a DevOps engineer role. Some even say the word DevOps doesn't exist. It goes on and on like that as if DevOps is a conspiracy meant to confuse everyone.

Jeff Sussna: For me, the meaning of "DevOps" is right there in the word itself. We have to start thinking about development and operations as part of one larger unified entity. The guiding principle I used to come to that conclusion again returns to this idea of service. The way we deliver service is digitally, and the thing about service is that the *way* you make it is part of *what* you make.

If you look at some of the public relations nightmares that have occurred in the airline industry over the last couple of years, flights are being canceled because reservation systems are going down. There was one incident recently when an airline couldn't check people in because their computer systems went down, and they were trying to use their cell phones to check people in.

> *"For me, the meaning of 'DevOps' is right there in the word itself. We have to start thinking about development and operations as part of one larger unified entity."*
>
> —*Jeff Sussna*

Viktor Farcic: I think that everyone takes software for granted these days. We are impatient and expect things to happen immediately, and if things fail, users just move somewhere else. There's no loyalty anymore.

What many have not yet realized is that it's not only about the features a piece of software offers, but also the stability of its systems. Would you agree with that?

Jeff Sussna: More and more, what's happening is that the user experience of the customer is very powerfully impacted by operation successes and failures, as much as by features and functionality. The example I like to use is that we imagine there's a new restaurant in town. You try it on a Saturday night, and when you come to work on Monday morning people ask you how it was, and you say, "Well, the food was great, but the service was awful." People are a lot less likely to try the restaurant because they think of the food and the service as part of one overall experience. In my opinion, DevOps reflects the idea that we have to think about functionality and operability together.

It doesn't matter how wonderful your design or how well coded your website is, if it's very, very slow or if people are constantly getting 500 errors, their level of satisfaction will drop.

You have to think about system architecture and application architecture. You have to think about how deployment happens, and you have to think about security all as part of one equation. In my mind, DevOps is a portmanteau, which means that we took two words and smashed them together, and the reason we smashed them together is that we started to understand that they're really part of one thing.

Viktor Farcic: Like one big theme instead of departments?

Jeff Sussna: Yes, and one thing that's important to me is the idea that smashing DevOps together doesn't necessarily mean that everybody must work for the same manager or VP. Everybody has to think about their work as part of something larger. You have to think about your code in terms of, "how will this code get deployed, how secure will this code be, how efficient will this code be, and how well will this code scale?"

That doesn't necessarily mean that you have to be the person who deploys it into production or answers the pager, whatever the case may be. I work with a lot of enterprises that have this notion of segregation of duties, and the idea that developers aren't allowed to push code into production doesn't mean that they can't do DevOps. If you're a large organization, whether it's a multinational insurance company or Netflix, with a lot of layers and a lot of pieces of technology, then maybe there are a lot of microservices. If not, there's still a lot of applications.

The idea that you can have them all as part of one big department with one big giant foosball table and one big giant open office space doesn't really make any sense.

You have to think about DevOps in terms of collaboration among groups that don't necessarily report to the same person, don't necessarily sit next to each other in the office, or don't necessarily even work in the same city, and there's no problem with that. The problem comes when each group thinks, "Well, this is my job, and I worry about my job, and anybody else who wants something from me has to get in line, and I'm just going to think about my part of the puzzle."

> *"You have to think about DevOps in terms of collaboration among groups that don't necessarily report to the same person, don't necessarily sit next to each other in the office, or don't necessarily even work in the same city."*
>
> —*Jeff Sussna*

DevOps in the team environment

Viktor Farcic: I often see the same thing happening, with people saying, "This is my job, but *that's* not my job." With that being said, how do you prevent this type of thinking if different managers are giving different teams different objectives, especially ones that are not necessarily in line with the global vision because everybody thinks only, as you said, of their part of the puzzle?

Jeff Sussna: The way that I coach teams to do it is by getting them to think of each other as the customers, in the same way that the company thinks about people who pay the money to their customers. The network team has customers, and it's really funny because in DevOps, we engage in this little bit of magical thinking where we're all thinking, "Well, one key component of DevOps is the cloud." The cloud solves a bunch of problems, and I agree with that, but if you think about an AWS, Azure, or Google Cloud Platform, it's the ultimate silo. There is no bigger silo than the one between your organization and AWS.

AWS won't even tell you where the data center is, let alone who works on your code, your systems, or whatever the case may be. The thing about these organizations is that they understand they're in the service business and their job is to help you succeed, and they're continually innovating in order to help you succeed. I think exactly the same model applies inside the organization; whether it's split, whether you have two pizza teams that are cross-functional, or if you have departmental breakouts – it doesn't really matter. The question has to change from how do we *run* the network to how do we help people *use* the network, and that's a very, very subtle but very important and really significant mind shift.

If you're thinking in terms of how do we run the network and somebody wants an IP address, a DNS entry, or a firewall change, they'll have to get in line behind your process. But if you put them at the center, and you say, "Okay, our job is to make sure that these applications can successfully run and scale on top of our network," then things such as IP addresses,

DNS entries, and firewall changes become the core of your job. So, through that, your job becomes primarily one of thinking about who are the people who need to use our services and answering the traditional question of, "Well, how do we make sure the router doesn't fall over?" It doesn't go away, but it becomes an implementation detail as opposed to being the core of your job.

Viktor Farcic: That makes perfect sense. Everyone's work becomes user-centric, no matter whether those users are external or internal. Meanwhile, everyone's job is to help someone, even when that someone is a colleague from a different department.

Empathy in DevOps

You've both written and spoken a lot about empathy. I'm not sure whether you coined the term EmpathyOps, but can you elaborate on what you mean by empathy?

Jeff Sussna: There's a lot of confusion and anxiety about its meaning, and a lot of people tend to misunderstand it. Sometimes people think empathy means wallowing in someone else's pain. In fact, there's actually a philosopher from Yale University who is now putting out the idea that empathy is actually bad, and that it's the cause of all of the world's problems and what we need instead is compassion.

From my perspective, that represents a misunderstanding of both empathy and compassion, but my favorite is when people say things like, "Sociopaths are really good at empathizing". My answer to that is, if you have a sociopath in your organization, you have a much bigger problem, and DevOps isn't going to solve it. At that point, you have an HR problem. What you need to distinguish between is emotional empathy and cognitive empathy, and I use cognitive empathy in the context of DevOps in a very simple way, which is the ability to think about things as if from another's perspective.

If you're a developer and you think, "What is the experience of deploying and running my application going to be?" you're thinking about it from the perspective of the operations person. If you're an operations person and you're thinking in terms of, "What is the experience going to be when you need to spin up a test server in a matter of hours in order to test a hotfix because all of your testing swim lanes are full of other things, and what does that mean for my process of provisioning servers?," then you're thinking about things from the tester's point of view. And so, to me, that's empathy, and that's empathizing, which is really at the heart of customer service. It's at the heart of design thinking, and it's at the heart of product development. What is it that our customers are trying to accomplish, what help do they need from us, and how can we help them?

> *"I use cognitive empathy in the context of DevOps in a very simple way, which is the ability to think about things as if from another's perspective."*
>
> —*Jeff Sussna*

Viktor Farcic: So, everyone has a customer, and we all need to start thinking about whether our work makes our customer's life easier or better, no matter whether that customer is internal or external. We shouldn't hide behind artificial objectives anymore.

Jeff Sussna: I'll give you an example of that. I actually got a little grief about this recently because I tend to be a bit of an AWS fanboy, but the reason for that is that I think they understand the idea of user-centered innovation better than anybody else.

A number of years ago, I was helping a client port an application from a colocation center to Amazon. It was a fairly simple app, and it was primarily a forklift port. It was running on old hardware that was starting to fail, and they didn't want to manage their hardware anymore. So we said, "Okay, let's just put it to Amazon." In this case, we were not going to try and do anything fancy like re-architect the application or anything like that, but we should take advantage of some of the more basic Amazon capabilities, like being able to run the web server auto-scaled across multiple availability zones.

It's a pretty straightforward thing to do, and there's no reason not to do it. We then came to one piece of our architecture, which was a Memcached server, and we couldn't figure out how to cluster it. It turned out that in those days, it was fairly hard to do. There was a product available that was very expensive, and we weren't sure if it really worked. So, we went around for a while, before we finally decided, let's not worry about it; it's a cache, and if the cache falls over, the application is smart enough to fall back and go straight to the database. Yes, it'll be slow, but it'll survive until we have a chance to tip the cache back up. Let's not sweat it, let's just go on with our work and finish.

We finished, and I think it was something like a few weeks later when AWS announced a new service called ElastiCache, which was – guess what? – a clustered Memcached server that ran across data centers. All you had to do was push a couple of buttons and type a few things into the console, and you could spin it up as a service. I remember thinking that it was as if they had been reading our emails.

The point of the story is that Amazon wasn't just resting on their laurels and saying, "We do infrastructure as a service, and we do storage and VMs and networking." They were looking at what it was that their customers were struggling with and how they could help make it easier. I think that is the essence of what we're talking about with DevOps: how do I, as a developer, make operations' lives easier and better, and as an operations person, how do I make development's life easier and better?

Viktor Farcic: But then what prevents companies from applying this type of thinking? Is it that they don't want to take this approach, that they don't see value in this line of thinking, or is it something else?

Jeff Sussna: I was talking with a client just the other day about this blockage in their process, to do with deploying code to a test environment. I started the conversation by asking, "Why can't developers deploy their own code? It's not production. There is no segregation of duty issues." They just hadn't thought about it. We talked it through, and they said there were no underlying reasons they couldn't. We would need to make some technical changes but there were no rules that say they shouldn't. It's a simple example of making available that which would make developers' lives easier. I think that expands out from there.

It has to do with the relationship between development and design, product and development, development and operations, and security and development. We all need to think from the perspective of, "How do we help each other better accomplish what we're trying to accomplish?" Empathy is what enables you to do this. But empathy is also thinking in terms of, "Forget about what I'm doing, what is it that you're trying to accomplish and how could I use my expertise to help you accomplish it?"

Viktor Farcic: When you visit companies, do you see any recurring themes, or any commonalities between them? Are they facing the same problems, apart from the obvious of one company is smaller and the other one is bigger?

The big DevOps guy versus the little DevOps guy

Jeff Sussna: I'm surprised at how common they are, regardless of the size of the company. For example, pretty much every single client that I've had, regardless of size, has compliance issues.

Maybe they're a start-up, but they're a healthcare start-up, which means they have to deal with HIPAA (The Health Insurance and Accountability Act of 1996); or maybe they process credit cards, which means they have to deal with PCI (Payment Card Industry); or they provide services to the Federal Government, which means they have to comply with FedRAMP, which is as draconian as any of the other compliance rule sets as you can find. Issues about audits, and segregation duties and access control; all of those things are common across my clients, regardless of their size.

> *"Pretty much every single client that I've had, regardless of size, has compliance issues."*
>
> —*Jeff Sussna*

I see the challenges between development and operations as being surprisingly universal. I think the main difference is that in the big companies, the dysfunction tends to be structural, as in, "I don't like your organization because we have different VPs and the VPs are competing for power," or something like that. Or maybe they're not competing for power, but they're just sort of separate and they're in competition with each other in some fashion.

There are institutionalized boundaries that keep people apart. In smaller companies, it tends to be much more personal. For instance, "I don't trust you because two and a half years ago, you broke things in a major way and so I don't ever want you deploying to production ever again," but these sorts of struggles to trust and to understand are surprisingly universal.

It's funny because in both Agile and DevOps, we talk a lot about feedback loops and how we can learn faster. If you look at the three ways of DevOps, you have flow, feedback, and continuous learning. It's surprising how difficult feedback is.

Viktor Farcic: I think that people tend to adopt practices, but where they fail is in understanding the goals behind those practices. As a result, we implement practices but fail to connect with them and gain any real benefits. Almost everyone collects feedback these days. The real question is, how many use that feedback to learn and adapt?

Jeff Sussna: I did a workshop with a client, a whole section of which was dedicated to feedback loops. The client was a very mature Agile and DevOps organization, and at one point I gave them an exercise, which was to take some linear processes they had and reimagine them as circular, feedback-driven processes in order to see what was different. They all chuckled and nodded wisely at me. Someone raised their hand and said, "We don't really have any linear processes anymore; we've made them all circular," and I said, "Alright, well, indulge me – just try and see what happens, this may be a very fast and easy exercise."

I'd split the group into four teams, and three of the four teams independently came to the same conclusion, which they reported to me very sheepishly after the exercise. They all came to the conclusion that they were very, very good at collecting feedback but they didn't actually do anything with it. They realized they were wasting an incredible amount of time and energy because they had this whole feedback loop mechanism that they never really closed all the way. If there's a danger that I see both with Agile and DevOps, it's that we get really focused on how fast we can get stuff to production, and we see it as essentially a push problem. One of the misconceptions I see about DevOps is that DevOps is about deployment automation.

> *"If there's a danger that I see both with Agile and DevOps, it's that we get really focused on how fast we can get stuff to production, and we see it as essentially a push problem. One of the misconceptions I see about DevOps is that DevOps is about deployment automation."*
>
> —*Jeff Sussna*

The problem with that is it's one-way, and you don't actually learn. If you push stuff to production and then all you do is go and pick the next thing out of your backlog, how are you really going to know that that's the right next thing to take out of your backlog unless you pay attention to what's happened to the thing you've just deployed? I would say the struggle to really get beyond this sort of an industrial-age approach, of the kind of pushing products out the factory door, is a universal challenge.

Viktor Farcic: Isn't that an example of blindly following processes without understanding the reasoning behind them? The idea behind short sprints is not to be able to do more work but to get that feedback sooner and better decide what to do next. If we just pick up a new item from the backlog, we are missing the point.

With that being said, let's change the subject. When you work with teams or companies, what is the approach? Are we starting from the top, from the bottom, or in the middle?

Jeff Sussna: I start all over the place; it really depends on the client. I mean, generally, it's anywhere from the CIO to some director of operations or director of development. It very much depends. It's an interesting question because what I find is that at some point, the two have to come together.

There's this interesting question about whether DevOps requires an executive buy-in or whether it should be a grass-roots thing. In my experience, it doesn't matter where it starts, but at some point, it needs both.

I've seen places where, particularly with Agile, a CIO comes back from a conference and says, "We're doing Agile now," which is great; the process of actually going from that to an organization that implements it really doesn't require a lot of on-the-ground activity. Some of it is very grassroots: propagation of new behaviors and activities. One of the places that I focus on more and more is what the adoption process looks like, and in my opinion, in my experience – and I think this is another place where organizations struggle – changing how the organization behaves is no different from changing how your website works, or changing how your continuous integration pipeline works.

It's something that has to happen over time, and it has to happen in an Agile way. What I mean by that is that there has to be learning based on feedback; you can't just drop a plan in and do it, because what happens is people interact with that plan, they struggle, they resist, they learn, they make mistakes, and you find out that your plan maybe needs a little adjustment based on your corporate culture, so it's something that really has to unfold.

Changing the culture around DevOps

Viktor Farcic: When you try to change the culture, do you have a plan? I remember someone told me that you could not really predict a complex system; the only thing you can do is poke it and see what comes out.

Jeff Sussna: You're correct in thinking that you can have techniques that you use to introduce people to your system, and then you have to relate to what happens when they interact with those techniques. Everybody is a little bit different.

I teach, and when I do a coaching engagement, I always start with, depending on the size of the organization, anywhere from a week to a month spending a lot of time doing an embedded observation to really understand who and where they are. From there, I start introducing new techniques; whether it be stand-ups, continuous integration, or automated server provisioning, it really doesn't matter.

Then the fun starts when we're introducing Kanban. We're thinking, "That's straightforward – we simply show people how it works and explain the principal tool." But what actually happens is that when people start to work with it, they struggle in ways that are very unique to who they are, what their personalities are, and what their corporate culture is. And that's where the real work starts, trying to actually relate to those. I don't think you can really predict that. That's something that's very emergent.

Viktor Farcic: Right, we cannot blindly adopt anything since each of us is very different, as is the culture of each company, and our projects. To think that we can have such a vast difference and yet hope that a single solution will solve everyone's problems is childish, in my view. We all need to gain experience, understand ourselves, and use that knowledge to discover what works best for us.

I'm curious about design thinking, which is something you've mentioned a few times now. Can you elaborate on that?

Jeff Sussna: Design thinking is quite simply the notion that you can take something about the way designers solve problems, whether it be graphics, industrial, or user interface designers, and you can extract that into a methodology that you can then apply to other problems. For example, how would you introduce DevOps to a new company?

At the heart of design thinking is the notion of user-centered design, which is based around empathy, but it has particular techniques for helping you empathize, which are all based on observing and interacting with your customers.

One of the things that I tell teams even deep within IT is that if you're going to redesign something – for instance, you're the database team and you want to redesign the process that application teams use to get new database instances – start by just observing how they do it, and actually go and sit with them and just watch; and then from that you come up with a solution, prototype that solution, and get feedback on it.

> *"Current Agile and DevOps practices are incomplete because we don't really have a mechanism to incorporate true feedback from the people we're trying to serve."*
>
> —*Jeff Sussna*

Too many times IT does this thing where we sort of figure out what the right solution should be, we build it, and then we send out these emails saying that we're going to roll it out over the next three months with training. What we've failed to do is take the time to understand how well our solution actually works for the people who are going to be using it.

The idea of design thinking starts with empathetic observation. It can get more or less formal in terms of how it actually does that, and from there uses a very iterative process of prototyping, user testing, redesigning, and re-implementing to, almost in an Agile way, find its way to a solution.

Part of why I talk about design thinking so much is that I think current Agile and DevOps practices are incomplete because we don't really have a mechanism to incorporate true feedback from the people we're trying to serve. But validating our ideas, beliefs, solutions, and strategies with them is the reason why I think it's important to incorporate design thinking into what we're doing.

Viktor Farcic: How about Agile and DevOps, then? Are they separate things that you adopt, do they extend across each other, or are they different names for the same thing? Because from what you've said, there are things that sound similar about the two.

Agile versus DevOps

Jeff Sussna: DevOps completes the Agile equation. Agile talks a lot about delivering value and working code, but the problem is that by itself, it doesn't actually deliver anything. Instead, Agile kind of stops when you have code that's been written and tested, which nobody can use, so it doesn't do anybody any good.

The reason for that is Agile grew up in the product age when you would take your code, put it on a CD, and send it to your customer, who were the ones responsible for actually deploying and operating it. Those days are pretty much gone now, so that development and operations elements are really part of the same equation. Agile can't actually deliver the value unless that code can be deployed, and that deployment environment can be operated, and the problems can be fixed, including where new code can be deployed, and so on.

I don't think development without operations is meaningful anymore; and again, to clarify, when I say "operations," I mean in the largest sense of overall operability, so that includes not just running servers or running infrastructure, but also security, which is an integral part of that.

If your code or your infrastructure isn't secure, that's probably worse than if they don't scale. If your code doesn't scale, your website is slow, or your data entry application is slow, and that's annoying.

Viktor Farcic: Being slow is definitely better than not being available at all due to a security exploit that someone has used to bring your whole cluster down. If my data gets stolen from your system, not only will I not be your customer anymore, but I am likely to sue you as well. The part that confuses me is the talk about DevSecOps, because I come away feeling, like, why are we even talking about security? Isn't security something that is mandatory anyway and therefore part of DevOps? Or, did it somehow become optional and now we need to talk about including it as a separate practice?

Jeff Sussna: If my personal health data, credit card, or social security number gets stolen, then that's a lot more than just annoying. I know that when people talk about DevSecOps, they talk about rugged DevOps, which is the idea of DevOps with security built in. But the thing is, would you ever want to propose doing non-rugged DevOps? I certainly wouldn't.

I certainly wouldn't want to go to my CIO and say that we don't want to do rugged DevOps, we're just going to do unrugged DevOps, and that we're not going to worry about security. I wouldn't think that would go down very well. But, going from there, I think I would say that if we were trying to be Agile, at this point, you can't really be Agile without extending that into your operational approach to things.

I think it's more and more questionable how meaningful Agile and DevOps are without each other. I look forward to the day when we have a better word that just encompasses the whole thing, and we don't even worry anymore about whether there's a division. I mean, if you think about it, the dividing line between Agile and DevOps is still this strange space between development and operations, which is what we're trying to get rid of with DevOps. You could say that if you take DevOps seriously, you can't really believe in a fundamental separation between Agile and DevOps.

> *"I think it's more and more questionable how meaningful Agile and DevOps are without each other."*
>
> —*Jeff Sussna*

Viktor Farcic: In your experience, are there expertise groups that are more or less willing to adopt this line of thinking, or is that a universal problem for everybody?

Jeff Sussna: I think that more and more people are comfortable with the idea of joining Agile and DevOps together from the perspective of how fast we can get something from the product manager's brain into production. I think the backside of the feedback loop is a lot harder, and I think most people are still struggling with that, and that's a sin. As I've said before, I think both Agile and DevOps discussions often share the same sin, which is we think it's one-directional.

I'll give you an example: I worked with an organization where I was told by the head of development that they did sprint demos to show people what they were going to deploy before they deployed it. The point of a sprint demo is information; it's gathering feedback, it's making sure you're about to deploy the right thing in the right way before you deploy it. This head of development was approaching the sprint demo in a pure sense: "well, we're done, and we're going to let you see it before we ship it, but don't expect us to make any changes or listen to your feedback." I see that problem all over the place.

Viktor Farcic: It's almost as if I'm giving you permission to see it but whether you see it or not doesn't matter much to me.

Jeff Sussna: That's exactly right, and I think part of the benefit of infusing design thinking is that at the very heart of it is the idea that you're going to show it to somebody, and then you're going to make changes based on their response to it.

Viktor Farcic: If I understand it right, that means that even if we go years back, in many places Agile didn't work, because if it did then that type of thinking would be engraved already, at least, in parts of an organization.

You mentioned complex systems, and I think that's actually worth talking about a little bit.

You hit the nail on the head when you said that complex systems are ones that you can't predict. So, in that sense, you can't plan for them; you can only really probe them and interact with them based on what you learned from that probe.

Jeff Sussna: The systems we are building are complex systems, so even in enterprises where there are very legacy environments, I see more and more that they'll have outages that are caused by interactions between the application, database, network, load balancer, and firewall.

In order to understand the outage, you have to understand how all of the components interact with each other, and if any of those had been different, then the outage might have been different, or it might not have happened at all. What digital business and the digital economy and all that the fun stuff is doing is breaking down the boundaries between these different systems.

Viktor Farcic: When I see things like this whole idea of bimodal IT, to me it doesn't actually connect to reality, because what I see is customer-facing applications that, in order to work properly, have to interact with ERP, or Enterprise Resource Planning, systems, and the lack of agility in the ERP system becomes a blocker to agility in the frontend system.

Nowadays, we have to think about our whole organization and all of our systems together as this one complex system.

Jeff Sussna: If we can't predict or control complex systems, what do we do? Do we just give up? No, we have to have the ability to continually learn. So, why do we need Agile? Why do we need DevOps? Why do we need design thinking?

Because when we approach them correctly, they give us the ability to very efficiently, and effectively, continuously learn from each other, from our customers, from our systems, from our incidents, and I think that's ultimately what we are trying to accomplish with all of these new practices.

Viktor Farcic: In my experience, when I dig a bit deeper, beyond what people tell me, I find somehow that the blame is always the biggest obstacle because when those things happen, like what you said – for example, an outage – somebody needs to be blamed for that, and that means nobody's going to give me enough information so I can learn from it.

Jeff Sussna: Even beyond that, the idea of blame assumes that you could isolate causes.

Viktor Farcic: Right, which brings us back to the complex system.

Jeff Sussna: Exactly.

Viktor Farcic: I think that gives us a nice place to wrap up unless you have anything else to say, Jeff?

Jeff Sussna: No, I don't, but it's been great talking to you, Viktor. I can't wait to see what everyone else thinks about DevOps.

2

Damien Duportal

Træfik's Developer Advocate

Introducing Damien Duportal

According to Damien, being a DevOps engineer is all about the people, culture, and tools. Alongside his work at Træfik, Damien is a training engineer at CloudBees, where he focuses on the CloudBees Jenkins Platform and Jenkins OSS. You can follow him on Twitter at @DamienDuportal.

Viktor Farcic: I'm going to ask you a question that I want to use as a springboard into our discussion of DevOps. Simply put, what is the Duportal definition of DevOps?

The Duportal definition of DevOps

Damien Duportal: Today, DevOps is a trendy buzzword that is used to try to achieve focus on value, and not only for the technical or cost concerns. At its core, DevOps is really about how we should work together in the IT industry. I'm not just talking about the process, but also about the culture, tools, and the people involved in it. This is why I said it's a trendy buzzword because there is no strict definition as you could have for IT service management.

> *"DevOps was focused not on the tools themselves but on the way these tools could achieve either a new way of working or a breaking down of the barriers between teams and departments, which means working and talking to each other, in order to generate cross-team awareness."*
>
> —*Damien Duportal*

More recently, DevOps has been taken over by a different sphere of influence, but initially, for me, it was a movement that started around the idea of tooling. DevOps was focused not on the tools themselves but on the way these tools could achieve either a new way of working or a breaking down of the barriers between teams and departments, which means working and talking to each other, in order to generate cross-team awareness.

I define DevOps as empathy, which I think is the main key here. DevOps is a way of bringing empathy back into our work, and the tools—Docker being the most famous, but by no means the only one—that can help you to do that. But it's important to understand that when I say empathy, I mean empathy with your other colleagues, not just between the two sides of DevOps—development and operations—but also between engineers and salespeople, executives and employees, and all of the local departments of an organization that should focus on the *global* optimum and not on their *local* optimum. You need to be aware of the issues that your other colleagues could be facing and not just those issues affecting you or your local departments. The tools are just one way of achieving that, which appeals a lot to engineers because engineers love their tools.

Can DevOps bring empathy back?

Viktor Farcic: So, DevOps is really using tools to help bring empathy back?

Damien Duportal: Yes! If you have a tool that helps you to share empathy, then you have a great foundation for starting the conversation. Even if this seems boring to engineers, at least they'll start talking and listening to each other. I mean, once they've stopped debating sterile tabs versus spaces or JavaScript versus Java—or whatever sterile debate it is—they'll have to focus on the value they're going to provide. So, this is really how I would sum up DevOps, which again is about how you bring empathy back and focus on the value creation and interaction side of IT.

> *"I would sum up DevOps as how you bring empathy back and focus on the value creation and interaction side of IT."*
>
> —*Damien Duportal*

Viktor Farcic: But why is that particularly important?

Damien Duportal: Because of the different human behaviors. But more than that, empathy is one of the most advanced bricks you can have for building human interaction. If we are able to achieve so many different things—with different people, different opinions, and different cultures—it's because we, as humans, are capable of having high levels of empathy. As soon as you have empathy, you can understand why you provide value. If you don't, then what's the point of trying to create value? It will only be from your point of view, and there are over seven billion other people in the world. So, ultimately, we need empathy to understand what we are going to do with our tools.

Viktor Farcic: That's a good one. You mentioned that Docker is one of those tools; could you expand on that?

Damien Duportal: Before I went freelance, I worked as a developer, but because there were only a few of us, I was quite close to those working in operations. Despite taking Java development courses as an engineering graduate, I was always interested in how we could start coding the infrastructure from very early on. I can't remember who said this, but I believe it was someone at Netflix—*If you build it, you run it*. I love that mindset and it's what brought me to provisioning tools such as Docker, SaltStack, Chef, Puppet, and Ansible.

Overcoming the fear of change

We used a lot of these tools to help to bring operations teams' concerns to developers. Bear in mind that a lot of developers didn't want to learn these tools, and what I quickly discovered was that this was because of fear. Developers were driven by fear because they didn't understand these new tools and, because they lacked a lot of knowledge, they were closed off. They were terrified by the idea of operations knowledge and failed to actually see that these tools presented a lot of new things for them to learn and try. But what the developers didn't realize was that that fear was also present in the operations people on our teams, and that was just locally.

Viktor Farcic: That fear of change is a really great perspective, but did you ever manage to remove that fear from both the development and operations teams?

Damien Duportal: I should add that I can't generalize to other contexts, but that's how I understood things and behaviors from our end. In response to your question, it took me three to four years of trying to build a bridge between both parties and convincing them not to be scared. That bridge was me saying that we can work together and choose pair programming, even something as simple as sharing a beer after work or a coffee before, or doing sports together outside of work. Was it successful? Well, it was helping, but not completely solving the problem because at the time I lacked the ability to bring empathy to the team.

When Docker landed, it was as if I had seen the light at the end of the tunnel because, finally, I had a development tool produced by a person who shared the same concerns of those in operations at the heart of the development. That's really the reason why I used it. The good thing is that whenever a person started with Docker, they had the same learning curve. Why was this important? Because it made it visible for everyone that we all had a lot to learn.

Docker managed to be the bridge because it successfully broke down the barrier of fear because operations not only saw what they had to learn, but it turned out that they really liked learning the new tools. The only thing missing now was the time to learn. But the time issue was also seen as a potential investment opportunity, with those in operations thinking that if they spend time learning Docker, then gradually, the developers would follow us or our recommendation. At the same time, on the other side of the bridge, the developers were starting to think along the lines of: "Hey! That tool Docker sounds good! It could help us. It's easy to use, and it works very fast." Docker was just a way to turn a lot of this scary-sounding technology into a fancy tool. So, with that thinking, even marketing got on board and helped spread awareness of it everywhere.

> *"Docker managed to be the bridge because it successfully broke down the barrier of fear because operations not only saw what they had to learn, but it turned out they really liked learning the new tools. The only thing missing now was the time to learn."*
>
> —Damien Duportal

Viktor Farcic: But apart from building a bridge between the two teams, how was Docker able to create a feeling of empathy between them?

Damien Duportal: What Docker did was make the learning curve linear. You were able to start with just a few lines of code and get something done very easily. Through this, you could then see that if the coding worked, then it's already gained value. The teams were able to choose the moment when they would learn and add more quality or more completeness to what they wanted to achieve with Docker. This method was quite linear when compared to whatever tools you could have used before for finding the gaps. But back then, you had to learn Linux and Linux configuration, and possibly even Unity or systemd—all of the distributions—which were all learned in big steps. This was how I discovered and was subsequently convinced, in a very short time, that these tools brought empathy.

It reminds me of situations we, as an industry, have been completely locked on for years, such as an operations person coming to the development team and saying: "Hey! Nice application. Do you know where the application is expected to write files on the filesystem?" Because, by saying that, it implied the intention was because we have an issue in production right now, a performance and/or security issue or an audit, and we needed that information because it's valuable. But in that case, the communication was just: "We need this, and it's mandatory." But all the developers heard was: "Oh, yeah. We want information that's really boring, and we don't want to search by ourselves."

Viktor Farcic: So, did Docker remove that barrier?

Docker, containers, and the rate of adoption

Damien Duportal: The message was totally transformed. By using Docker as a support for the base communication, we just removed that barrier. In Docker, you can just say: "OK. Let's use the read-only flag," and by default, everything will be forbidden in writing except when you have an exhaustive list of the data volume. This is technical stuff, but once you've tackled the technical problems, you remove the stress, and then you can start talking. We were in need of Docker because we needed to remove that stress. You just removed the engineering part and focused on the discussion of needs in advance, and that's why Docker was a big game changer here, but it stands on the shoulders of giants.

In earlier years, this work was being done by the likes of Puppet and Chef, who were already bringing the development mindset back to operations. Operations people are just developers for the system. For example, all kernel developers are developers, and their operations people help. So, *there is no such thing as operations or development because, at the end of the day, we are all doing the same job.* It's just that the amount of knowledge required for each area is much more than one person can handle on their own, so we have to partition that knowledge. But still, the daily job is editing text files, planning, and testing that that change locally, and then globally, is the same for everyone. We just have to be reminded of this, and Docker was a great aid for that.

Viktor Farcic: That's interesting because, if I understand you correctly, what you said is that Docker made it possible to implement DevOps without companies having to plan the change. Basically, Docker made it happen naturally without any enforcement of the idea that you need to talk to this guy. Otherwise, the consequences are going to happen.

Damien Duportal: I used to say that Docker was just uncovering the dust that you hide for a year under the carpet, and suddenly, you put Docker somewhere, and you can use it as a maturity indicator. If you put Docker somewhere and everything explodes, then you don't know how to monitor Docker, or even how to build an image. If that's the case, the real question then is what were you doing before Docker? Were you just covering your eyes and throwing code into production without thinking about it?

> *"I used to say that Docker was just uncovering the dust that you hide for a year under the carpet, and suddenly, you put Docker somewhere, and you can use it as a maturity indicator."*
>
> —Damien Duportal

Generally speaking, the issue was that the knowledge was partitioned across all of the different departments and no one was sharing. Docker is just there to underline that point. It would say: "OK. If you're having issues, it's because you are not able to communicate with each other efficiently. You already have the knowledge, you already have the skills, but you need to bring awareness and empathy," and that was a much better indicator for me.

Viktor Farcic: So, how big do you think the adoption of containers is these days? Is everybody already using it, or is the full acceptance of it still pending?

Damien Duportal: I would say it's still pending.

Viktor Farcic: What's stopping everybody from adopting it?

Damien Duportal: I don't have enough experience to give a definitive answer as I haven't seen that many cases, but what I have seen over at least the last two years is a failure to take the time to embrace the change. In layman's terms, this means DevOps teams are saying: "We're scared of doing that. We are always on edge in terms of timing. Stop focusing on what is our value, what we could bring, and what we should remove on our path, and instead tell us what we should focus on." So, then, you could say that we might use a container, and this could help us. It's an investment; we can spend some time now so that we don't have to spend time later on. That issue is more about being totally on edge, and not being able to stop, focus, and breathe. This can, of course, be caused by a number of things such as a large number of people leaving the company, culture issues, or a big increase in the workload, but they're all things that shouldn't last for any significant amount of time.

The other thing I saw, mainly with smaller companies, or where they have people that are already efficient in empathy, is that, by sharing and being empathic, they don't see the container as bringing them value. Let's say you have three big metal machines: what's the point of installing Kubernetes or Docker Swarm if you already have a load balancer and a few applications? I would be interested to ask the same question in two years' time because there are things in motion that cannot be stopped. I wouldn't say container is the de facto standard; it's just that things that were in one direction three years ago have totally changed. But I'm not scared by this because that would mean you have the mindset of saying, "should we do that?" Yes, because of blah, blah, blah, or no, because of blah, blah, blah. If that's going to happen, expect to spend the next six months, or even years, evaluating your options based on your current context.

Viktor Farcic: But the idea is that containers will become the de facto standard, so do we just need more time, or is something else coming down the line?

Damien Duportal: One thing that containers don't bring to the table is resource management as we used to have it. I have an example from the CI/CD world with Jenkins, where it has been a challenge to use Docker in the same way over the past few years, and it's still because what you want is to allocate resources when you need them, and deallocate resources when you don't need them anymore.

Back then, containers were thought to be the golden solution, providing you with an immutable environment that you could easily start and stop within a few seconds, and then use the implied infrastructure for running the container, which could bring you these facilities of scaling horizontally or vertically. Right now, we have a cloud solution, and this is how they make money in the cloud by providing a platform on which to run these containers. So, I think this will be the big kick in the backside, in the sense that now that everyone is selling platforms for running containers on all of the big guns in the market, the rest will just follow. It's exactly like where virtual machines were a decade ago.

Viktor Farcic: Out of interest, what system did you grow up with?

Damien Duportal: I'm too young to have known the transition to virtual machines. I just know my history. I started with a PowerPC Mac, and everyone told me that I was running a virtual PC, and because of that, I was wasting resources. But two years later, when I started engineering IT boards, everyone was like: "Oh, look; this metal provides a virtual machine, so it's easier as I can change it during a run." History is a repetition. Virtualization concepts have existed for 40 years, so a container is just one way of reusing this concept, and this technology is just improving the usage.

> *"What's missing in order to have containers as the de facto standard? Just a bit of time for everyone to be convinced that the system is good for them."*
>
> *—Damien Duportal*

What's missing in order to have containers as the de facto standard? Just a bit of time for everyone to be convinced that the system is good for them. But there are also other factors, for example, the recruitment and subsequent hiring crisis, which is resulting in it being difficult to find good engineers. So, that's not the person with the diploma who solves problems in the IT area—say, someone like an IT engineer or software engineer because we already have a lot of them—but it's not enough. What we require is people with different backgrounds, because as the container becomes the de facto standard platform, it will create the required blueprint for everyone to build something, whatever language, culture, or way of working you come from. I think it's more a matter of time than anything else.

Software companies, vendors, and conferences

Viktor Farcic: You've mentioned companies. I know that you go to conferences every once in a while, so I'm wondering what do you think about software vendors nowadays? Whenever I go to a conference, I always see every product being labeled as DevOps, and I'm getting a bit confused by that because it's got me thinking, what do they actually mean?

Damien Duportal: It's just a way for those vendors to find a business model in a fast-changing sector. There are the debates about the open source or closed source business models. As you said, everyone at conferences today is selling DevOps because everyone understands that selling just a single piece of software is not sustainable. It might have been in the 1980s or 1990s, but not today. As a developer, you need to grow the value of what you are providing, or someone else will build the same software and will just totally roast you in their wake. When I grew up as an engineer, the pace of new development was years, but now it's months.

You can start with whatever legendary product you want, but in a few months' time, someone else will be able to duplicate it even more successfully, or at least for a cheaper price. So, DevOps is a way of not closing yourself off on the business marketing side.

It's a loose coupling between the marketing people and engineers because they're not totally sure, so they shove the DevOps between those two. Maintaining the lines of communication between these two departments should bring cross-departmental awareness because the engineers have the ideas, some of which have sales potential while others do not, but they are valuable internal assets, and marketing need to sell things.

I'm not a marketing person, but at the point where you need to market the product to someone that doesn't have the engineering background, you need to have some synchronization between teams. It's much like databases. If you do synchronization or meetings all of the time, you are locked in, and you can't go fast. But if you go too fast, you'll have desynchronization between both the organization and the local optimum that are not the global optimization of the organization. So, by using DevOps in marketing as a tight coupling, you say: "OK, let's put in that blocking keyword, and then we'll see."

Viktor Farcic: You've spent a lot of time teaching. It's got me wondering: what challenges do you face when you try to teach people something?

Damien Duportal: It's all about the diversity block word. I said "block word" because it can have a lot of meanings based on your intention, but the main barrier here is that we are in desperate need of skilled engineers, and right now, we have a few ways to teach people how to be engineers and problem-solving people. What we need are developers, not those that aren't at that engineer-grade level, but those who are able to build stuff.

I've lived through the very cool change that saw people coming from web development who then started to work next to Java developers, who used to be the backend of the organization. You had just enough cases where they were fighting each other. Those frontend developers with their just-enough typed language—JavaScript—where you can do whatever you want in JavaScript, and that's catastrophic. Everyone was focusing on that, but there were a lot of situations where people were starting to learn from each other.

> *"JavaScript went untyped and took the good things from the other world, and this is exactly what we need: more people coming from different backgrounds and different work cultures."*
>
> —*Damien Duportal*

JavaScript went untyped and took the good things from the other world, and this is exactly what we need: more people coming from different backgrounds and different work cultures. Just to be able to say: "OK, well, you used to do things that way, but I would have done it this way." We could learn a lot from each other, because it's not only about the person that knows and the person that doesn't know, it's also about the person who thinks differently; and that can help you to focus again on the value, because our brains are all different, and the bigger barrier in education is teaching to different profiles.

The education system

Viktor Farcic: So then, what's your view of the education system? How do we get it to teach to so many different profiles?

Damien Duportal: Some people prefer hands-on practice over reading. For instance, if someone says that they don't understand your slides about the network OSI model, that's actually OK. What you should do then is give them a Raspberry Pi and a keyboard and make them learn by configuring a TCP/IP, and then they'll go back to learn the OSI model. We know it's a requirement to have that foundational knowledge and, for now, it's OK. But do you need it after working in IT or networks for a few years, or do you need it upfront before doing anything else? It depends, and if we say we should teach all people like this, we are already in the wrong.

The main challenge is finding teachers who are adaptable, and are able to talk to the people in front of them and say: "OK, you don't understand what I'm saying? I need to find something else, or I need to ask for help from someone else, someone in the group maybe." It's not only about being a teacher or a student. It's about sharing knowledge and learning from each other. I think I learn as much as my students do each time, which is fine, and I think we need people that are not scared of that fact.

You just have to look at what's currently happening where I grew up and where I live—in Western Europe: the educational system creates that fear. You are the teacher; the students must address you as a grown-up adult, which I am not at all and will never be. But that's the case for a lot of people. I feel the best place for people to learn and share knowledge is in a less formal environment, but we have some work to do in order to safeguard that. Only time and experimentation will help to solve this issue. Because again, almost all teachers have the skills and the knowledge. But their ability to share this knowledge is blocked by their fear of not knowing everything, of not always having the right answer, of feeling ashamed to say when they don't know something or that they need help from someone else. Sometimes we just need to figure out a solution together. There's absolutely no shame in that.

Viktor Farcic: Because what you're now describing in education to me sounds very similar to what you described initially with the empathy problems faced in companies.

Damien Duportal: Well yes, it does, and that's because, once you are adaptable to unlearning what you've learned, you can start solving problems by saying: "OK, let's take a deep breath and focus on what the problem is that I need to solve." You might try different ways until you solve it, or equally, maybe you don't solve it. But whatever you do, you at least learned something and maybe, along the way, you solved the issue. I mean, that's the natural cognitive pattern for humans, and because of that, we need to have it in both education and work, and not only in the IT sector.

I mean, we know how farmers are doing things. For instance, you cannot be a farmer for 40 years and always have the exact same routine because the climate is constantly changing. You don't know whether you'll have ice next year, whether it will be too sunny, or whether you'll have enough water, and so, you have to adapt; that's the natural way.

Viktor Farcic: Do you ever get requests from people asking you to teach them how to become DevOps engineers?

Damien Duportal: No, never. I mean, how should I answer that question? Talk to each other, and say: "Hey, you're almost a DevOps engineer"?

Viktor Farcic: The only reason I'm asking this is that I don't truly understand what a DevOps engineer is. I see the word everywhere, and in fact, I get DevOps engineer job offers all of the time. But at the heart of it, I still don't understand what it is they would be expecting me to do.

Damien Duportal: In my first company, I was a DevOps engineer for one year, and I still don't know what my role was. So, I agree with you in that there is no such thing as a DevOps engineer, or even a DevOps team. The main purpose of DevOps is to focus on value, and by that I mean finding the optimum for the organization and the value it will bring.

> *"In my first company, I was a DevOps engineer for one year, and I still don't know what my role was. So, I agree with you in that there is no such thing as a DevOps engineer, or even a DevOps team."*
>
> —*Damien Duportal*

So, if you build an organization that only has the support of the organization focusing on the value, then what's the job of the other? What are they doing? You just put the keywords in, but in fact, what you need is someone who has the speaking skills and empathy. So, maybe a good place to start would be with an empathy engineer?

Viktor Farcic: Whenever something new comes along and becomes popular, there is always a hype around it. And then, even before that hype has diminished, there's a new product or a new tool right behind it that's generating even more hype. But right now, I don't know what's next. What's the next big thing? Is there anything coming after DevOps?

What's next after DevOps?

Damien Duportal: Not yet, but to be honest, I still haven't gained enough experience in my professional life to be able to make that kind of prediction. I would not have been able to predict Red Hat being bought by someone else. When Sacha Labourey did that, I was like: *that guy is completely crazy*, though in fact, he just has way more experience than I have.

Right now, in the technology sector, we have the Internet of Things stuff, and so maybe a security engineer will be the next big thing, because when the smart fridge that everyone owns gets hacked, all of the milk and beers you had in it will be ruined. So, maybe this could be the new trend? It's like the Ghostbusters; it would be the security engineer coming out because your fridge has been hacked.

Viktor Farcic: I mean, when IoT, and I'm not saying even if, but when IoT is all around us, we might see the same pattern.

A long time ago, we had people coming to our house to fix our computers, but now we don't do that anymore because we have laptops that we throw away when they don't work. But maybe that will come back, kind of like a person that fixes your house, in a retro way, bringing back the old school stuff of someone fixing your home.

Damien Duportal: People that were thrown by force outside the IT world—for example, people building a house—might be able to come back into the hype because you, Viktor, might need someone to break down the wall of your house because no one can unhack your door. So, you'll need someone with a hammer to deconstruct the wall.

Viktor Farcic: Let me out! I cannot go through the door!

Damien Duportal: Ha! I think we're all going to have a lot of fun with the new trend.

On Amazon, Microsoft, and Google

Viktor Farcic: There's one last question before we go, which is based on the way companies such as Amazon, Microsoft, and Google are working. Are they eating away the need for skilled people? I mean, we're in 2019, and you don't need to develop your own machine learning now as Google gives it to you. Likewise, you don't need to transcribe as Google does it for you, and that's just two of multiple possible examples. So, what is the relation between the services and what we're doing?

Damien Duportal: For me, it's like drying a river. Those companies need skilled people, and the few that they've currently hired are being paid a lot. But right now, the question is: why are these people skilled? It's because they gained experience and knowledge over the years. But how did they do that? Because the companies that hired them gave them opportunities.

It's like the COBOL time. At this moment in time, a skilled person—unless they build the new Terminator or supercomputer—will want to focus on something else in their life before they retire. But when they stop, what are we going to do at that moment? Because if we dry the river, we don't have water anymore. I think that's exactly what is happening.

But since things are changing a lot, I think there will be an ever-growing number of Red Hat-type companies or new companies that will emerge because, on the other hand, we have increased capabilities to build whatever we want. So, a lot of new, differently skilled engineers will emerge and will build alternatives. I really trust human nature to do that.

> *"But since things are changing a lot, I think there will be an ever-growing number of Red Hat-type companies or new companies that will emerge because...we have increased capabilities to build whatever we want."*
>
> —Damien Duportal

But the last thing I'll say is that you always have resistance. We were talking earlier about the transcript for this interview. In my case, I'm willing to pay you a few bucks to have it done because I don't want to spend my time doing it. But at the same time, I know a bunch of people that would say, "Oh no, I'm going to use AWS! I'm going to buy a Raspberry Pi and do it with no network at all."

I'm sure if you go to DevOps functions all across the world, you will find people that will build things themselves, and one of these people will be the next Alphabet executive. The issue is that, right now, they are drying out, but it's short term, and we have enough resilience for solving that problem.

Viktor Farcic: Let's end it there. It's been great talking to you.

3

Kevin Behr

Chief Scientific Officer – PraxisFlow

Introducing Kevin Behr

As CSO of PraxisFlow, Kevin Behr spends his time working with clients who seek to develop their DevOps process. His 25 years of experience have been driven by a passion for engaging with the complex problems that large IT organizations face, and how we can use DevOps to solve them. You can follow Kevin on Twitter at @kevinbehr.

The journey to DevOps

Viktor Farcic: Hi Kevin, you've been involved with many topics that have become central to DevOps since your early childhood working with your father. How did your father's work prepare you for DevOps?

Kevin Behr: Well, it's exactly 30 years since I first got formally involved in the world of computing. In my earlier years, I had the fortune of growing up with my father, Harold Behr, one of the cofounders of the Association of Field Service Managers, or AFSM. For those who don't know, AFSM was one of the first global groups dedicated to global service managers. AFSM would discuss topics that are still related to DevOps today, such as how mainframe computing was going to be serviced, as well as discussing availability and continuity of value for customers.

I was seven years old when I started building small digital computers, working on vacuum tube equipment. I was about ten years old when I started working with midranges and mainframes, in the context of repair. My dad ran a team that would charter jets to fly to their customers whenever their mainframes went down, and they would fix them at night, so that they'd hopefully be ready and working by the time morning came. If they had an outage happen on a Friday, I would often go with them if they flew out in the evening. Even back then, it was a fun thing that I could do with computers and with my father.

Viktor Farcic: You were fixing mainframes at ten years old?

Kevin Behr: My job would be to hold the solder and heat sinks. This was a time back when you could actually service and fix these beasts! One guy would be on the phone with IBM Armonk, or whatever mainframe company they were dealing with, and they'd be getting traces to test for certain voltages and impedances on the boards. Then, they would solder and replace the bad components. I was better at soldering than most of them, because I had small hands so I could get into places, but they mostly had me hold on to heat sinks and make RS–XXX cables while they chain smoked, muttered fresh obscenities, and squinted through reading glasses while soldering.

Viktor Farcic: And by the time you graduated high school, you were in business with your father servicing mainframes. How did all that sit with your education commitments?

Kevin Behr: Yes, when I was about 18, we were taking vacations in Moab, Utah. But, like a lot of places where you'd go for a vacation, there was no work. In our case, that meant that there were no computer services or consulting companies or anything like that. So, my dad and I started a small computer consulting company. We went out to businesses, government and schools, and we built computers! It was just becoming possible back then to build cloned computers for the first time, and so we went right ahead and manufactured our own computers. And we serviced them, right along with any mainframes and minis that needed servicing in the area. I also picked up some work with a company that had a contract with the state. I had a pager, and when they gave me a call, I would go fix the mainframes and Wang OIS systems.

A few years later, my CS professor asked me how much I made in those years; I told him it was anywhere between $35,000 to $40,000, which was pretty good in the 1980s. My professor then grabbed me by the arm and said, "Leave and get out!" When I asked him why, he said something important to me:

"I'm not saying this because you're a bad student, Kevin, you're an exemplary student. And I'm not saying this because you're asking a lot of questions about who is going to manage all these people we are teaching. I'm saying this to you, Kevin, because you're right: somebody needs to go and write this curriculum. But to do that, they have to do it from empirical experience. Somehow, Kevin, you have to work your way through these organizations and write your learnings."

And while I didn't set out with that purpose, I did drop out— and I've taken the exact path that my CS professor advised!

Viktor Farcic: What did you do right after dropping out of college?

Kevin Behr: Over the next several years, I held every job in an IT operation. I got to know what it's like to be a network engineer, and what it's like to be a system administrator, and what it's like to be the lowly guy who checks the disk array fault lights, the fans, and the filters on the air-conditioning. From rotating the backup tapes to programming firewalls. I did all those jobs.

I also went to school to develop software. I'm a lazy and slow developer, but I made sure that I understood *everything*, from the bottom of the stack to the top of the stack. I started with the B language as we used to joke—as in assembler—which means staring at a lot of binary, which is hard for us dyslexics.

I found during this period that the more I worked, the more disillusioned and confused I became about the folks who were managing the technology. It seemed like companies were just promoting technical people who had been there for a while up into management positions. In many cases, those people were not very good at what they were doing. They were not trained to do those things, and they often didn't want to be managing those things.

> *"The more I worked, the more disillusioned and confused I became about the folks who were managing the technology."*
>
> —*Kevin Behr*

Viktor Farcic: But if you want a raise in your salary, then you need to become a manager. It's like for a long time you might want to continue being a coder but then, five years later, you need more money, so you think about becoming a manager.

Kevin Behr: But back then, there was literally no help or support for the people going into technical management positions. There was nobody to mentor these technology managers, nobody to answer their questions, and there was no documentation for them to read. There just wasn't anything for them at all, and I found this very strange, especially when you reflect for a moment on how much emphasis there is around most executive positions to prove competency, education, and experience; and to provide training and documentation to ensure professional standards.

This was very strange, and it affected my view of CIOs profoundly, because I didn't see CIOs making any decisions on their own. I stopped seeing it as an equal partnership between CEO and CIO as the parents of a company. The CIO job looked more like a babysitter than a parent.

Viktor Farcic: That's a great way to describe it.

Kevin Behr: In my view, the CIO wasn't a peer with a real position in most companies during the 1980s and 1990s. The CIO essentially worked for everybody else.

The management of information systems during the early 1980s involved a lot of finance people, and, of course, technology originally came into businesses through finance—to help them calculate numbers and construct books and records. The first computer from IBM was a time clock that was designed to track people's working hours. Technology solutions had always had the backing of finance groups.

It was therefore very interesting and very curious when finance proceeded in the 1980s and 1990s to kick technology out of finance! I remember seeing this happening when the PC first came out. At that time, I was a mainframe guy, so was biased, but, like a lot of people at IBM back then, I believed that desktop PCs were just business cards for the mainframes. So, I just sat in front of them every day. Computer. IBM. Computer. IBM. I didn't believe that PCs would amount to much.

Then, suddenly, we had client-server computing in the 1980s and 1990s. As far as I'm concerned, client-server destroyed computing and set us back 40 years. The issue with client-server was that we already had all those capabilities in mainframes, but they worked better, faster and were actually less expensive by the time you counted all the people, weird contractors, and vendors that you would need. But finance made the mistake of only looking at the purchase price of the computer.

Viktor Farcic: You could say that finance became its own worst enemy. But a mainframe cost a lot more than a PC, so the client-server idea must have been very attractive?

Kevin Behr: Yes, sure, but then there was another false assumption: that you could run the PC all by yourself because... it's personal. The reality is that when you have 100,000 personal computers, it is not personal anymore. You then need to manage all those PCs, and they are all distributed!

So, I kept seeing this disconnect between technology and organizations, and the disconnect between CIOs and CEOs, become greater and greater. It was not until some years later, through the 2000s and 2010s, that DevOps was working to heal this disconnect.

Bridging the CEO–CTO gap

Viktor Farcic: It's interesting how those first phases of your career related to a history before DevOps, including those tensions and disconnects you talk about that DevOps tries to address of course. Did your next career step, as CTO at IP Services, take you closer to DevOps as we talk about it today?

Kevin Behr: Yes, in the 2000s, I was the CTO at a company called IP Services, which could best be described as an early MSP and outsourcer for infrastructure. It provided mission-critical infrastructure for large fortune and global 500 companies. While I was at IP Services, we had to develop ways to manage across various systems of control, because we would have auditors from every client wanting to come in and inspect our operations.

At this time, I started collaborating and working with Gene Kim, another kindred DevOps mind. We were both CTOs reporting to a CEO, and we both experienced a very specific process of adopting and adapting our thinking to meet the challenges in our work.

Viktor Farcic: Did this experience help the disconnect you mentioned earlier, between CTOs and CEOs in organizations?

Kevin Behr: Yes, we noticed how CEOs often describe things with word pictures, using primary colors, and numbers from 0 to 9. On the face of it, this CEO language can feel super-reductive and oversimplified, and that's certainly how it would sometimes feel for Gene and myself, because we were both engineers at heart. And the point here is that, as CTOs, it took a *lot of work* for us to learn this CEO language and its associated CEO mental frameworks. But that's what it takes sometimes.

I also remember Gene and I agreeing how humor can help

heal a disconnect. Gene found this great book called *Throwing the Elephant*, by Stanley Bing, and together we began to appreciate how Bing discussed "managing up" in a tongue-in-cheek way, like humor, from a Zen perspective.

Listening and finding common links with other people was another important lesson for us during that time. Gene and I would often meet at a restaurant/bar called Pazos in Portland, Oregon, where we would each describe common scenarios about our respective executives and clients. We found that we had a lot of passion and many common questions about our industry.

Viktor Farcic: Such as?

Kevin Behr: Well, we might say "How come Client A has all of these problems?" They have the same amount of money, and a lot of the same talent as Client B; and yet here we are, with Client B doing so much better. Why?

Gene and I were very passionate about these types of questions, and we convinced our bosses to let us put our pith helmets on. As Gene used to like to say, we were like old explorers cataloging plants and animals for the first time. Our world was business of course, and so we would study high-performing companies to see what they did differently.

We shared a lot of what we learned at the first *Security and Audit Controls That Work* workshop in 2003 that Gene and Stephen Northcutt chaired, and I gave the talk *Blood, Sweat and Visible Ops*, which was later memorialized in a book with Gene Kim and George Spafford called *Visible Ops*, which came out in late 2004.

Viktor Farcic: Why did you decide to use ITIL in your *Visible Ops* book?

Kevin Behr: We decided to use the language of ITIL because ITIL was a standard process language that a lot of people understood. We'd also mapped into ITIL all the actions that we'd been watching those different companies doing.

Our objective was to be able to compare the patterns of activity between successful and less successful companies using ITIL. What we discovered was that a lot of companies were doing things completely differently from the others—most critically, around how they managed risk and change. The more successful companies usually had the most effective change management processes.

A great example of the positive effect of good change management was at a client where we went in to change what was called a WAR, a work authorization request. The management of this client didn't like change because it was dangerous—and they happened to run one of the largest financial institutions. But the funny thing was that this client made way more changes than low-performing clients, and I was like wow! Their risk surface was much greater, and yet, they had almost no failed changes. Or, if they did, they were reversed very quickly and there was almost no impact to production.

We saw such high-performing clients as this one, and we saw low-performing clients, where both would be similarly skilled, and have similar budgets. The ITIL analysis showed that the key difference was the way that different clients were managing the change process that was integrated with release and incident processes. It turned out that 80% of failures were caused by things people did, and so the incidents are the results, and the changes are what we intended. We therefore started measuring things such as change success rate, and how do you know your process works? Is it successful?

But one of the things that we found about high performers is that they tended to have fewer controls than low performers. That was a big surprise. We were like "Hey! Wait a minute here!"

Viktor Farcic: Do you mean less control over people?

Kevin Behr: No, it was all about fewer process controls, such as from a management intersection or audit standpoint. So, we're there thinking our client has like 15 controls in here, while the other client has almost 40 from COBIT. And I'm like... this doesn't make any sense at all!

As we looked harder at this, we saw that the people with fewer controls were building purpose-built processes: they knew what their process had to do and where the risks really were. Meanwhile, low performers were reading best practices and they thought more controls were better for the auditors. And the lower performers treated every change the same way: they'd get a bunch of people in the room, and they'd talk about it, but that didn't make the outcome any more reliable.

The high performers were seeing changes as releases. They were looking at their whole infrastructure as if it were a platform; and as though they were releasing a new piece to this platform. They were looking at everything more holistically, and so they would track the interdependencies. They were doing a lot of things that were really and simply just in the change process, the incident management process, the release process. They had these processes integrated in such a way where you knew the outcomes of every step, and it was all very tightly integrated.

> *"[The high performers] were looking at everything more holistically, and so they would track the interdependencies. [...] They had these processes integrated in such a way where you knew the outcomes of every step, and it was all very tightly integrated."*
>
> —*Kevin Behr*

So, let's say you had an incident. You could see the last problem that somebody had on the ticket, and you could see the last change that was made on the ticket because 80% of the outages were caused by changes. But, 80% of the time it took to solve a problem was spent just figuring out what had changed, with the other 20% used to do the work to actually fix it. What we discovered was that a lot of these high performers were eliminating change as a causal factor in the first minutes of the problem, giving them a much higher chance of a very, very low mean time to restore service and have a better shot at staying within their SLO error budgets.

Viktor Farcic: And so, you discovered a first DevOps pattern?

Kevin Behr: That's right! What distinguished high-performing clients wasn't anything to do with them having fewer failures in those scenarios. We discovered that it is what companies do with their failures that tests their organizational resilience; and, more importantly, how resilient they really are in small teams.

Making it safe to fail

So now, we started to notice these DevOps patterns in our studies, for example, where people were willing to focus on learning together versus blaming and co-designing resilience. Designing systems that are safe to fail is borrowing thinking from flight simulators. The average learner needs to crash several planes in the simulator before flying in real life. The point is to decouple deployment from activation so that we can learn for free without affecting our customers' experience.

When you look at continuous deployment and continuous delivery, we're putting code out there faster. In some cases, code is on a unit test, and then committed, and then through static code analysis, integration tests, fast regression stack and—Bam! Production! Well, why do we do that? Because we know that we have options: blue green deployments, dark deployments, feature toggles, flags, and switches. So, we can turn something off in production if it causes a problem by itself, and effectively flip it back to the way it was. Many have adopted blue/green deployments, which let the teams run the old system at the same time as the new system from the same database. They don't cut over to the new system until it's working and there's zero downtime.

With these new patterns, ideas can arise for engineers to fail safely. That's quite the opposite to what the industry had always said before, which was that we must rely on fortification, such as redundant data centers. Sure, all the metal, namely the big servers, can make us feel good, because everything's fault tolerant. But the DevOps generation says that it's all going to fail. So instead, give me a resilient and safe-to-fail system so we can move at will, break things, and learn fast!

> *"Give me a resilient and safe-to-fail system so we can move at will, break things, and learn fast!"*
>
> — *Kevin Behr*

Viktor Farcic: Saying that everything fails sooner or later is admitting the truth!

Kevin Behr: Right, so what do you do when it fails? How fast can you make it invisible? So that it doesn't matter. Because Cobb's thinking, along with DevOps, starts to make a different set of possibilities appear!

The heart of DevOps is democratizing the work

Viktor Farcic: Are you saying that DevOps patterns are the heart of DevOps?

Kevin Behr: While those DevOps patterns are vital to DevOps, what I *really* believe to be the heart of DevOps, and what I think we've lost touch with today, is what, in the 1940s and 1950s, was a movement and a discipline called STS, or socio-technical systems.

Social-technical systems started with some sociologists, and it was one of the big-funded projects immediately post World War II. I do actually give a talk about STS, called *DevOps and Its Roots in Coal Mining*. It's kind of a joke, but one of the big things that they had to do after World War II was figure out how to make more coal to help power the war recovery. There was a conflict because all the coal companies wanted to keep the price of coal high, while the British government wanted lower coal prices so that coal and oil could power post-war reconstruction. It was in the national interest to get as much out of the mines as possible.

To help achieve this, the British government hired two sociologists, Eric Trist and Elliott Jacques, to look at all the mines and figure out which ones were the most productive and what made them more productive. Trist and Jacques discovered that all the low-productivity mines were highly automated, and that automation didn't create the expected returns on productivity. Across many different styles of mines, they found one mine design that really stood out, because it put out more coal per day than any other design—by many multiples. This most highly productive mine design also had fewer significant injuries than any other mine type, and had iron-clad, strong team morale!

Trist and Jacques also found that this productive type of mine had 100% attendance, and people were coming in every day. And that was odd, because for most mines, 30% of the workforce wouldn't show up on any working day, because coal mining was dangerous and there were a lot of other jobs available most days in post-war Britain.

To find out why this highly productive mine had 100% attendance, Trist and Jacques talked to the people after their shifts, but they still couldn't find anything different. So, they went down the mine themselves with the coal miners. At the top, the shift leader would meet all the coal miners to talk about everything they were supposed to do. But then, as they were down in the mine with the miners, Trist and Jacques immediately noticed something different: the group democratized the work.

Viktor Farcic: Okay. That's a twist.

Kevin Behr: What the miners were concerned with was: "What is the whole task?" Not what is the thing I'm supposed to do, and the thing you're supposed to do... but what is the whole thing that we're supposed to get done?

In one particular case, this might mean saying that we're going to need somebody to do the dynamite, or that we've got to blow up some holes here, and we need a safety person to make sure everything goes okay; or that we're going to need someone to do the jackhammer. They all had these different roles, and so their conversations sounded something like, "Hey, who didn't drink last night? You? No? Okay, you're doing explosives today."

Through this dialog, they would figure out how to divide the whole task into role-based work. They became self-organized and self-regulating based on who was the most capable person on the day to perform each important role.

In addition, another priority they had was to teach each other enough about each other's job so that if they got hurt in an accident, the team could pick up and still do what it needed to do to save everybody. So, they all learned a little bit of each other's job, enough to where they could do it. My question to you, Viktor, is, are you seeing the piece of modern DevOps here?

Viktor Farcic: You're talking about self-sufficient teams?

Kevin Behr: Yes, and you know what? They did it! The funny thing is that their bosses never knew the difference, because their bosses were above ground where it was safe; they would never come down into the actual mines. So, when the miners knew what the whole task was, they literally self-organized based on capability. Like actual democratization of work.

But it wasn't only that; they were also cross-training each other. Are you familiar with the Pareto principle?

Viktor Farcic: Yes, it's the 80/20 rule to most of us.

Kevin Behr: Now, the *inverse* Pareto principle is very powerful. It says that there's 20% of something you can learn that will allow you to do close to 80% of the task. The inverse Pareto principle often works both ways, and so, what these coal miners were doing, I theorize, is that they were learning the inverse Pareto of each other's jobs. And that is what DevOps is!

We talk about people who are full-stack, but very rarely are we going to find someone who could actually do everybody's job. So, why not spread that out? What's really there isn't the tools or the technologies that they use, but the way they decide to interact around the day's work.

> *"DevOps is [...] helping each other understand enough of each other's work, so that we can think about what's next."*
>
> — *Kevin Behr*

I listened to Patrick Dubois give a talk about his work on a contract, I believe it was with a government agency, and he developed a piece of code that he needed to get into production. He talked about how hard that was. There was a small job to do, but the operations people made it so hard, and Patrick was saying "Why can't we work together?" And so, to me, that's what DevOps is.

DevOps is working across those lines, helping each other understand enough of each other's work, so that we can think about what's next. But the key word is empathy. Caring across boundaries.

Empathy and culture in an organization

Viktor Farcic: You're not the first person in this book I've talked to who has said that empathy is so important to DevOps.

Kevin Behr: What do we mean when we talk about empathy in DevOps? We're saying that we understand what it feels like to do what you're doing and that I'll never do that to you again. So, let's build a system together that will allow us to never be there.

DevOps to me has evolved into a lot of tools because we're humans, and humans love tools of all kinds. As a species, we've defined ourselves by our tools and technologies. And, as a species, we also talk about culture a lot, but, to my mind, culture is a rearview mirror. Culture is just all the things that we've done: our organizational disposition.

The way to change culture is to do things differently. Let's not wait for culture, because culture is in the rearview mirror: it's the past. If you're in a transition, then what are you transitioning toward and what does that mean about how you need to act?

The very interesting thing about DevOps is that while frequently, its mission is to create a change in the culture of an organization, this change requires far more than coordination: it also requires pure collaboration, and co-laboring. These can be particularly awkward to achieve given the likelihood that we haven't worked with the people in an organization before. And it can become intensely awkward, when those people may have already made villains out of each other because they couldn't get what they wanted. The goal of the DevOps process is to create a new culture, despite these challenges.

Viktor Farcic: Yes, part of the DevOps puzzle is how we can achieve pure collaboration in the middle of very awkward situations, with people we don't know very well.

Kevin Behr: What people don't understand is that DevOps is hard. Working across those lines is hard. We don't have to do DevOps, it's optional—and so doing DevOps is hard. But changing culture means changing the way we do things in organizations. If we keep doing things differently, then we'll look back and we'll see that our culture has changed.

Viktor Farcic: Exactly, but these things also take some time.

Kevin Behr: Yes, if we do things differently for two weeks and we then look back and conclude that this didn't change our culture, the issue is certainly that people didn't understand the relationship between what they've always done versus what they're doing now. DevOps empathy enables cultural change because it enables behavioral change.

Viktor Farcic: And DevOps also enables collaboration.

Kevin Behr: Yes, collaboration is beneficial to both parties. From a game theory perspective: if I maximize my utility, then you do too. But also, from the non-rational and relational standpoint of human beings, there is the benefit of building strength through diversity. When we look at technology teams, we can tell from a DevOps standpoint whether they're together, as a team, or apart.

> *"The goal of the DevOps process is to create a new culture. [...] But changing culture means changing the way we do things in organizations. If we keep doing things differently, then we'll look back and we'll see that our culture has changed."*
>
> — *Kevin Behr*

Viktor Farcic: Are most technology teams you see together or apart?

Kevin Behr: In America, many large enterprise companies have adopted DevOps, but what we tend to encounter there in reality are "special teams" within those organizations; or technology groups that are "paramilitary organizations" as it were. These types of technology groups don't have to follow the same rules as everybody else, and so they tend to be successful in their short term because they have fewer constraints. And, of course, we can make pilots for them that have low bars; and can set very easy things for these teams to jump over.

I've talked to a lot of CIOs and enterprises, and they love this idea of DevOps having agile infrastructure, and agility all the way through their value stream. The main issue is that those

CIOs just don't know how to manage DevOps. Do I have teams? Do I have a VP? My response is always the same, and I say, "Listen, I think of DevOps more like this: you can now have teams working on projects together."

But consider volunteer fire departments. Do you have those in Spain?

Viktor Farcic: I know they exist.

Kevin Behr: So, in America, some towns can't afford to professionally pay for firemen, and so they have volunteers that all wear radios. If there's a fire, they'll all get a signal on the radio that's very loud, and they'll go driving like crazy to the fire station, get in the trucks, and go out and deal with the fire.

This is called a crew, and in a crew, there's a very important set of understandings. The first is that these people have a day job, and so one minute they might be doing some accounting, but in the next minute, if they get the signal, then they run: now they're a firefighter. The second understanding is that when they are being a firefighter, perhaps on their way to a fire, they already know what to do; they are pre-trained. Much like the scenario with the miners, when they need to be firefighters, they already know their roles and responsibilities.

My point here is that many of the successful DevOps interactions I see also involve a crew that assembles. There's some infrastructure, some developers, and some security people, who all get on the team; they know their roles, and they know the mission. They get it done. Bam!

Viktor Farcic: And then you want to start spreading the success of that team!

Kevin Behr: Yes! Every five times that the team is together, you should add another crew. They won't be great at the start, but they'll be learning.

The broad idea here is to create a playbook of signals so that we can let an organization know when collaboration is important. Of course, it takes some level of ability to make sense out of what's happening around you. This means that, as engineers, we sometimes have to look up from the keyboard, or take off our headphones, and notice what's actually happening.

> *"As engineers, we sometimes have to look up from the keyboard, or take off our headphones, and notice what's actually happening."*
>
> — *Kevin Behr*

Viktor Farcic: You believe that DevOps has a social component then?

Kevin Behr: Yes, the idea with socio-technical systems is that people come before the technology; and that the technology serves the people. This is in contrast with when we talk about techno-socio, which means the machines dictate how we organize, how we work, and how we even lay out the *way* we work.

What I observe is that DevOps has its roots in socio-technical empathy. This comes from individuals such as Patrick Dubois saying: "Why can't we work together?" Likewise, individuals such as Andrew Clay Shafer, who suggests that all our infrastructure should be agile, and essentially code.

I remain close to Andrew, and I talked briefly to Patrick on Twitter quite a while ago. To me, their work is certainly part of a socio-technical system: where people work together and share. We're going to automate stuff on the machines, so we have more time to experiment, learn and collaborate on the important things.

Viktor Farcic: In that sense, tools have an important place in your idea that DevOps helps to create a socio-technical system?

Kevin Behr: Yes, it's obvious how important tools have now become in DevOps, and the reason for this is because people are learning how to perform many of the techniques that DevOps people tend to like to do—from continuous delivery, continuous integration, continuous deployment, or automated testing. In many cases, we've now got tools in front of people.

So today, when you see people talking about how to do DevOps, the first thing that they mention is a toolchain; and I'm saying to myself, "So now you're organizing your team around the tools?" This doesn't seem right.

Viktor Farcic: Is that *the* fundamental misunderstanding of what DevOps is about?

Kevin Behr: Yes, it's like the difference between Brandy and Courvoisier. All Courvoisiers are Brandies, but not all Brandies are Courvoisier.

You can be working with some teams, across boundaries, on a very technical project. And everyone may even be collaborating in a DevOps style. But the teams are usually too focused on the tooling, and the tooling is dictating how the teams are working together. The tooling may even start to create divides.

Sometimes, when I'm working with an organization, I talk about archetypes, or stereotypes. When I do this, I use the Winnie the Pooh story. I believe that all of Christopher Robin's friends... Pooh Bear, Rabbit, Tigger, all of them, are different manifestations of Christopher Robin himself. It's kind of an interesting way of exploring different parts of Christopher Robin's personality. And then I like to say that product managers are like Tigger because they're very excited about the thing I'm going to do. The developers are more like Rabbit, while the infrastructure people are like Eeyore, because they walk around saying "thanks for noticing me." My point is that teams are a mixture of different personalities.

In most teams, you've got a group of people who are very excited about new things, and a group who are not so excited, because all those new things seem to hurt them. For example, people in operations are often very skeptical, because they've been told a lot of things about how great everything is going to be, and yet they get pager calls at 02:30 in the morning to fix something they just deployed. Naturally, operations people tend to develop skepticism over time.

When you manage to introduce empathy to a team, the development and the operations people seem finally to come together. You suddenly hear someone in operations say, "Oh, can we do that differently? When you threw that thing at me last time, it gave me a black eye and I had to stay up for four days straight!" And the developer is like, "It did? How did it do that? Next time, if something happens, please call me, I want to come help." That empathy of figuring out what went wrong, and working together, is what builds trust.

Trust is key to successful DevOps

Viktor Farcic: So trust is key to your vision of successful DevOps teams?

Kevin Behr: Yes, trust is vital. I'm convinced, for example, that the US military operates on the principle that you will move at the speed of your collective trust. You'll see this same principle at work within your company or in your own team. When you're frustrated that you can't get things done, you should immediately assess the level of trust around you. Ask yourself, "Are things transactional here?" For example, if you place an order, do I then give you a plate? Or do we have a relationship, and do we have trust?

> *"That empathy of figuring out what went wrong, and working together, is what builds trust."*
>
> — *Kevin Behr*

I have a story I use to explore trust. I read an article where there was a conversation between a US General, who was in a foreign country, and a General from that poorer country. The General from the poorer country says to the US General, "You're not a very good General!" The US General is curious to know why he's not a very good General, and the conversation went something like this:

US General: *"Why don't you think I'm a very good General?"*

> **Second General:** *"Because when you hand your soldiers weapons, you know that they're not going to shoot at you."*
>
> **US General:** *"Yes, we build, and have trust."*
>
> **Second General:** *"And when you give people 30 tanks, they're not going to sell them on eBay."*
>
> **US General:** *"Yes. We have trust."*
>
> **Second General:** *"So, you don't have to do very much—and so you must not be very good at this!"*

Viktor Farcic: I love that!

Kevin Behr: But then you know what the General said? He said, *"I guess you're right!"* So now, the US military operates on a different principle: mission command. It's no longer command-and-control at every layer. With mission command, the leaders state what they want the outcome to be, but not how we can do it. The leaders define signs of success and failure, and then they get their people to back-brief them, so that they all stay in sync.

Staying in sync is vital of course, because when the situation changes on the ground, the plan isn't necessarily going to stay the same. The team are able to improvise because they understand the intent of the commander, so they can find new ways of fulfilling that goal.

Viktor Farcic: That's brilliant.

Kevin Behr: Right, and so when we use an intent style of management, it allows DevOps teams to figure out how to do things themselves; and they know better, because they're closer to the work and they are guided by the intent and signs of success and failure.

With an intent style of management, we're also doing something that Reed Hastings, CEO of Netflix, talks about, which is developing team judgment. We're not just telling the team to go here or there and then just having them check to see whether they've arrived. Teams don't learn anything that way; they tend to just stop while people are shooting at them or until their leader tells them to move.

Viktor Farcic: There's a lot of pressure for teams to be efficient, of course. Managers want certainty, but we know from the military battlefield that the best plans will not always go as expected. Mission command does fix uncertainty. It's a way to try to deal with it, right?

Kevin Behr: Yes, what the managers want to know is exactly when the plan is going to work! In organizations where we have resilience-based engineering, the expectations are, of course, that things *will* break. The first step is to acknowledge that things break, and the second step is to recognize that it's very important how we deal with things when they do break—both during, and afterward.

First then, how do we solve the problem in front of us? Then, as we fix what is broken, we regain our morale and our strength. Sometimes, this involves taking a couple of days off after we've been up awake for two nights straight.

The next step is, how do we get our passion back? We need to apply that passion to make sure these things never happen. It's a constant process of celebration, defeat, victory, celebration, and defeat.

In the United States, this process tends to create a lot of burnout. We have a lot of pressure put on people, and they work a lot of hours that they shouldn't need to work. Technology jobs are not only difficult technically, they're also a difficult lifestyle. If you are alone and isolated in a hard job, and you don't have people to collaborate with, and you have impossible deadlines, and unreasonable coworkers, then you're going to be depressed. You're not going to do your best work, and you're going to leave the company... which leads to even bigger issues, because we all know that software developers and good infrastructure people are hard to find.

Viktor Farcic: Those people can find another job in a week, so they will leave.

Kevin Behr: I try to explain this to company leaders, and they're like: "Well, we're going to cut costs." But there are a lot of ways you can cut costs; the first thing is to become more effective, because only then you can become truly efficient. If you're trying to be efficient before you're effective, then, in the long run, it will always cost more.

It doesn't have to be this way. I have found that when these teams begin to work together, and as people get drawn into new levels of collaboration and coordination, those people who were alone, those people who were depressed, and those people who have been working too hard, they get empathy from the people around them. Suddenly you start to hear things like, "Oh, I know what that feels like," and "Oh, I know that woman, and the next time that happens to her like that, maybe we'll go get a coffee together so we can encourage her to keep at it."

> *"...as people get drawn into new levels of collaboration and coordination, those people who were alone, those people who were depressed, and those people who have been working too hard, they get empathy from the people around them."*
>
> —*Kevin Behr*

Viktor Farcic: When I was a developer, I don't think I ever even met an infrastructure person. How could I have ever possibly developed an empathy with someone when I wasn't even sure that person existed? For all I knew, there could just have been a script running that was making me wait for a long time!

Kevin Behr: A human "for-next" loop!

Viktor Farcic: Yes, because for all I knew, I've never met an infrastructure person.

Kevin Behr: That's such a good point, because if we don't even get to meet someone, how can we build empathy? And it's not enough to only meet people during problem situations, or on conference firefighting calls, because those are not the places to build empathy.

Viktor Farcic: I've met some people only when they yell at me.

Kevin Behr: Yes, which creates negative reinforcement and deprecates social capital. One of the first and most important things you do with a new situation is ask your key vendors to support company social events for the teams. You'd be surprised; a lot of teams want to engage. Organizations can find creative ways to get people together.

Earning the right to be heard

One very subversive way to get people together is to start a Lean Coffee approach to meetings. If you can convince a grumpy Eeyore to come to your Lean Coffee meeting and you just ask and listen, then you're already creating change. The change issue you're solving when you do this is that people want to be heard and they want to feel some interest or empathy from other people before they want to listen. But it's important, during change, to earn the right to be heard among each other—by first listening.

> *"It's important, during change, to earn the right to be heard among each other—by first listening."*
>
> *—Kevin Behr*

If somebody who has dealt with the operations and infrastructure side can come to the Lean Coffee, then everyone can listen to what that operations person is saying. People in both the development and the operations groups are likely to be cynical at first. To make progress, somebody must be able to start trusting. Team members must trust at first, and listen, and listen, and continue to listen. People need to remove their filters, and they will find it helpful to imagine that the other person has positive intent in what they're saying, even though it may not sound like it at first. This is something many have been able to do in Lean Coffees. You put all your topics out, and you vote on the topics. If we have a new member, I have a bias to make sure new members talk and get it.

If it's your first time on a Lean Coffee, you get to talk about what you want, and everyone will listen. I think when people feel heard, they are usually more apt to listen to you. Honestly, have you ever noticed how much people talk over each other? We're so busy trying to show each other that we know what we're all talking about and that we're smart that we often missing the point. I see that creep into a lot of things. So yes, you're right, Viktor: getting together when you're not having a problem is massively important.

Viktor Farcic: How else can we help people collaborate?

Kevin Behr: I like to use Toyota Kata to help people learn how to collaborate. Toyota Kata was first established in 2009 by Mike Rother. It's a simple way to improve a problem situation, and it gives us a scientific method to do this.

You begin the Toyota Kata method by defining a target condition, something that should be in good order to have an optimum or positive result. Only then do you look at the actual condition you're starting with.

Next, you say: "If we are going to solve this problem, what's the first obstacle we're going to run into when we try to achieve the target condition?" You make a small list, and then you think about the people that are involved in that problem.

What I'll often do then is bring some infrastructure people

and some software developers together, and we'll give them a common problem. We'll ask them to use Kata together to solve the problem. They will then run experiments together, and typically the first one won't go so great; the second one—hmm; and the third one—no fights.

Viktor Farcic: Nobody's hurt.

Kevin Behr: Correct! They start solving some problems together, and they start to appreciate each other's abilities to solve problems. The operations and development teams may speak different languages to each other, but what I found is that Kata standardizes the language and the patterns around the problem. This allows the operations and development teams to enter a collaborative problem solving sequence, because the language barrier is smaller.

The Improvement Kata is a great way to teach infrastructure people about Agile and Lean. I once ran an Improvement Kata with a group of product managers and software developers. The problem was that the product managers were just making up things for dates. This had led the developers to think "This has to be done here, and that has to be done there." Then on the other side, the product managers thought the developers were overestimating everything to build themselves safety—which is a pretty common problem.

While I was working with that group, I said to them, "Your goal is that you want a measurable target condition. You want an average cycle time for a story, and your average story is one day size." I then said, "You want your cycle time for these sprints to go down by 20 percent." The infrastructure people said things such as, "So what does that have to do with us?" Meanwhile, the product managers said, "How can we improve? That's up to them!" And the developers replied, "You set the deadlines!"

So, the team went immediately into conflict. But I told them that none of that was important right at that moment, because the reality was that both teams contributed to hitting the target condition. So, using the Improvement Kata, we looked at obstacle one; what is it, and what's the first thing we're going to run into?

Engineers are usually awesome at finding problems, because they tell you all the problems you're going to have; and so, once you get them focused on the problem, they will obliterate it. If engineers have got a problem in their head, they take it home, and they can't stop thinking about it; they can't let go of it until they crush it.

Viktor Farcic: That's something I agree with from my own experience as an engineer.

Kevin Behr: Once engineers have put their heads into an issue, they come back with an idea, and then we want to tell somebody. But while a lot of that is about personalities, and perhaps who is most outgoing, it's also about making space for the person who is quiet, so that they can say what they need to say.

In the situation I just mentioned with the product managers and developers, a product manager finally came back and said, "Listen, I realize that what we've been doing is asking you to estimate something, and then turning your estimate into a commitment, which isn't fair because I don't like it when people do that to me."

That doesn't seem fair does it? To hold someone to an estimate, when they've never previously done the thing that they're being asked to do. In which case, would it be fairer for me to ask you, "How long would it take if everything went right?", and then I checked in with you when that time happens? That way, you don't build a buffer, I'm not holding you to this, and all I'm going to do is check in with you. So, what would that do?

Let's think about this some more. If a project manager came up to you like in the old days and said, "How long does it take you to do this?", you may reply, "Well, I've never done that before. But I did something kind of like that, and it took me two days. The thing you're asking me to do today is a bit harder, so maybe I'll say that it's three days. And then, to be on the safe side, I'll say that it will take five days." The person you're talking to in those old days then says to you, "Okay, I'll come and see you on Friday then," and they'll know you'll be done when they arrive. So, the project manager comes back on the Friday, and you say to them, "Ah, it's going to take me another day, maybe two." Now at this point, the project manager must go back and move all the things around on the plan. It pushes the date out, which often causes a lot of fear.

Now, let's try that differently. This time, the project manager says to you, "Tell me what you can do if everything goes right, and I'll just check in with you, there's no commitment." So, the project manager comes back on day two, and they ask you, "How is it going?" You might say, "Well, I'm going to need another day and a half." The project manager replies, "Okay, that sounds great, but you're pretty sure about that?" And you're like, "Yes, that's a commitment. It's time now for me to do this, and I know what I'm doing." The project manager comes back, and it's done. Please take note that in this second sequence, the project manager finds out that you need more time on day two—instead of day five!

Viktor Farcic: Exactly.

Kevin Behr: If you're a project manager, or if you're running sprints and you're a scrum master, then naturally you add the usual buffer that people will incorporate in almost every task. Then, as long as your due date is after your buffer, all you need to do is manage every little instance where you lose some time by finding some extra time somewhere else in the whole project.

What you're doing in that sequence, most often, is finishing ahead of time! This is called Critical Chain, which Goldratt invented. Critical Chain basically asks you to identify your most constrained resource in a project, and it then subordinates all the other project elements to that constrained resource.

We called it the Brent Paradox in *The Phoenix Project*. What we encountered there was a very fortunate situation where one of the product managers had read *Critical Chain*, the book by Goldratt. This project manager was like: "It's so unfair that developers get yelled at when they can't meet an estimate." And suddenly, we saw all these things that we hadn't seen before: we had no estimates, and we had all these different groups of people reacting to that problem. We also had different people thinking about their management style in various ways, and different people interpreting in their own ways what it was that we were even trying to commit to!

Viktor Farcic: That's a very divisive situation you're describing.

Kevin Behr: Yes absolutely, because when something unexpected happens, all those groups of people will feel pressure to take the blame or the credit.

There is an alternative, of course, which is that you give people the ability to trust each other through experience of working together. Then, when problems do happen, people are a lot more able to withstand the blow of the problem, because socially they have a basic understanding of who can do what. They will then know what you're good at, and what I'm not good at, and begin to cooperate. I don't know about you, Viktor, but I would rather be in a terrible problem with people I know and trust!

Viktor Farcic: That's not just you, Kevin! I think that's true for everybody. You would have to be a real psycho to face problems with people you don't know or trust.

Kevin Behr: Right! So, you'd have to be a management person, because, at the end of the day, a lot of things that people in higher management do are without compassion, or empathy. They have no idea what difficulties that causes for people below them.

> *"In DevOps, we ask ourselves how we can create an environment that's resilient."*
>
> — *Kevin Behr*

In DevOps, we ask ourselves how we can create an environment that's resilient. We don't all need to be best friends, but we do need to have a working relationship together, and it needs to not focus on blame.

The Yin and Yang of DevOps

A key part of building a no-blame culture is about how to do the postmortem. How do you do the retrospectives correctly, so that blame is not an issue? How do you create the environment where, if somebody makes a mistake and it causes an outage, that they raise their own hand and say, "Hey that was me, I did that, and what do I need to learn because that happened?" Through that kind of attitude, the whole team will learn.

What you do in the postmortem *stays in the room*, because the team trusts each other, and they'll solve it. I find that a lot of organizations don't build trust this way, and people in those organizations tend to be focused instead on building security for themselves in their jobs. The result is that those people will sometimes be opposed to each other.

Viktor Farcic: This is surely related to what you were saying at the very beginning of this discussion: that companies were, or still are, too much focused on how to prevent problems from happening, and how problems will be solved? To me, what you just said is the human side of the same coin.

Kevin Behr: Exactly right. It's a Yin and Yang situation. To me, watching what's going on with DevOps and the confusion about its meaning is astonishing. I recently read that 80% of IT managers are interested in DevOps. They then asked those same people if they were confused about what DevOps means, and 80% of them again raised their hands! That's a bad combination—but, you know, we do this in all kinds of other aspects of life as well; it's a human quality!

Viktor Farcic: Yes, wherever I go, in most cases, I see a complete misunderstanding of DevOps, at least from my perspective, and, like you, I happen to think that the problem is in human nature itself.

DevOps isn't as easy to understand as an idea such as Scrum, because with Scrum, you just come in every day at nine o'clock and stand on your feet for fifteen minutes. The Scrum is very precisely defined: what you do, when you do it, and how you do it.

When it comes to DevOps, you hear people say, "You need to solve problems together to do DevOps." And that's all they say, which leaves everyone wondering what it really means to solve those problems. You then hear, "Should I buy Jira? Is that what you're telling me?" So, they go and buy Jira, and then say, "Now we're DevOps."

Kevin Behr: "Now we're DevOps," exactly! That's the joke! I did an engagement in Germany, and they were having this same problem: those people *thought* they were doing DevOps! They had a very, very detailed plan about where everything should go, with procedures and policies. But when I asked them, "What happens when you say you are doing DevOps," they replied, "Oh, that's what we do when there's no playbook." It's just like you describe, Viktor—they completely misunderstood what DevOps is.

Gene Kim and his team wrote a book called *The DevOps Cookbook* to show people how to do some new things in DevOps, but also to introduce some of the thinking behind DevOps. As I've already said, what I feel is often missing is that basic empathy and compassion, and if you go to a *DevOps Days* conference, you'll hear about empathy. Empathy is still my number one priority.

So, if you're doing DevOps, then the job of leaders is to enable empathy, learning, and judgment. If you're doing DevOps, then leaders can spend less time managing how people do the job, and less time seeking evidence about the way people are doing and thinking about the job. If I'm a leader, and I can help you develop your mind, then I don't have to keep checking on you. I'd rather have fewer people with fewer rules, and people who have better judgment. The more rules you need to have, this is a sign that maybe you don't trust people or trust people's judgment. We already talked about how important trust is.

> *"If you're doing DevOps, then the job of leaders is to enable empathy, learning, and judgment...then leaders can spend less time managing how people do the job, and less time seeking evidence about the way people are doing and thinking about the job."*
>
> —*Kevin Behr*

Viktor Farcic: The whole point would be that we enable people to use their brain. Like they would take the approach of saying, "From now on, I'll allow you to actually solve the problem—instead of just applying steps A, B, and C."

Kevin Behr: Yes, because then you enable people to turn the more holistic, problem-solving parts of their brain on then. You don't just want their lizard brain, or limbic brain, turned on—because it's not just about survival.

In fact, one of the early pioneers in the socio-technical systems approach, a guy called Eric Trist, went as far as to say that learning on the job is a *human right*, and that if you don't practice this right, then you're a machine, and you should really be replaced by a machine. But if people cannot provide an environment for you to learn while you're working, you might as well get a job somewhere else.

The good news is that many technology professionals are very fortunate in this sense. Not everyone is so lucky of course, but there are ways to learn no matter where you are, and even if the company or its managers hinders you, you can still learn. If the company helps you and you have the desire to learn, and maybe you happen to have someone you can collaborate with, then—suddenly, you have a real chance to learn and maybe to solve something together.

This is something that people do not understand, the higher up you move in an organization. As Russell Ackoff says, and I'm paraphrasing: the lower you move in an organization toward the line workers, the more they know about fewer things. And yet, the higher up you move in the organization, the less you know about more things!

Engineers always love that joke, but it's true. As you move up an organization, you must generalize more, and you must have a lot more knowledge. But the other thing is that when you're an individual, you can solve the problems yourself in many cases—because you can work on something. When you're a manager or even a director, you find that you must instead build consensus, collaboration, and teams to solve problems. You realize that your problems are not problems you can solve by yourself.

For instance, I have to go talk to marketing if I'm in sales and I want to run a promotion, because I need them to tell people about it; and I need the permission of the CEO, but I also need to talk to the CFO to make sure we have money. There's a natural path of collaboration to get something done.

Toyota, the Taylor Principles, and Kanban

Viktor Farcic: This reminds me of Taylor, back in the late 1980s and early 1990s.

Kevin Behr: Yes, the division of labor, right? Now Taylor got us a long way. Taylor got us to Toyota, and Toyota started with Taylor principles. A lot of people do not realize how much of Toyota's management system was scientific management.

Viktor Farcic: What I'm surprised about is how nobody stopped to consider whether it was actually a good idea to apply Taylor's principles to software development. Because if I'm doing the same thing today as yesterday, which is the only way to apply Taylorism, then I really suck at my job.

Kevin Behr: Oh, I'm not saying that it was good. What I want to say is that it was better than what was there before, even if it was optimized around the idea of mass production.

Viktor Farcic: Exactly.

Kevin Behr: Right now, we're in a different era of mass customization, with totally different thinking. But you're right, the thinking that was in place when the Taylor management style was a fad was very different from today. Nonetheless, Taylorism did get us to the beginning of Toyota, and to the mass production we saw in Ford.

What a lot of people don't know is that Toyota's whole production system (TPS) came out of a period of bankruptcy. Toyota hired Taiichi Ohno, in 1950, when the bank owned them. The bank had said to Toyota, "You cannot make a car unless you have an order," to which Toyota had replied, "Why not?" The bank's point, here, was that Toyota had made so many cars that nobody wanted to buy, that they'd now spent all their money, and were now bankrupt. The bank was saying to Toyota that the only way they could really know that a car they built would sell was if that car had already been sold. So, what did Toyota do? They developed the pull system, and one-by-one flow, as a system goal.

Viktor Farcic: That's certainly one way to think about it.

Kevin Behr: But the important thing is that Toyota did all that at the lowest cost, because the one-by-one flow is not cheap at the beginning. By the end, they'd figured out how to make it cheaper, and continually cheaper, and cheaper, and cheaper, and cheaper. Toyota did not have any big bang moments during this sequence—they achieved everything through the daily application of Improvement Katas.

Viktor Farcic: Including the invention of Kanban, though?

Kevin Behr: I mean, there was a point in the 1970s where Taiichi Ohno was running around saying, "The point of Kanban is to not need Kanban," and people's heads were exploding! His point was that if you're constantly looking at a board, or looking at a card, then you're not looking around you. But Kanban is intended as a problem-solving method, for a specific problem, for a while; Toyota would then use the Kata to grow out of that.

One day, Toyota realized that Kanban was powerful, and so... *everything* was Kanban! There were all these cards flashing around the Toyota plants, and all these signals, and Taiichi Ohno would say, "This is too much motion and waste." In the end, Toyota figured out how to have *a lot less* motion and waste. I think we go through that cycle in all kinds of technological breakthroughs.

Viktor Farcic: Where, if something is good, then a lot *more* must be better?

Kevin Behr: Yes, and I think we're there with DevOps right now. You see people trying to add things to the portmanteau of DevOps, such as DevSecOps—with more and more things coming soon.

The optimal environment for DevOps

This is all cross-functional collaboration, and so the management questions become: What can you do to get out of the way? And how can you make it possible for people that don't normally talk to talk, and under good circumstances? When they hear the vision, or when they hear their direction, you can bring people into working groups, and say to the infrastructure people, how are you going to help developers? Or developers, how are you going to help infrastructure people to do this, right? That is leadership.

Viktor Farcic: But DevOps has been largely a grassroots movement, and leadership hasn't known what to do with DevOps, right?

Kevin Behr: No, management doesn't know what to do with DevOps. They come back after a random meeting and say, "I want three DevOps, give me that! And now we need a VP of DevOps!"

Viktor Farcic: The funny thing is that this isn't even a joke! I've really met one of these "VPs of DevOps"!

Kevin Behr: Oh, I've met several of them! I must, of course, respect the fact that they're in a leadership position, but I don't necessarily understand why they exist. The DevOps idea is that you're supposed to be building teams with higher and higher levels of trust and judgment, and that's supposed to move through the organization too!

> *"Management doesn't know what to do with DevOps. They come back after a random meeting and say, 'I want three DevOps, give me that! And now we need a VP of DevOps!'"*
>
> *— Kevin Behr*

Organizations don't understand the environment that DevOps requires in order to flourish. In our corporate HR- and finance-driven models, structures, and organizational charts, we can feel trapped in those positions. We must understand that those positions are social constructs.

For example, I point out to people in HR that their organization chart is just a hypothesis. I ask them, "Is this your best idea of how to organize the office work? How do you know that it works? Where are the tests?" Because if an organization chart doesn't work, then someone should change it.

One of the ways I look for flexibility in an organization is by looking at how long it has been structured this way. Who can change it here? Could somebody, say a developer, walk up and say, "We have a problem. Our organization is keeping me from talking to this person, but I need to talk to this person, because we have a problem." And will anybody listen to them when they say this?

Viktor Farcic: Chances are... probably not.

Kevin Behr: And because we like our boxes, and our pictures, and our compliance, and our work councils, and all those kinds of things, we then feel forced to participate. But what I've been showing people is that the organization chart is only an idea. The organization chart does not know about the project you have right now, nor the problem that you have right now. If the organization chart is preventing you from taking the correct actions, then maybe it's time to sit back as a team and ask whether there's a better way to do things. Maybe you don't need permission to just get it done, or maybe you say, "Oh, sorry, I didn't know that I couldn't work with my neighbor."

Viktor Farcic: Exactly.

Kevin Behr: I think a lot of times, we assume that the way we can work is based on boxes and charts, and I think we need to test and raze those assumptions. People who control organizational structure need to be more fluid around the possibilities for the organization. After all, organizations are always in transition toward something; they simply can't and won't remain the same.

> *"People in the DevOps community are starting to see the larger organizational system. And once you see DevOps in the larger system picture of business, you see everything differently."*
>
> —*Kevin Behr*

Viktor Farcic: Are you optimistic that organizations can therefore improve?

Kevin Behr: Yes, I have strong hope for DevOps in organizations, because the environment in which DevOps can thrive also exists in other systems. I believe that people in the DevOps community are starting to see the larger organizational system. And once you see DevOps in the larger system picture of business, you see everything differently. I'm hoping that the DevOps community starts to look up and see that they're in this larger system, and how that system is itself part of an even larger system. I'm hoping that more organizations see that our only chance of steering our systems is by doing so together.

4

Mike Kail

CTO at Everest

Introducing Mike Kail

Over 25 years, Mike Kail has experience in a wide range of IT fields, including scalability, network architecture, security, software as a service, and cloud deployment. His DevOps area of focus includes empathy, integrity, teamwork, and resilience. You can follow him on Twitter at @mdkail.

Viktor Farcic: Hi, Mike. I want to start with what may seem like a really silly question: what is DevOps? Everyone I've spoken to has given me a different answer, with some saying it's a process, others saying that it's a tool, and others that it's being a DevOps engineer. What's your view?

What is DevOps?

Mike Kail: I certainly don't view DevOps as a tool or a job title. In my view, at the core, DevOps is a cultural approach to leveraging automation and orchestration to streamline code development, infrastructure and application deployments, and subsequently, the managing of those resources.

> *"I certainly don't view DevOps as a tool or a job title. In my view, at the core, DevOps is a cultural approach to leveraging automation and orchestration."*
>
> —*Mike Kail*

Viktor Farcic: You've spoken in the past about DevSecOps. Is that the next iteration of DevOps?

The next iteration of DevOps

Mike Kail: As the industry has evolved, there are companies that have transformed into a culture of DevOps. In that situation, the question is, how do we shift left and bring them into the continuous integration and deployment pipeline? We need to inject security testing earlier on in the process from CodeCommit to the building and delivery stages. Security needs to be treated as a continuous loop instead of as a periodic approach to testing and compliance.

Viktor Farcic: Does that mean that by evolving toward including security, the industry is almost falling behind by not including it from the very beginning?

Mike Kail: Unfortunately, for the most part, security has always been a periodic set of tasks or processes. For example, when you did a pen test once a quarter, you might have done static code analysis every now and then, but they're all done manually. You need to think about how you start leveraging automation to make it part of that continuous CI/CD (Continuous Integration/Continuous Delivery) pipeline, ensuring you use the best tools to do that.

You'll also require security engineers to start better understanding the software development process. They don't have to be developers themselves per se, but they need to understand at least what's going on. Developers also need to have some awareness about security, although it's never going to be top of mind or top priority. They have features and other reasons as to why they want to do high-velocity development, but they at least need to understand the security aspect and to start thinking about it as early on as possible.

Viktor Farcic: In other words, you're baking security into your process and not treating it as an afterthought.

Mike Kail: Exactly! It's similar to the grandparent or parent test that we can implement when we're using Microsoft Word or Google Docs to write a long document. As you're typing, the program will do the spelling and grammar checks for you so you don't run the risk of having your project delayed because of errors that you need to correct when you're about to publish the document.

The same can be applied to security, SQL injection, and cross-site scripting, which are always in the OWASP Top 10 set of vulnerabilities that keep surfacing over and over again.

Viktor Farcic: Brilliant, I love it. Depending on whom we ask, it's been a couple of years since DevOps really became a thing. This gets me thinking: as an industry, would you say we are at the top of the hard cycle? You've worked with a number of companies, so I would love to know if you see companies as part of the story of whether we're adopting DevOps, or whether it has already been adopted.

> *"I still think it's early days for the cultural transformation within DevOps."*
>
> —*Mike Kail*

Mike Kail: I still think it's early days for the cultural transformation within DevOps. We've seen the early adopters and leaders show the benefits of DevOps and what it can do to transform your business. But right now, everybody's trying to figure out how they get to that place, and I think that's why we still have a lot of misconceptions about what DevOps really is.

Look at it this way: if I just call my team of engineers DevOps engineers, then I'm doing DevOps. You have to approach the idea from the cultural perspective, and then, from there, leverage one of the core tenets of DevOps—that being measurement—to see where you are and how it's actually helping transform your business. DevOps is not a panacea.

Viktor Farcic: That's my impression of the situation, because when I visit companies, I always get the sense that in most cases, a random team was renamed "DevOps." What was once the tooling or CI/CD team is now a DevOps team, and when I ask people what they now do differently, quite often they don't know how to answer me.

Mike Kail: A long time ago, I was a Unix system and network administrator. I've seen through my work there that title inflation can take place. If I wanted to make more money, I wouldn't be a system administrator; I'd be a systems architect. Both site reliability engineers and DevOps engineers only exist to justify more pay without the benefits of the cultural transformation.

A true DevOps culture, with a team of engineers, means that they can articulate what they're doing differently, as well as actually show you because they measure it. They have metrics around the efficiency of how many deployments they are doing today versus what they were doing several months ago. However, what benefits the business from seeing these metrics versus just piling on more deployments won't necessarily equate to whatever is actually driving the business. To achieve that, they have to have that business focus as well.

Viktor Farcic: Does that mean that people who want to be in the DevOps industry need to learn new skills, or do we need people with different abilities?

The evolution of DevOps culture

Mike Kail: I think the evolution of DevOps culture is an ongoing thing. It's not like, all of a sudden, I go from being an operations person to a DevOps person because I did some automation. We have to understand that everybody needs some software development skills, whether it's scripting, pair coding, or implementing proper tooling in the CI/CD chain. But at the end of the day, you have to have an engineer mentality, and I think that's probably what we're saying.

The technology landscape is always evolving, whether it's through new infrastructure, or a new CO tool coming out to help you manage your fleet better. It understands Kubernetes, Mesos, or the myriad of other container orchestration platforms out there. It's also the wider question of how you make those platforms more efficient by the standard of DevOps cultural components.

> "The technology landscape is always evolving, whether it's through new infrastructure, or a new CO tool coming out to help you manage your fleet better."
>
> —*Mike Kail*

Viktor Farcic: I recently spoke with a friend on a similar subject, and he described it as the DevOps industry needing to remove the silos between departments. It's not because they're inefficient, but because when people start working together, they begin developing a level of empathy and start feeling each other's pain that in the end leads to better collaboration on different solutions.

Mike Kail: Exactly; otherwise, it's this "us versus them" mentality, which gets DevOps either implicitly or explicitly put into the culture. You're then not working to move the business forward. Instead, you're working on looking better, or having your team be more efficient, and at the end of the day, that doesn't really matter. What matters is your company's metric, whether it's revenue, customer delight, or something else.

First you break down the silos, flatten the organization, and eliminate the hierarchy, which is disarming for many, and then you figure out if you have the right people from a personality and collaboration perspective versus those with pure engineering skills. Softer skills like empathy matter, as does proper communication, owning your failures, not punishing mistakes, and learning from those mistakes and failures quickly.

Viktor Farcic: That's a really good point. People often ask why they can't have DevOps where developers, those testing the products, sysadmins, and all the different people from different silos work together. But on the other hand, there's that story about infrastructure being a commodity, and not mattering that much anymore. Is that something you agree with?

Mike Kail: I still think you need to understand the various components of infrastructure and where different CPU, memory, or disk configurations matter.

Infrastructure, cost, and the cloud

You need to think about infrastructure as a set of components. How do you assemble those components and then interact with them? In addition to that, how do you keep everything evolving? Infrastructure is much more elastic—to use a cloud term—than static, as it was before. Applications that live on top of that used to have the monolithic stacks or classic three-tiered architecture, but nowadays with containers, VMs, and microservices-based architectures, that's changed rapidly. It's why everybody needs to understand from an engineering perspective how the application or a set of services behave. It's also why they keep tracking that and looking for anomalies, because that's how you make sure that the site or your service is more reliable.

Viktor Farcic: What prevents companies from going to the cloud? Many of those that I've communicated with still tend to reject it, or maybe I'm just unlucky with the companies I work with.

Mike Kail: No, it's not just you. I think it's a classic combination of fear, uncertainty, and doubt. People fear insecurity in the public cloud for various reasons, whether it's a fact or a rumor. For example, there's a fear of jobs going away. If I manage the metal in a data center, how do I now do that in the cloud? Is it more self-service? This is the exact reason why you have to keep evolving your skills to be more engineering-centric than just a maintainer of pets.

Other factors are at play here as well: doubt and cost. You get a shock when you receive the monthly bill from your public cloud IS provider because while you may have shifted your application, you failed to do any proper refactoring of it. Your on-premises was overprovisioned—which is also something you didn't factor that cost into—and is now running on expensive, virtual machines in the public cloud. You're wasting a bunch of resources.

> *"People fear insecurity in the public cloud for various reasons, whether it's a fact or a rumor."*
>
> —*Mike Kail*

You should use that opportunity to move to the public cloud and look at re-architecting how you can make your deployments more efficient, because there's a bunch of other cost levers. Having managed a dozen or so owned-and-operated global data centers, I know there's a lot of costs that people never factor in. There's the obvious cost of employing people 24/7, but you also need to factor in the cost of power cooling. You'll find that, typically, you've overprovisioned the metal because you're a large, successful company, and you have to manage the peak. You can't just deploy rack and stack servers on demand, much like you can deploy cloud infrastructure on demand. There's really a lot of implicit costs that have never been shown in a Total Cost of Ownership model of on-premises versus cloud.

Viktor Farcic: I have the same impression that whenever

I discuss prices, people somehow compare the cost of cloud versus the cost of only having servers.

Mike Kail: From my experience, it's always the apples-versus-oranges comparison. Companies just look at that monthly bill, and fail to understand the shift from CAPEX to OPEX, or they haven't articulated that with their CFO well enough, if at all. You can't just say, "I'm moving to the cloud, and I'm done," and then get the bill, because you don't understand the security controls in place, or how to manage them properly.

Whether true or perceived, lack of visibility is also a challenge. I can't see my servers, and I can't just walk into the data center. I may have people doing shadow cloud deployments, so there are more instances running than I know about. You also have to have proper governance around cloud usage, and I think people don't go into that with their eyes wide open and prepared.

Viktor Farcic: I get the impression that DevOps is moving away from being operations-based and becoming more development-oriented as we're developing data centers. Nowadays, everybody's becoming a software developer, not only those coding your applications.

Mike Kail: Yeah, it goes back to Marc Andreessen's manifesto of software leading the world, because we're moving to software-defined everything. Software-defined infrastructure, networking, and security. There are a few companies now doing software-defined power, power leveling, and load leveling. I think everything is becoming programmatic, which is why—once again, going back to my common thread—everybody needs to have an engineering or a developer mindset.

> *"Everything is becoming programmatic, which is why—once again, going back to my common thread—everybody needs to have an engineering or a developer mindset."*
>
> —*Mike Kail*

Viktor Farcic: That might then be similar to what we were experiencing a while ago with testing. The idea that when automation became a thing, testers who don't know how to write code became very defensive or scared. Maybe something similar is happening with operations right now.

Mike Kail: That and security as well. Because at the base of the stack, both QA testing—classic QA testing and security testing—are very similar. You're looking for anomalies and issues, whether there are security vulnerabilities or there's other application issues or bugs. Those have all been manual processes, and they delayed the overall deployment process, which causes that contention, which leads you to be defensive of what you're doing, instead of being collaborative.

Viktor Farcic: That's like moving from acting as a gatekeeper or a policeman to being more of a collaborator.

Mike Kail: It's about moving from being a blocker to an enabler. How do you still provide your testing—whether it's security or performance—as fast as possible to not add friction to the deployment and delivery processes?

Viktor Farcic: True. No conversation these days can exclude Kubernetes containers in some regard. Do you have any opinion on that? Is Kubernetes really going to become the one ring to rule them all?

Mike Kail: I'm a big believer and supporter of Kubernetes in general, I'll start with that. But if you take a survey, many, if not most, enterprises are still struggling with virtualizing and moving to cloud virtual machines.

The leap across the chasm to get to containers is a long one. You can't just deploy your application in Kubernetes, Mesos, or whatever your container orchestration environment is. Now you magically have microservices, an auto-scaling application that is resilient, performant, and cost-effective. There's no magic. I think there are very few container-native applications, especially outside of Silicon Valley.

Jumping into the valley

Viktor Farcic: Does that mean companies should not jump into whatever is "today"? If you're not into virtualization, don't jump into containers. If you're not into cloud-native applications, don't think about deploying to cloud.

Mike Kail: I think you first have to ask yourself, "Why are we doing that, and why does that matter for our business?" You need to tie that to potential results versus it being the newest and coolest technology that's going to make you cooler than Facebook, because that won't happen.

As developers or DevOps cultural employees, we tend to become overly enamored of technology. Just look at how Kubernetes is so cool or how containers and clouds are so great. But you need to tie that back to why you are doing this. Why does it matter for the business, and what benefits is this application going to have from being cloud-native or container-native?

I'm a big pro-cloud, pro-software-defined person, and I think there's plenty of ways to justify that. But you need to make sure that your culture is ready for that technical transformation, and that you have the right people to handle the process and technology components.

> *"As developers or DevOps cultural employees, we tend to become overly enamored of technology."*
>
> —*Mike Kail*

Viktor Farcic: How often do you think that companies actually even understand the reasoning behind it? Do they jump into those things because they really understand why they want to do it or is somebody coming and saying, "Thou shalt become Agile!"

Mike Kail: I think there's probably a lot of dictatorships that take a stick-versus-carrot approach. You have some people, or a team, inside the company that says, "Look. We're going to do Agile," or, "We're going to do DevOps." This is not the right approach.

Much like a start-up trying to raise funding, you have to go in and do a proper presentation. You go to the higher-ups and tell them what you're proposing and why. You show the efficiencies and keep making sure that it's not a one-and-done situation and that everybody's on board for this continual transformation and evolution.

Viktor Farcic: In other words, people should come to you, rather than you telling people where to go?

Mike Kail: I think it's asynchronous. It's not me or somebody internally preaching at people. It's actually getting them engaged and collaborating, which is the biggest part of a DevOps culture. Without collaboration, you don't have anything.

Viktor Farcic: You mentioned Silicon Valley a couple of times. Do you see a big difference inside and outside of the Valley?

Mike Kail: I do. I think in the Valley, we're the first to hear about the latest hype. For example, Docker's been around for some time, but in the last two years of my travels it seemed that no one really understood what a container was. I went to a group of executives at an organization and asked them to give me a definition of a container. If there were 15 people in the room, I'd get 12 different answers, including some arguments as well.

Viktor Farcic: But if there's a big gap, do you think that those running behind can actually catch up? I'd really be interested in knowing if there's hope for digital transformation. Is there a chance that big enterprises will really become competitive, or is it a lost battle?

Mike Kail: It's somewhat of a religious topic because it really comes down to the internal workings of the given company. I've seen too many large enterprises get in their own way, and they're still mired in this annual budgetary cycle mentality. I'm pretty sure Amazon doesn't operate that way. I'll put my hands up and say I've got no intimate knowledge of Amazon's inner workings, but as fast as they move, they're not doing an annual budget cycle and kicking the can down the road when it comes to new transformation and transformative initiatives.

Too many enterprises are just content with the status quo or the soundbite because, mentally, that's the way they've always done things. Until you remove or change that mindset, there's no amount of technology that can help you.

Viktor Farcic: It reminds me of that truism: every company is a software company. Now, assuming that you think that's true, how does this coincide with externalizing your world? Because, obviously, nobody externalizes core business.

Mike Kail: Are you talking about open source initiatives?

Viktor Farcic: No. Not open source—for example, say you're a big bank or insurance firm that outsources all your software development to a third party. I'm trying to figure out how somebody can say that software is important when they don't develop it in house.

Mike Kail: I think you need to keep the core IP or crown jewels of your business close to your chest, and not outsource, offshore, or nearshore them. You need to protect, to some degree, the core features of your business, or at least what gives you strategic differentiation. Maybe you can then rely on third-party developers for everything else.

I think a lot of people believe that offshoring or passing work to third-party developers is less expensive, but I think given time zone challenges and, in particular, language and cultural barriers, that's not often the case. It's like on-premises versus cloud: people don't compare apples and apples.

Viktor Farcic: True. Is that because it's like counting the price per head, not per the outcome?

Mike Kail: Exactly!

What's next after DevOps?

Viktor Farcic: So, what's coming next? I don't know if you want to look a month down the line or even several years, but where are we going as an industry?

Mike Kail: We hear the word "bubble" mentioned a lot, but compared to the real bubble of 1999/2000, today's technology is pervasive in all of our lives in Silicon Valley. If I look at buzzwords, I think blockchain will start becoming more and more prevalent. Once people understand where it's applicable, it will be a game-changing technology in a bunch of different sectors. However, there will be scaling and growing challenges that I don't think a lot of people have thought about.

Not to conflate blockchain with cryptocurrency, but I think we'll see cryptocurrency becoming much more well-formed, as we've seen more recently. For example, only the other day, the payment company Square announced they're allowing trading in crypto, which will allow new businesses and opportunities to be built around that.

> *"I think we'll see cryptocurrency becoming much more well-formed, as we've seen recently."*
>
> —*Mike Kail*

The other area, which is still in its early stages, is artificial intelligence. How do we leverage AI in positive ways for business and humanity in order to remove biases from them?

Viktor Farcic: Theoretically, that should actually also affect engineering. Are we moving in a direction where we'll end up programming AI so AI can program everything else?

Mike Kail: I think every role I've had in my technology career has eventually gone away. Again, as we mentioned before, there's that fear. Realistically, I think it's still a long way before AI eliminates all our jobs. Quite the opposite, actually: I'm more of the mindset that AI will create more opportunities.

We want to eliminate the menial tasks by leveraging some machine learning—which is a component of AI—to make your job more efficient. Then you can spend time on higher-order things. I think that's what we'll see, and when people understand that, they'll be successful. The ones who sit around worrying about their job or position going away are the ones that are probably not going to be long for that position in general.

Viktor Farcic: As we wrap up this interview, is there anything you would like to add that we haven't covered yet?

Mike Kail: I think my closing message is that we're all still early in the DevOps transformation. There are still plenty of cultural opportunities out there to make a difference and actually make things much more efficient.

Viktor Farcic: It's not really a standalone project then, but more a never-ending story.

Mike Kail: I'd describe it as transformation or continuous evolution. You're never done transforming the DevOps sector. There's always an area of the business or aspects to improve upon with respect to performance.

Viktor Farcic: That's why I don't like the term "digital transformation." For some reason, it sends a message to my brain that this is something with a definite start and ending.

Mike Kail: It's not a project with a finite endpoint. I'll go back and use the Amazon example. I would guess that they're always thinking about digital transformation, and there's plenty of inefficient parts of our society and world that could be improved by digital transformation.

5

James Turnbull

Chief Technology Officer – Microsoft for Startups

Introducing James Turnbull

James Turnbull leads a team of "CTOs in residence" at Microsoft who help start-ups build the right architecture and teams in order to be successful. A seasoned engineering and infrastructure author, James has published a series of books on those subjects. You can follow him on Twitter at `@kartar`.

What is DevOps?

Viktor Farcic: Hello, James. I wanted to start our discussion with a question: what does DevOps mean to you? It's a question that I find fascinating because everyone I've interviewed for this book has given me a different answer.

James Turnbull: I'm not sure that there is a single description for DevOps anymore. I started talking about DevOps in 2009, and although I wasn't at the first DevOps event in Ghent, Belgium, that year, I was at the next one.

I think when it first started out, DevOps was really about trying to build bridges between operations and their functions and developers and their functions, which largely focused around the moment of handover where the code goes from being in development to being deployed and in production. Then from there, we analyzed a lot of the problems with that particular challenge and identified that some of the issues were cultural, some were technological, like automation and tooling, while other issues were process-oriented.

> *"These days, I think DevOps is a lot of different things to a lot of different people."*
>
> —*James Turnbull*

These days, I think DevOps is a lot of different things to a lot of different people. I think if you work in marketing, there was a time when you just relabeled all your tools as your DevOps toolkit. It's 2019, and you still see a lot of companies with a DevOps page, or they outright call themselves "DevOps something" – as to whether those tools are DevOps or not, I'm not sure.

At the end of the day, DevOps is about ensuring that applications and products are built in a cross-functional way, so that product engineers, designers, operations, security, and business people all have a common understanding of their mission, which is to build products for their organizations that hopefully make that organization money.

Viktor Farcic: That makes sense. You mentioned DevOps tools, and at least when I visit companies and attend conferences, every single tool has the word DevOps attached to it. It's kind of as if nobody can sell anything without DevOps, which leads me to think: is there even such a thing as DevOps tools?

James Turnbull: No, I don't think there is. I believe there are tools that make the process of being a cross-functional team better. I would argue that for many companies, Slack is a DevOps tool because it's an easy way for companies to communicate across teams.

I would also say Puppet might be a DevOps tool, even Chef, Salt, Ansible, or Docker, because they all enable automation and workflow that makes it easier to manage and move assets and code around. Any tool that facilitates building that cross-functionality is probably a DevOps tool to the point where the term is likely meaningless.

What's the best stack available today?

Viktor Farcic: You're a very technically oriented, hands-on person. All of your books, at least those that I've read, are highly technical, which gets me wondering whether you have a favorite stack. I saw that you wrote a lot about Puppet and Terraform. Is one replacing another? Moreover, where do you see the industry moving to now?

James Turnbull: I'm probably less technical than I used to be. I've moved between a lot of different roles; these days, I'm primarily a people leader. I'm a CTO, and I've been a VP of engineering for a number of years, so I dabble in this space in my spare time, but I wouldn't consider myself a practicing SRE or a practicing Systems Engineer anymore.

In terms of things like Puppet and Terraform, I think they do different things. Terraform is clearly an infrastructure build tool, and if you want to build a virtual private cloud (VPC) and a bunch of Amazon EC2 instances and a bunch of other things hooking them all together, then Terraform is the ideal tool. If you want to configure those assets and deploy the application on top of it, then I think Puppet, or another configuration management tool, is a more appropriate choice.

Viktor Farcic: How about the O'Reilly conferences? Do you see any trends there? Can you predict what's coming next, at least within DevOps or infrastructure-related subjects?

James Turnbull: We've changed the purpose of Velocity considerably over the last couple of years. The future is really in distributed systems. I think that monolithic applications that are based in a single geography are the dodo of the infrastructure and architecture world. They have a long tail, and it will take a long time for them to go away, but people who are building new systems really need to think about whether that is the most appropriate way to develop their application or their service.

I think there's a couple of reasons for that, one of them obviously being that monolithic applications tend to move slowly, and speed to market really matters now, as does your ability to deploy a new feature, a new capability, or a new offering of some kind that actually makes a marked difference, as does performance, and scaling, and availability. Monolithic applications are notoriously not great at that.

> *"Customers have very high expectations about the performance of applications and services, which are significantly changing the way that data is distributed."*
>
> —James Turnbull

The second reason is that I think customer expectation is much higher now. The last couple of generations of folks, who are probably the third generation who grew up as sort of internet natives or cloud natives, have never known a time where they didn't have data on their phones. Customers have very high expectations about the performance of applications and services, which are significantly changing the way that data is distributed. For example, no longer is the optimum model for a lot of applications a large centralized data center; it is, in fact, an edge computing-centric distributed application where the data for a particular cohort of customers is closer to those customers rather than your core infrastructure. I think, overall, what we see now is that, for the next two or three years at least, distributed systems will be the focus of infrastructure and application development, and certainly the backend.

Monoliths and microservices

Viktor Farcic: You mentioned monoliths and microservices. Can you explain why they've only become popular now? I mean, obviously, microservices have existed for a number of years. Is that because our needs changed or the tools that we have access to changed? It's not that that concept didn't exist for a long time, but everybody only started talking about them recently.

James Turnbull: When I first started out in the industry, there was a concept called service-oriented architecture. Primarily, it was a way to break services into individual fault domains that allowed them to scale, manage, and interact on their own. The definition of service was pretty broad. It generally didn't resemble a microservice.

But I think a couple of things have happened, namely that virtualization, the cloud, and containers have enabled microservices architecture. They're very easy tools to allow someone to build those services.

I think the reason those services have also become popular is that if you are building an application that is designed to be retail and customer facing, and you want that application to be able to move fast, then building independent services that are easy to iterate on is significantly easier than building a giant monolith where, at some point in time, you'll lose the ability to reason about the model. You will lose the ability to understand the model as a whole, and you will lose the ability to make changes to the model without potentially impacting other things, whereas microservices with appropriate protocols and APIs can be versioned and managed, and canary-deployed and rolled out.

Viktor Farcic: Do you have any contact or experience with security in that model? Because I hear security is kind of a concern, especially when joined with containers.

James Turnbull: I was a security engineer for a few years, so I see containers as having some security challenges. Obviously, a container is not as robust as a virtual machine in the sense that the walls between compute resources are considerably thinner. For example, in most cases, a container represents a process separation versus a hypervisor separation. But I think that, realistically, a lot of it comes down to how you deploy your services, and how you build your environment.

If you put security architecture up front and apply security in depth at both an application and infrastructure level, and you design it into your environment, then a lot of the common issues that have tripped people up in the past start to become less of a concern. There's a lot of work being done around building zoned security models and deploying like-risk-level workloads together. You deploy your cluster of marketing web servers together, but not on the same host as your payroll system. There's a lot of common-sense stuff that has been done for years and years, and that, I think, makes a large number of the security concerns in that space not as severe as they look.

Viktor Farcic: When I look at the software, at least as you describe it in the books you've written, it's always open source. Do you see that as the death of closed source? Or does closed source even exist anymore?

James Turnbull: I think the same thing that's happening to the customer is also happening to software in other places. I like open source software because I like the ability to control my own destiny. I also believe in composable applications. The fundamental principle of a Unix application is small, composable tools that I can put together and build a stack of, and I'm very attracted to that model. For myself, and a lot of other people who are probably reasonably experienced engineers, I like choosing a stack where I can take a bit of Kubernetes and a bit of Prometheus, and maybe a bit of this and a bit of that, and I can combine them together to provide me with a stack that I like and can work with.

> *"I like open source software because I like the ability to control my own destiny."*
>
> —*James Turnbull*

I still think a lot of companies, particularly enterprise companies, want someone to talk to if something goes wrong with a product or an application. They want a neck to choke, or someone to be able to provide them with support and indemnification, so I think there's definitely still a market for closed source enterprise software. But I'm not convinced that the demand is as large as it used to be. More and more people are building things that are primarily open source. When there's open source at the core of it, they're selling additional bits of technology or functionality that is either closed source or commercial in some way on top of that. If you look at a significant number of the movements happening around orchestration tools, then at the heart of it, a lot of them are Kubernetes and then other things are built around or on top of that.

Kubernetes, RHEL, and Ubuntu

Viktor Farcic: You mention Kubernetes. Do you think Kubernetes will affect operating systems? Are we going to continue seeing RHEL and Ubuntu dominating the market?

James Turnbull: I don't think so. I personally think the operating system is dead; I don't see a purpose for it. I want to build composable things that just use the system-level resources that I care about, whether they are disk, CPU, or memory. I want to be able to take libraries or middleware from a selection of stuff and then combine those without needing a huge surface area of other materials. I think that we'll see more and more things that are shaped like Alpine and CoreOS, where the operating system is largely a black box, or you're getting a piece of the operating system where you don't configure any of it, as a lot of it's not exposed to you.

I still think that people will want some sort of support. They'll want somebody to be able to talk to when something breaks. I just wonder if it might be at a different level of abstraction that they wish to support. Do they need a RHEL support account or do they need a support account for a particular workload, application server, or a stack running on, say, OpenShift? Again, this is a long tail problem, so I suspect it'll be a number of years before this is over, but I don't see the operating system market having a long future.

Viktor Farcic: Do you think that it will be replaced with new operating systems like CoreOS, or will it be the do-it-yourself unikernel type?

James Turnbull: I think unikernel is a possibility. With serverless stuff, you don't really care about the underlying hardware, or whether you should run AWS Lambda or Azure, for example. It doesn't really matter whether that's Ubuntu, Fedora, or RHEL – it's not relevant to you. Therefore, I think we'll see things where it's either hidden from the end user because it's a black box to them, because they never need to change anything in it, or it's a segment, a slice of the operating system rather than a whole operating system.

Viktor Farcic: You mentioned serverless. I often hear concerns about people being vendor-locked-in. Do you feel that's a valid concern?

James Turnbull: I mean, that's what those cloud vendors want you to do. They want you to buy all of the pieces of their product and lock you into their ecosystem, so I do think that's a concern.

Over time, we'll see more and more things look like standards, like, to a large extent, a RESTful API, GraphQL API, or a function of some kind where it's very easy to create sort of patterns for. Whether that runs on top of Azure Functions or Lambda, it might just be a bit of deployment functionality rather than changes to the core code of the function itself. I'd be curious, because I haven't written very much outside of Azure and AWS to see if you could write a function that had multiple backends and multiple deployment paths that were essentially identical. I suspect it would be pretty easy.

Viktor Farcic: How about schedulers? I mean, with Kubernetes, I saw 2017 as being more about schedules. Do you think that's over, or are we going to continue seeing multiple solutions? Right now, is Kubernetes the only thing or is there is still Swarm and Mesos?

> *"You still need a reasonable amount of infrastructure-centric knowledge to run Kubernetes, and scheduling is not a trivial tool to build.*
>
> —*James Turnbull*

James Turnbull: I think that's a hard question to answer because I don't think the market has shaken itself out yet. I like Kubernetes, Mesos, and things like Nomad, but I suspect for the vast majority of people, these tools are at the wrong level of abstraction. You still need a reasonable amount of infrastructure-centric knowledge to run Kubernetes, and scheduling is not a trivial tool to build. I think there's a long way to go before you can think about Kubernetes or any of those other orchestration tools as more platform as a service where a developer can just push the workload at a black box like Heroku, and it'll just work.

I think that'll happen as some of the clouds start to roll out tools like the Amazon, Azure, or Google Kubernetes services, where if you take something like Amazon's EC2 Fargate product, where you don't manage the instances anymore, combine that with AKS, their Kubernetes product, and suddenly it's heading very close to a continuous delivery and integration model where I just push container images with some metadata about how many of them, and maybe wired into some metrics or something to scale or shrink them, and then it's fine. I think that's probably where we're going, but I think we're a little way off from that being a realistically useful tool for a vast audience.

Viktor Farcic: Are there any other subjects you would like to discuss or comment upon?

James Turnbull: I think there's a fascinating discussion happening at the moment about the definition of monitoring. Monitoring has traditionally been very infrastructure-centric, where you'd have a machine out there that monitors the CPU and the memory and the disk, and maybe some transactions and error rates.

Today, though, we see two things happening: one, we see much more framework-oriented monitoring; for example, things like Google's four golden signals or Brendan Gregg's USE method, Utilization Saturation and Errors. Then, we are also seeing observability-centric things like tracing and end-to-end analysis of performance. I'm really interested to see what tools will emerge in that space in the next couple of years.

Viktor Farcic: I get the impression that they are not catching up with the increase in services we are running today.

James Turnbull: I agree. I think that it's an aspect of monitoring that has always been a bit of an afterthought or a reactive thing that happens after something goes wrong. I believe we are now starting to see that injected a bit earlier into the development process, so the monitoring, metrics, and exposing metrics can be consumed by health checks, which are happening more often, in which case it'll be super interesting to see what tools and changes in infrastructure emerge out of that.

I think a lot of people still have legacy Nagios installations, and it will be interesting to see what replaces those in the next five years.

Viktor Farcic: Do you think then that tools like Prometheus are already getting there, or we are going to see something even more radically different?

James Turnbull: I think Prometheus is an exciting avenue, for certain types of services like microservices, container-driven applications, and Kubernetes.

However, I'm not necessarily convinced it's a very good fit everywhere. But then again, I don't think any tool is a universal panacea, so I think we'll see a lot more from Prometheus. It has a bright future.

I think we'll also see a lot more of tracing-style tools. In addition, we'll see a second or third wave of SaaS tools. The first wave tools, which were simple things like probing tools where you would connect to a service, and if it returns an HTTP response with a 200 exit code, then it's up, and maybe you sample a little bit of data to confirm that it's doing the right thing. And then in the second and third generations there are things like New Relic and Dynatrace, which were more APM tools.

> *"I think we'll see a lot more from Prometheus. It has a bright future."*
>
> —*James Turnbull*

In the next wave of SaaS services, we'll see a combination, a hybrid of infrastructure-level monitoring, middleware application-level monitoring, performance-level monitoring, transaction-level tracing, and then layered on top some business-level monitoring. I don't know what those tools are yet, but I think there is definitely some interesting stuff that will happen in that space.

Viktor Farcic: Since we talked about Prometheus, it might be worthwhile mentioning that you wrote a book about it. Where can we get it?

James Turnbull: The book is called *Monitoring with Prometheus* (https://prometheusbook.com), and there's a discount code, TALKINGDEVOPS, that'll give the readers 25 percent off.

Viktor Farcic: I think we can agree that the future will be a fascinating space. Thank you.

6

Liz Keogh

Lean and Agile coach
and trainer

Introducing Liz Keogh

A holder of the Gordon Pask Award, given by the Agile Alliance, Liz Keogh specializes in Cynefin, and putting Agile at Scale in context. Liz embraces the many risks inherent in software delivery, driving collaboration and transparency between teams. You can follow her on Twitter at @lunivore.

Viktor Farcic: I want to start by asking what exactly do we mean when we say DevOps? I was also wondering though if you could touch upon the relationship, if there is one, between DevOps and Agile.

The relationship between DevOps and Agile

Liz Keogh: DevOps used to be when you did Agile with a small team; back then, it was just developers in small, cross-functional teams who were writing code directly for the customers. The customers would give the DevOps team their requirements; the developers would then develop the code and give it back to the customers. Now you've got much larger enterprise organizations where operations is a separate department, and possibly even a separate company within the larger group, and yet you still want to ship stuff. I always say that DevOps is a good start.

> *"DevOps used to be when you did Agile with a small team; back then, it was just developers in small, cross-functional teams who were writing code directly for the customers."*
>
> —Liz Keogh

Agile generally starts with the development teams. You've likely got some business analyst types, testers, and developers all writing the code, and then they think they're done. Except they're not done, because they still haven't actually shipped the product yet. Operations is the next stage of that.

The way you engage with your customers hasn't really changed, but if you can actually get to the point where you can ship stuff reliably to the customer and get feedback from people on how it's going, then you're doing well. It's the difference between changing direction within the team and actually changing direction with whatever you put out there. I'm personally a massive fan of the Agile Fluency Model.

Viktor Farcic: Does that mean that Agile somehow excluded operations, or is that why DevOps was not Agile?

Liz Keogh: I don't know quite what's happened, except that Agile has generally always been a development-focused thing. The Scrum framework talks about cross-functional teams, but I guess it's because of the nature of enterprise that we've always put things into these horizontally sliced departments within both large-scale enterprises, and even some small-scale companies who've got their little fledgling departments.

As soon as you compartmentalize, you've created a gap between development and operations that needs to be bridged.

When I was working with ThoughtWorks, a community of individuals whose purpose was to revolutionize software design, creation, and delivery, I had rudimentary Linux admin skills, and I mean *really* rudimentary. I actually started as a sysadmin, but it was within Windows in 1998, so it wasn't as though much advanced skill was necessary. But now you look at all the specialist skills required to get stuff shipped, plus what it takes to make things maintainable and to be able to monitor things, to be able to back them up, and all the rest of the things you need, and it's generally beyond my skills as a developer.

Nowadays, you've got Puppet, Chef, Docker, and Kubernetes; these are all tools I've never even touched because they've come along in the time since I've stepped away from doing hands-on development. I only tend to do hands-on development as part of my consulting work now, but you look at these specialist skills that they've got and it's really tempting to say, "Okay, well, that's your bit—we'll do our bit as development, and then we'll give it to you, and you'll ship it for us, and that'll be great."

When you actually look at what's needed to make something reliable, and maintainable, and to stop those people having phone calls at 4:00 a.m. because something you wrote as a developer broke, then there's a ton of things that you can do to help each other. Operations can talk to developers about what they need, and developers can speak with operations about what they're going to do to help. That's really what DevOps is: adults talking to each other and working together.

I've spoken to people in enterprises who say, "I can't do DevOps because operations is a separate department." But if you're reporting a bug in production, all you need to do is put your name on the bug report, and you've started off well: you're in operations.

If you're a developer, you just have to say, "Hey, if you have any problems with this bit of code, come and talk to me—don't just write a report, we're up here, why don't you come and talk to the team, and we'll help you fix it?" It's that attitude to shipping software. That's what DevOps really is: an attitude change and the building up of a relationship.

> *"That's what DevOps really is: an attitude change and the building up of a relationship."*
>
> —Liz Keogh

Viktor Farcic: That's a brilliant point. It's as if you went back in time and replaced the word "Ops" with "a tester of the problems we're trying to solve with Agile." Those guys don't speak to each other; they live in different departments.

Liz Keogh: Exactly!

Viktor Farcic: I've heard you speak quite frequently about the Cynefin framework. Could you explain what it is?

The Cynefin framework

Liz Keogh: The Cynefin framework is very much about making sense of different situations and how you approach them. For that reason, it's called a "sense-making device." Think of it this way: there are five ordered domains – simple (or obvious), complicated, complex, chaotic, and disorder. The boundaries between them are fuzzy. In the simple, or obvious, domain, problems are easily solved because the solutions are obviously apparent and easily categorized.

Take a landlady in the pub. I say, "What do you do when the beer runs out?" She responds by saying, "Well, I change the barrel, obviously."

When problems enter the complicated domain, they require expertise. A watchmaker can fix your watch, a car mechanic can fix your car, and that's great—both of those have predictable outcomes. In the complicated domain, problems can be analyzed and solved only if you've got the relevant expertise.

The problem is that human beings crave certainty. We want predictability. We like knowing what's going to happen next. In all of our evolutionary experience, unpredictable things typically spell disaster, and that's chaotic, which, within the Cynefin framework, puts us in the chaotic domain. Chaos is accident and emergency, it's your house burning down, it's people bleeding to death. Chaos is a transient domain, however, which means it resolves itself really quickly. It doesn't like to stick around for long, but, unfortunately, it might not resolve itself in your favor. Chaos is also the domain of urgent opportunity, but it's normally a really bad place to be, and that's the problem, because there's a bunch of stuff that isn't predictable, or chaotic either. And this is the complex domain within which a lot of software development takes place.

We have to allow things to emerge. We know where we've got to when we look back with hindsight. This is called "correlated in retrospect." You can see where you've got to, but you couldn't have predicted the outcome. Anybody on Agile projects working in combination with the business, getting their feedback and changing direction, will be experienced with that, to an extent. Take, for example, the fact that you're working in a very high-uncertainty environment. You're doing product development or creating new products. One of the things that Toyota frequently does, for instance, is concurrent set-based engineering. They'll try three different types of engines at the same time, and from that, they work out which aspects of their engine they want to settle on for that new car. The complexity thinkers, or particularly the Cynefin thinkers, call these "parallel probes."

Viktor Farcic: Could you explain what a probe is and how it relates to DevOps? I mean, how does this fold into the world that we live in today?

Liz Keogh: A probe is something that's safe to fail. As you get more and more innovative, you'll get higher and higher levels of uncertainty in what you're doing. Your variance increases, as do the chances of getting something wrong. You're guaranteed to make discoveries, though you won't make them in the safety of the team anymore. Many of these discoveries will take place in production, and you can't help it because things are so new and unpredictable.

> *"I regard DevOps as absolutely essential for innovation, at scale certainly."*
>
> —*Liz Keogh*

What you need to be able to do then is to change direction really, really quickly, and this is where my focus in DevOps is. A lot of people think of DevOps as a path to predictability rather than a safety net that allows you to do unpredictable, high-discovery things. I regard DevOps as absolutely essential for innovation, at scale certainly.

You need to have those automated tests, like the probes, not just because they're catching things, but because they provide living documentation and they keep the code easy to change. What's probably more important is that you want monitoring in place; you really want great relationships with operations, so that when those discoveries do come along, and when you do have a bug in production, and something does go haywire, you can spot it really quickly and you can roll back. This is where this idea of phoenix servers comes from, where you can release these bugs to one server, see how it goes, and if it doesn't work, you just trash your server. This is where the world is going now, where we can actually just play and see what's happening out there. We're used to playing as children in safe-to-fail places; this is how we learn as kids. Now we're kids in the playground of production, and it's still important that it's safe to fail out there. That's why I love DevOps so much.

> *"It's still important that it's safe to fail out there. That's why I love DevOps so much."*
>
> —*Liz Keogh*

Viktor Farcic: DevOps kind of allows you to deploy to production and fail fast. Effectively, you're validated in production instead of in a testing environment.

Liz Keogh: The thing is, there's a balance between getting it right and making it okay to get it wrong. I always say if it's something that's reasonable for you to predict, then you should probably try and get it right. As an example, you should use a production-like environment where you can run your tests using production-like data.

You won't be able to do it for everything unless you're actually going to have exactly the same customer base, data, and software landscape, which you never do; then you're going to end up testing some stuff in production. There's no way around that, so then you've got to have really good stuff in place to spot when it goes wrong.

Viktor Farcic: You would then have to have exactly the same users as well if we follow the same logic, no?

Liz Keogh: Exactly!

Behavior-driven development (BDD)

Viktor Farcic: You're big on BDD. Can you explain to us, for those who may not know, what it is?

Liz Keogh: BDD came about as a replacement for test-driven development (TDD). TDD wasn't really about testing, because anyone who's done TDD would say that you wrote the test before there was even any code. Essentially, you're not really testing anything; you're describing how the code you're about to write is going to work, why it's going to be valuable to you, while coming up with some examples of how you want to use it.

When we actually start thinking of them as just examples

of behavior, that's class-level behavior. You would say, "Here's an example of how my class behaves." But then you've got your system: "Here's an example of how my system behaves, here's an example of my application in use," and we call those scenarios. It's the same. You take your scenarios, and now you've got an example of how you think your system is going to work.

When things are predictable, they require expertise, and having the conversation around those scenarios is a really great way of gathering that expertise yourself and picking up a language that people want to use around it so that you all have a common language, which they call a ubiquitous language. When things are really uncertain, those scenarios provide what we call coherence, so it's a realistic reason for thinking that what you're about to do is a good idea. You might decide that that example doesn't quite match what you're thinking, or it might turn out that customers don't quite want to use it that way, and then you'll have to change your scenario. The more uncertain you get, the more important it is to have the conversations that just explore, and the less important it is to put the automation around them, because automation is a commitment, and if you're committing to stuff that's changing, it's an over-investment on your end.

You want to commit as little as possible until you reckon you have a good understanding of the problem that you're trying to solve, and then when you understand the problem, you can start writing those scenarios, automating them, and having a stab at what you think the solution ought to look like. But sometimes it takes learning by doing, and you actually have to try something out and then you understand it.

There's a lot of spiking and prototyping these days compared to when I started doing software development.

Viktor Farcic: I'm guessing you started on Waterfall. Could you take us through your experience with that?

> *"There's a lot of spiking and prototyping these days compared to when I started doing software development."*
>
> —Liz Keogh

Liz Keogh: So, yes, when I started, I was on a Waterfall project, and we had three years' worth of development, and I believe before that, there was a year and a half's worth of analysis. I was in a basement for three years working on this thing, and we did not ship at all in those three years, but now we're able to ship. Diana Larsen and James Shore, the people behind the Agile Fluency Model, call it to release at will. In this model, you're able to release when you want to if you get this stuff right, which means you can change direction really, really quickly. This also means that spiking and prototyping is probably more important than it used to be, while automating is actually less important, though the conversations you have are still important.

These conversations around those scenarios—around what you think this might do for people, how they might use it, what other stakeholders need to be considered and how it's going to work for them, what other outcomes we need, and what contexts are going to be in and out of scope—are still really crucial, while also being very lightweight. They don't take long to have.

I always recommend starting with the conversations and only moving to the tools when you've gotten really good at having those conversations. It only takes about a month to retrofit scenarios around a small code base while you're still developing it; obviously, it's not a month of full-time work. If you started with the tools, put them down and then have some conversations. You'll come back having a better understanding once you've had those conversations around the scenarios.

Viktor Farcic: If we're inviting operations to the party, does it mean that BDD is extending in that direction as well?

Liz Keogh: A little bit, but you're still going to want to talk through examples of the kinds of things they want. Generally, their examples will focus on monitoring; it will be, "What if we have a bug like this? What should we do?" They're going to be examples of how you want to use that relationship.

The best conversations I've had are not about what the software should be but rather how we as teams are going to work together to quickly solve any potential issues that might come up after the software's release. It's the human aspect that I really enjoy. This is where the complexity stuff—Cynefin— really comes into play, because human systems are what we call complex adaptive systems. They're systems in which the agents of the system can change the system itself.

While you might be able to look at the behavior of software and go, "Okay, that's relatively predictable," as soon as you've got two groups of people working together, you'll need to be a bit more forgiving and a little more mindful of how that relationship is building, what's going on with it, what's not working, and how you fix what's not working.

I really like it when the conversations and the scenarios switch from how the software is going to behave to how we're going to behave as human beings. Having said that, if you've been diligent in how you monitor things, you'll have examples of the kinds of thresholds at which you're going to trigger your monitoring, and can ask questions about what it's going to look like: "Are you going to email me or am I going to get a notification on my pager?" You can have those conversations as well, but BDD isn't the only way to develop software, and it's certainly not the only way to test things. There are tons of great testing practices that have nothing whatsoever to do with BDD. When people think of testing and BDD synonymously, they miss out on all the other things that testers do.

I love my testers because they make it safe for me to fail. I think it's the inherent nature of humans to pick one thing and then go with it. For example, I adopted BDD, and it used to be BDD and nothing else. The same thing happened for almost everything else; everything needs to be a container today.

Viktor Farcic: How about the relationship between Agile and DevOps? What are your thoughts on that? Does DevOps replace Agile? Does it complement it, or is it conflicting?

Liz Keogh: Agile is just an anchor term to help people look up different practices, knowledge, experience, stories, and to find a community. They're all related.

Is DevOps part of that? It's definitely related to it, and

if you've got a cross-functional team, then yes, absolutely, it's related to it. I'm a massive Kanban fan, and when we do Kanban, we start from where we are right at this moment. I've got people doing Kanban just in the testing phase of big Waterfall projects, so you don't need that cross-functional team anymore, and the advantage to that is that you can just start wherever you are. You don't need to rearrange the structure of the organization or worry about the line management; you can just start improving.

The way you do this is to look at the value stream and see where the parts are that you can improve. The big obvious one is development and operations working together. Your development team, which is probably cross-functional, and then your operations team. You want them working better, and you want them handing over more smoothly; that's the ideal situation. Even if they're a separate organization, or even if they are a completely separate department and they've got different line management or different KPIs, they can still work together.

> *"The way you do this [start improving] is to look at the value stream and to see where the parts are that you can improve. The big obvious one is development and operations working together."*
>
> —*Liz Keogh*

Consulting with Agile or DevOps

Viktor Farcic: When you consult for companies with Agile or DevOps, do you have a prescriptive type of approach? For instance, thou shalt do Scrum!

Liz Keogh: Thou shalt learn Cynefin because it's pretty much the first thing I teach. After that, if you want to start with Scrum, go ahead. I think Scrum is a great way to get started, especially if it's a new project and you don't have anything in play already.

Typically, large organizations have already done a bunch of analysis work. We talk about how great it would be if we had this flexible scope, but most organizations have already done three months' worth of UX research and analysis, and it tends to constrain things. So, let's slice it up vertically; let's work out what the most important bits are and deliver those first—where are the risky bits, where are the highest-uncertainty bits, and where's the new stuff?

Let's do those first and do it early. Let's spike it out and see what it looks like, and then see what it would actually take to ship this. What else do we need to get this new thing that you're really interested in live, but also, what's the smallest way we can actually deliver that?

Somebody on Twitter asked for a different term for minimum viable product (MVP), and I told them it means no smaller than the minimum functionality that you can ship because I'm yet to meet anybody aggressive enough that's actually shipping something valuable fast. You can ship really small things and learn a lot from them, or at least get them into a state where you could just click a button and ship them. I've had people say, "Oh, but, you know, we're not allowed to change our databases in production." Well, great, change them in your own environment and then provide the scripts to operations.

There are ways of managing this, and there are things that

operations need: there are places where they're having pain. I spoke to one team, and they'd been up until 4:00 a.m. fixing bugs, trying to work out why things were falling over, and desperately trying to get releases out. When there are five teams all trying to release at the same time, these poor people are not happy. There's a lot that we can do to make them happy as developers, and all I want to see is us reaching out going, "Hey, how do we avoid you being woken up at 4:00 a.m. again?"

There are some people who are really big fans of giving pagers to the actual developers and making them wake up at 4:00 a.m.—I don't really have the experience to deal with things at 4:00 a.m. and I wouldn't have a clue where to start, but just having the conversation around what it would take so that you didn't have to wake people up at 4:00 a.m., and what you can do to help—that would be nice.

Viktor Farcic: Indeed. Judging from what you've said so far, you seem to put a much bigger emphasis on transforming or improving the people and culture rather than relying on the tools.

Liz Keogh: This is about delivering software, and it turns out that focusing on people is the best way to do that. I don't want people to think I'm fluffy; I'm not interested in people for people's sake.

> *"This is about delivering software, and it turns out that focusing on people is the best way to do that."*
>
> —*Liz Keogh*

When I'm talking to enterprises and organizations, my focus is on delivering, and getting people to work together is part of delivering. It turns out that all the things that you reckon make a really great workplace—that motivate people and result in having some fun at work—are also the things that help delivery. If you focus on delivery, you'll end up doing the right thing by the people anyway. You can use it as a nice test; if you're finding that yelling at people is the way you're getting things done, then there's probably something wrong with your process.

Viktor Farcic: When you try to help organizations improve, how do you make certain predictions about how they'll behave?

Liz Keogh: Some things will be fiercely resisted. When that happens, don't worry about it; try something else. There will always be some things that you can change, and if you find the things that you can change—this is the heart of Cynefin and of what probing really means—focus on that and on the people who can help you effect that change. Don't worry about that which is out of your control.

If you find one person who's managed to get BDD working in a project, now you know there's organizational support for BDD. If you find that one person has also managed to have a conversation with somebody over in operations, you can get those two people to do a presentation on what they learned together. Anything you find that works toward positive change, support it, amplify it, jump on it, and make a big deal of it, because every little bit of positive change buys some room for positive change elsewhere, until one day you find that the bits that were resistant are now no longer, and everybody's cloud-based, and you're not even sure how that happened.

I spend most of my time now as a consultant just wandering around going, "Wow, that's awesome," and then asking how we do it more, how we do it bigger, and how we do it elsewhere, while spreading those good stories.

Viktor Farcic: Are there certain types of expertise, experts, or departments that are more defensive, or others that are easier to work with, or do you find it to be more or less on the same ground everywhere?

Liz Keogh: It depends on the organization. Every organization has their tribes. If you read *Great Boss Dead Boss*, by Ray Immelman, you'll learn about tribal behavior and organizations. I found it so absolutely true that anywhere where you see a tribe being threatened, that tribe has strengthened their borders.

I've had one situation where backend developers were learning to do a bit of UI work, and the UI developers strengthened their borders. In fact, I've seen this in about three different places now where UI developers strengthened the borders of their tribe. Now, for me at ThoughtWorks, that would be completely bizarre because I was a frontend developer working on Swing and desktop apps. I only did a bit of web, but I knew how to write some HTML, CSS, and some basic JavaScript.

I could correct a typo and change a color, but the idea that it's somebody else's domain seems so strange to me. But when you find that people feel threatened, and they feel like their expertise is being devalued, and then they'll strengthen the borders of their little tribe, and suddenly you've got, "UI developers are more awesome than backend developers," and you've got a schism within your organization. The trick is to make your internal tribes feel valued and secure.

You want development and operations to both feel like they can work together because they're both skilled professionals, and they both have deep experience. With DevOps, all you're doing is bridging those two groups; you're not tearing them apart, you're not chucking everybody into cross-functional teams because every team must have an operations person in it. This is one of the reasons why I think Kanban works better than Scrum in some situations and certainly when you're dealing with enterprises. You want to be mindful and respectful of those groups; you don't want the organization as a whole to feel threatened.

This is where John Kotter's sense of urgency really comes in. In his talks, Kotter discusses the need for creating a sense of urgency around your competition. He talks about how hard it is to go up against Amazon, Google, or Facebook. He also discusses how your threats are not coming from inside your organization, but outside of it. What you want is for everybody within your organization to be working together against the external threats and not against each other.

> *"You want development and operations to both feel like they can work together because they're both skilled professionals, and they both have deep experience. With DevOps, all you're doing is bridging those two groups; you're not tearing them apart."*
>
> —Liz Keogh

Viktor Farcic: I love that. I might be mistaken, but I remember once hearing you say that there's more to delivery than development and operations. What did you mean by that?

Liz Keogh: When I look at an end-to-end value stream in an enterprise situation, what I usually do is say, "Okay, let's put the development team in the middle."

The customers have a need, or maybe some customer representative has an idea about how to help them and how to make things better, or maybe even some stakeholder has something they want, who gets between them and the development team. Can they just go to a development team and say, "Hey could you do this for me?" Probably not, because there's going to be some level of prioritization.

I've worked for companies in the past where you wasted precious time jumping through various interdepartmental hoops to either get funding or be allowed to get a project off the ground or to move on to the next phase. You'd be getting your team of developers together while waiting for various board approvals. Six months could pass by before the developers even got a sniff at the code, and then on the way out—and this is typically what we see from Agile—by the time we get hold of the project, all of the previous work had already been done.

The reality is that there are all kinds of people who get between your development team and actually releasing something. If you've got a low-trust business who are not exactly used to getting what they want from IT, you've probably got some user acceptance testing group somewhere as well who are going to test the hell out of your software.

What I tend to do as a consultant is draw this on the board, and I say value streams are made of people. I identify all the different groups of people involved in getting something live, and then I get the person who brought me in to draw a dotted line around their area of influence.

Viktor Farcic: Getting people involved seems like a great way to make organizations aware, but surely implementing this between multiple teams and getting them to make the actual change takes a long time.

Liz Keogh: What I usually find if I'm being brought in for DevOps is that it doesn't go as far as operations. There's a bunch of other groups for whom it doesn't go that far as well, and usually operations is about 10 different teams that don't talk to each other. There will be one team for pen testing, another for monitoring, another for analytics, and yet another team for support.

You're going to end up being the people who bring those groups together as well, so, Dev and Ops: great start. If you can get those teams working together, you'll start finding that your portfolio and your governance needs to be addressed.

Now you also start finding your funding model, and then finally you'll get the business on board, and the business will go, "Hold on—if we can do these small things now, can we just do this experiment? Can we just do this one small thing?"

Then you're innovating, which is a point that it takes years for a large organization to even get to. I think that sometimes when people bring in things like the Scaled Agile Framework and large-scale Scrum and impose them on an organization and restructure everything, the habits of a lifetime are still there and the stories being told are still the same stories. You don't change the stories just by restructuring things; you change the stories by creating great relationships. And yes, Dev and Ops is a good start for that, but it is only a start.

> *"A good DevOps culture makes things safe to fail."*
>
> —*Liz Keogh*

Viktor Farcic: You mentioned innovation. How do you foster that? When I visit companies, I always get the same response: "We would like to do this and we would like to try that, but we don't have time."

Fostering innovation

Liz Keogh: There's a couple of things you can do: one is to make sure things are safe to fail. If it's not safe to fail, nobody's going to try anything that might fail, and so DevOps, at least a good DevOps culture, makes things safe to fail. If you can't get innovation, focus on how we make sure it's safe to fail, how we get good quality in production, how we get the things that you can get right *right*, and then make sure it's okay to get things wrong.

You can focus on continuous delivery and then continuous deployment, and that's great—get your phoenix servers up and running. Then there's the other thing you can do. There's a thing called the shallow dive into chaos, which Cognitive Edge teaches as part of their Cynefin training. It involves taking people and splitting them up so that you get a divergence of ideas, and the idea, like chaos, is to create an urgent opportunity, but it's also a place where you have nothing to lose. When you can't talk to other people, the ideas you come up with on your own tend to be crazier than the ideas that you come up with if you're in a group. When people are in groups, they want consensus. I actually spend a bit of time splitting up consensus cultures.

You need to make it safe to fail and then create a forgiving system where you have permission to try things. You do that by getting people to try things on their own or in very small groups, so that it doesn't matter if there's a bit of rework and duplication. Usually, the cost of delay eclipses the cost of rework, and I think a lot of people don't see that. People don't see how quickly they could move if you weren't waiting for everybody to agree on what the right thing to do is. So, you need to make it okay to do the wrong thing.

Viktor Farcic: Does anybody stand out to you in this situation, where they say it's okay to do the wrong thing?

Liz Keogh: Chris Matts does. He started the Real Options movement, and he's my guru for real options. He says that if you're faced with two different situations, and you're not sure which is the right one, rather than doing a whole bunch of analysis that doesn't work in complexity, pick the one that's easiest to change. If it turns out to be wrong, you can change it. But if it turns out to be right, then that's great.

It's that kind of thinking. It's about how we move forward without having to go to absolutely everybody else in the organization and pick their brains for what they think is the right thing. And again, once you get started with that, and once people realize that it's safe to do that and you start supporting them, and you start going around saying, "Wow that's awesome," other people will want to try things too, and you start building a culture where people will try things out and do the right thing as well.

Viktor Farcic: If I understood correctly, delivery is a team effort, but innovation is more individual?

Liz Keogh: Coming up with the ideas is certainly individual or small team-based. There's actually a great talk by Jabe Bloom called *The Value of Social Capital*, in which he refers to Ronald S. Burt's structural holes. The holes where people aren't connected is where innovation comes from. Everybody is too over-connected, and you get massive stability, but you can't try new things, so you have to shake it up—for instance, getting individual development groups to try things. If you want to move to Git, don't agree to move to Git as an organization; get one small team to try it out, and they can tell you whether or not it's worthwhile.

If you want to try a particular BDD tool, get two teams to try two different tools. You might end up having to rewrite one of them, or use two different tools for a few years until one of them dies out, but it's better than not moving, and it's better than six months of analysis to see whether it will work. Instead, you learn by doing. So, do some stuff. Fostering that culture is how you foster innovation.

Viktor Farcic: We've spoken quite a lot about including people and fostering collaboration, so I wanted to ask you why there aren't more women in the field.

Diversity, gender roles, and representation in DevOps

Liz Keogh: You know, I'm not the right person to ask. Every time somebody asks me what the difference is between a team with a woman on it and a team without one, I say I don't know because I've never been on a team without a woman on it. I'm not an expert; being a woman does not make me an expert on what it's like to be a woman in development—I couldn't possibly tell you. I do know that nobody told me I wasn't supposed to be there.

I started programming when I was seven years old because my dad left the BBC computer lying around with the manual, which was illustrated with beautiful colored robots. It was deliberately marketed to kids. So, I had an early start. For almost as long as I can remember, I had computers, and I think maybe that's the secret: it's just making sure that you're supporting girls as they come up through school, and making sure they have a role model as well. That's one of the things I've taken on board.

I always hated being the token female. Everybody says how they want more female speakers. But my response to that is, "How about you just get me because I'm really good at talking about DevOps and Cynefin or something? But no, you want a female speaker." It took me a long time to realize that having a female role model is actually important to girls, and to young women coming into the industry as well. However, I've taken that on board somewhat reluctantly, as I don't really want to be a speaker for quality and gender diversity.

> *"How about you just get me because I'm really good at talking about DevOps and Cynefin or something? But no, you want a female speaker. It took me a long time to realize that having a female role model is actually important to girls, and to young women coming into the industry as well."*
>
> —*Liz Keogh*

I want to be a speaker for Cynefin and BDD, but sometimes the gender diversity stuff, the sexism, and the sexual harassment becomes a thing because all of that stuff gets in the way. So, then I have to be a speaker about that as well. But it's not what I want to be speaking about. My passion is delivering software and doing it as a woman, but that means I've had to talk about these other issues too.

The difference between the self-taught engineer and the schooled engineer of today

Viktor Farcic: Switching gears, you mentioned that you started with computers when you were seven. Do you have any thoughts about the difference between the self-taught engineers or schooled engineers of today? More broadly speaking, how do you see education in today's world?

Liz Keogh: I didn't know what I didn't know. Back then, I was a little bit more disciplined than a hacker. I have a fairly ordered mind when it comes to programming, so I got taught how to test my software, and I very quickly realized I was second-guessing myself if I wrote the tests afterward. At first, I was writing the tests around empty interfaces, and just making them compile, which, of course, is a lot like TDD now. There were no IDEs back when I started professional coding. We were all working in whatever text editors we had. I think it was Vi or Emacs or something like that, and you compiled on the command line.

IDEs didn't exist, I didn't know about things like design patterns, and I definitely didn't know about domain-driven design. I didn't know there were communities out there where you could learn, and the internet was fledgling. It was 1998 when I graduated, so the internet was still in its infancy; companies didn't all have domain names, and they didn't have addresses.

Viktor Farcic: But that's all changed in the 20 years since then—the internet has exploded.

Liz Keogh: Exactly. Now the internet is everything, and you've got access to so much more information, and so much more around what good programming could look like. I've got some friends who are working in academia, and as part of their academia, they program, and by and large, they still haven't caught up with modern programming practices. They're not learning TDD or BDD, or about DevOps. But they know those things exist. All you need to do is reach out because there are people who will help you.

For instance, Stack Overflow and the Stack Exchange network is fantastic, and it's not even just true of developers and operations, or Dev and Ops; it's true of anybody in a leadership position. There's a PM Stack Exchange, places where you can learn about psychology. Wikipedia is phenomenal because there's so much free information on there. I used to have to go to a library and check out a book when I was at school, but you don't have to do that anymore. You've got the whole of human knowledge on tap, and all it takes is finding out what it is that you don't know, and what of that you want to know, because there's more than you can possibly learn in a lifetime.

Viktor Farcic: How do you know what you don't know? I think that that might be the problem, because if I've never heard about BDD, how do I know that I don't know about it? I'm inventing an example.

> *"You've got the whole of human knowledge on tap, and all it takes is finding out what it is that you don't know, and what of that you want to know, because there's more than you can possibly learn in a lifetime."*
>
> —Liz Keogh

Liz Keogh: You find somebody who is working in the space that you want to be working in, and you ask them, "What is it that I don't know? Where would you start?" If you're working in a new place and you don't have access to expertise, you learn by trying it out. I was there pretty much very early on in BDD, and I worked on the story of JBehave, which was the first English system-level BDD natural language tool. We learned by trying. JBehave 1.0 was not usable, nobody ever used it.

I very recently tweeted a blog by David Chelimsky, in which he took the Ruby version of JBehave that was written as RSpec Story Runner and converted it to plain text. That's obviously the precursor for Cucumber, JBehave 2, and all of the English language tools that followed. In that case, you learn by doing, and it's okay to get it wrong. It's okay to create something that nobody uses because maybe it will lead to something that people do use.

Viktor Farcic: To close this up, I'm going to ask you a question that I hate being asked. What do you see in the future?

The future

Liz Keogh: Mars. I want to go to Mars. I would love to see the human race on Mars, and I know Elon Musk is still chasing that.

So, what do I think we're going to see? I think we're going to see more cars in space, and more large-scale experimentation where it's safe to fail. I think that the future is going to be really exciting. I think companies are going to be held a little bit more accountable for their ethics, which means no more behavior like Uber, and no more Volkswagen emission scandals. That being said, I want to see transparency in organizations. I think that we're going to see some of the large banks dying off, and I genuinely think that you're going to start seeing mergers as banks die.

There's no way that people with money will support the level of waste that I see in some of the big enterprises. Capitalism will result in those things merging together, and I'm really, really hoping that that happens in a good way. I think that there's probably some space to make it happen in a good way, to make investment more transparent, to make the world a better place. I think we're probably going to see an economic crash in the next five years just because the wealth is so concentrated and it's such a level of concentration that human society just resists that.

In the last year or so I've also had a chance to look at the IPCC report on climate change. That's less exciting but more urgent. So right now, my focus is on that. I'm still hopeful that companies will step up to deal with it; that we'll see new emerging technologies that will help too. It's going to be hard, but there's a lot we can do from our end.

Viktor Farcic: So, you think that there's going to be a big blowout in the next few years?

Liz Keogh: I think when you have a sense of urgency, you have chaos. It buys you a lot of space for innovation and a lot of space for trying things out, because you have nothing to lose.

I have a feeling we're going to see some really exciting things in the next 10 years. We've got blockchain, we've got a bunch of new tools coming into play, we've got great DevOps practices, and we've got a whole open source ecosystem available that did not exist when I started programming. Java was free, and that was about it. I've been in IT for 20 years now, and I've seen so many changes already. I think the next 20 years is going to be even bigger than that. In another 20 years' time, I don't think the world's going to be recognizable from what I knew 20 years ago.

Viktor Farcic: Do you think then that the traditional, slow-moving, rigid enterprises will survive that future?

> *"In another 20 years' time, I don't think the world's going to be recognizable from what I knew 20 years ago."*
>
> —Liz Keogh

Liz Keogh: They'll survive the commoditized stuff, and stuff that's really boring and very, very predictable, but the way people provide electricity and provide water—there won't be a lot of money in it. Simon Wardley says it with respect to his mapping; everything moves to the right. You see it with Cynefin as well, and everything moves clockwise. It becomes stable, and then you build on the stable stuff. Everything's going to be stabilizing, so the innovative stuff that we're used to seeing right now—we think of DevOps as being innovative—it's going to be just the way that software is done. People will ask, "Why would you do it any other way?"

You'll have DevOps out of the box; you'll have Google servers that will be really cheap, and so why wouldn't you use them? Nobody's going to have their own infrastructure. If you build your own infrastructure and you're not working with Google, Facebook, or some other large company, people will be asking, "What are you doing? Are you genuinely configuring a server by hand? Why would you do that?" It will be that level of crazy. We're not there yet, but we will be.

Viktor Farcic: I might be a bit more skeptical than that, because I have the impression that when I go and visit enterprises, I get answers along the lines of, "We're all Agile," and then you spend the day with them and you realize, they've only just started Agile.

Liz Keogh: Try not using the word Agile. I don't use the word Agile when I do my consulting; I focus on delivery and talk about uncertainty and predictability and things like that. I focus on the awesome.

When you do see something moving—when you do see something really great—focus on that, spread it, and tell stories. Encourage other people to tell stories, because stories have power and are a really great way of getting change working.

Viktor Farcic: Is there anything else that you would like to share?

Liz Keogh: Somebody once asked me what my favorite thing and worst thing about working in software development was. I said the worst thing was the human tendency to see patterns in uncertainty that don't exist, and then move forward getting things wrong. The best thing is the human ability to see patterns in uncertainty that don't exist so they can move forward. Those two things go hand in hand. So, the same things that trip us up are the things that allow us to move forward, and I think it's worth just celebrating that.

7

Julian Simpson

Global Security and Platforms Manager, Fuel50

Introducing Julian Simpson

Julian Simpson worked at Neo4j until August 2018, where he helped deliver projects across both DevOps and continuous delivery. In August 2018, Julian moved to Fuel50, where he's now a Global Security and Platforms manager with a focus on building out the company's platform. Julian is also an organizer at DevOpsDaysNZ. You can follow him on Twitter at @builddoctor.

Defining DevOps

Viktor Farcic: I want to start by asking you a two-fold question. First, how would you define DevOps, and then how has that definition played out in your career?

Julian Simpson: I used to be a Unix systems administrator. In that role, I spent a lot of time during the dot-com boom building Solaris servers and arguing with developers. This conflict between system administrators and developers carried on for the next three to four years of my career.

During this time, two things became obvious to me. Firstly, the approach of building systems by hand seemed wrong, and secondly, it really seemed counterproductive to handle this conflict. While I can be sucked into a good fight, it didn't seem like a positive way to go about things. Eventually, in 2002, I discovered the CFEngine project and started building all my systems with CFEngine, in order to rebuild those builds.

This was combined with Solaris Jumpstart, which was an awesome technology to have at the time, because from the hardware point of view, I could just build a machine anytime I wanted to. I could also iterate over builds and store that source in version control, practices that evolved into DevOps. An important thing to add is that I discovered the Agile movement in 2004; I consider the DevOps movement to have evolved as a natural progression of the Agile movement.

> *"I consider the DevOps movement to have evolved as a natural progression of the Agile movement."*
>
> —*Julian Simpson*

Viktor Farcic: That's how I typically describe it too. While I agree that DevOps is an evolution of Agile, the conflicts you described are something that I see today between developers, QA, security and everybody else involved. What do you think are the causes of those conflicts?

Julian Simpson: I think it's all about structural conflict within organizations. To me, it seems insane that, as an industry, we set up teams that have conflicting goals and then expect them to resolve the conflict as if it's something about them rather than the game they've been asked to play. You're keeping the system secure, up, and available, and your job is to deliver it as fast as you possibly can.

I don't know if it's just folk wisdom or whether there's actual research we can rely on, but it seems that there are a lot of teams out there that go out of their way to deliver the wrong thing very quickly, but at the cost of security or availability. If all those things are causing you to sweat, then actually working together on the details of what features to deliver in a project and giving the entire team the incentive to deliver it securely and in such a way that you can keep it available, to me, seems like an obvious way to go about things.

The difference between DevOps and Agile

Viktor Farcic: Let's talk more about the evolution from Agile to DevOps. What exactly did you mean by that?

Julian Simpson: I came to the Agile movement reasonably late in its development. I wasn't around to see some of the earlier Agile projects, but my understanding is that we solved some of the problems of how we know what to build and how we should go about planning and delivering the build in an iterative fashion. Once you've solved that problem, there are engineering challenges, such as integration. There's no excuse for having a huge merge phase at the end of your project now because continuous integration has been a thing since at least the late 1990s.

> *"DevOps is the response to solving problems that you have when you're successful in the earlier stages of your project's evolution."*
>
> —*Julian Simpson*

You'll find other problems that you didn't have originally because you probably weren't succeeding anyway. I've only just tried to phrase this now, but maybe DevOps is the response to solving problems that you have when you're successful in the earlier stages of your project's evolution?

If you're getting better at writing both the correct and the most appropriate software at the time and deploying it, suddenly you have all these other operational considerations to think of. To me, if you have a deployment problem, it's probably a good problem to have.

Viktor Farcic: Exactly, and it changes if part of your pipeline suddenly becomes much faster. Then, as you said, you encounter the problem on the next page.

Julian Simpson: I'm a big fan of the theory of constraints, so that absolutely rings true. I believe that you need to optimize across the entire value chain rather than optimizing based on cost, which is what a lot of projects do.

Viktor Farcic: Cost per department, to make it even more complicated.

Julian Simpson: Exactly. I've worked on several projects for consultancies where the departmental politics didn't come into it so much as just the day rates of all these developers, which were obvious to the project managers. So, they would optimize for developer utilization rather than anything else.

Viktor Farcic: Something like an optimization Excel sheet, when you change two numbers and then suddenly, you're more optimized.

Julian Simpson: I saw that on projects where it was entirely feasible for the developers to run all the acceptance tests on their development systems. I think they should have been doing it at the time because we had a huge Continuous Integration (CI) and QA bottleneck, so the sensible thing to do would be for each pair to run those tests before they pushed, thereby easing up on the bottleneck later. This was a very hard message to get across to project managers.

Viktor Farcic: I recently discovered that you go by the name of The Build Doctor? How did you get that name?

Julian Simpson: I had a little niche between 2004 and 2008 where I would fix people's Ant builds. At the time, I was very proficient with Apache Ant, to the point that I'd written an article in a book about refactoring Ant build files. The tool isn't so popular now, but back then I was wondering if I was going to move on from consultancy, or if I would just build my own personal brand. I thought, okay, build doctor – I already fix this stuff for a living, so I'll build a brand based on that. But right now, it's kind of on hold.

Viktor Farcic: What are you up to now?

Julian Simpson: I've been working for Neo4j, formerly known as Neo Technology, since 2012. Within the company, I've worked in the engineering, marketing, and IT departments. I've found myself doing everything from working on the product to deploying our full-stack website on Amazon.

Right now, I'm working on internal IT projects and writing internal apps. In fact, this morning I've been writing scripts to delete Dropbox accounts.

Viktor Farcic: So, what makes Neo4j such a great company?

Julian Simpson: Simply put, the people.

Viktor Farcic: Could you elaborate on that? Because, relating this back to your field of work and the concept of DevOps, in your opinion, is there such a thing as a DevOps team?

Julian Simpson: When I started at Neo4j, I worked with the Swedish team. As a company, we tended to optimize for good people and good attitudes, and we've had an almost unconsciously very good selection of people in that way.

DevOps teams, DevOps problems, and configuration management teams

But can we have something called a DevOps team? I don't believe so. You might spin up a team to solve a DevOps problem, but then I wouldn't even say we specifically have a DevOps problem. I'd say you just have a problem. My original thinking about the movement from 2009 onward, when the name was coined, was that it would be about collaboration and perhaps the tools would sort of come out of that collaboration.

> *"Can we have something called a DevOps team? I don't believe so."*
>
> —*Julian Simpson*

I expected that a configuration management tool would be adopted by developers, so it was possible for a systems person and a developer to collaborate, but I didn't expect that a bunch of classic systems administration teams would just rebrand to DevOps because there were similarities with some of the tools. I didn't expect to have what I'd traditionally think of as a configuration management team become a DevOps team. To a certain extent, I think the only difference is with outsourced platforms now because we've always had someone running what you would call a platform.

Viktor Farcic: That's what confuses me. On the one hand, hardly anybody disagrees that DevOps is mostly about collaboration. But then you have a huge number of DevOps teams, which to me sounds completely contradictory. If you create another team, you're creating another silo that will probably not actually help in collaboration at all.

Julian Simpson: I don't see much difference between what you call a DevOps team now and what a configuration management team used to be. The only difference is that the DevOps team today takes on what a systems or a Unix administration team might have done back in the day: the same basic structure with a new name for the team in the middle.

If you're going to have that DevOps team, I would expect that you'd be able to take the developers and operations teams from the outside and rotate them through with the goal of downsizing or disbanding that team or just replacing it with one or two people who are responsible for running the infrastructure that your pipelines run on.

Viktor Farcic: My theory, judging from the companies I've visited, is that the DevOps team is the team who was the fastest to change the title.

Julian Simpson: It becomes a branding or a status thing rather than a useful exercise in collaboration.

Viktor Farcic: I've worked for a software company, and they don't help either. If you go to a conference, every single tool from 10 years ago is now a DevOps tool. They're all saying that if you buy this tool, you're going to become DevOps-certified.

Julian Simpson: Absolutely, and the incentive to do so is too strong. I even suggested that CITCON rebrand and at least talk about DevOps more, because I see them as one of these sorts of prototypical conferences.

One of the inspirations for Jez Humble and Dave Farley's book, *Continuous Delivery*, was that we had a DevOps team effectively via eight people, including myself, Chris Read, Dan North, Tim Harding, and several others. Our job was just to bridge the gap between a bunch of contractors on day rates, consultants, and the operations team, who were probably too overloaded to take much of that on. We're either paying back technical debt or working on how to get the code from CI/CD back into production, while passing all of the risk management and internal controls that they needed. That did disband; it scaled up to solve a problem, and then once most of those problems were solved, it became just me for a while, before even I left.

> *"It [DevOps] becomes a branding or a status thing rather than a useful exercise in collaboration."*
>
> —*Julian Simpson*

Viktor Farcic: Almost everybody gives me a different explanation, though I must say that I liked yours the most. I read in one of your blog posts that the full definition of DevOps is common sense. So, if DevOps is a theory and had existed, say, since the dawn of time, and we know there's a need for operations and development to collaborate in one way or another, why do you think DevOps became a thing so relatively recently?

Julian Simpson: I think that DevOps has always been a thing. I found it interesting that when I used to work at Thought-Works, Martin Fowler and Rebecca Parsons, their CTO, had both worked as system administrators at universities. I think DevOps used to be just a thing that someone on the team did. The developers that I used to work with were super competent at whatever Unix system you'd be deploying.

A lot of my experience is very geared toward Unix. I did a talk the other day at a company that was mostly .NET, and while I'm not sure my message really got across because their problems are slightly different, I think someone will always solve those problems. But then I think with the dot-com and the Y2K boom, we literally forgot because, remember, Linux on the desktop wasn't really a thing.

You still had a lot of people deploying on to Unix, and I don't think macOS was very popular in development shops at all, so there was barely any command line being done. My experience, at least, is that everyone wanted to be given a Windows machine and an IDE and be told to get some code delivered, and they didn't even have the tools to work on the problem in a different OS. I believe a lot of my conflict with developers stemmed from the fact that they pretty much just needed

Java. I think the marketing of the "compile once and run everywhere" mantra contributed to the problem as well. Microsoft's "visual everything" mantra also contributed to a lack of understanding of what was going on.

You had this incredible demand for developers to be solving important problems such as, "Will airliners fall out of the sky on the turn of the millennium?" or less important problems like Pets.com. Lots of inexperienced developers joined the industry and simply didn't have the skills to work on those problems, so they tended to be thrown over the fence even more frequently to an operations team.

Conveniently, the Y2K and dot-com boom era ended after I started working on software projects. I used to work tech support, so I may be totally ignorant of a couple of decades before that, but my feeling is that we made it very bad in the early noughties.

Viktor Farcic: Back when everybody became a programmer.

Julian Simpson: Exactly! We always joked about those people who would go back to selling life insurance once the dot-com boom was over. For them, it was possible to cram in some certificates and then start contracting for a daily rate that wasn't huge but was a huge advantage over a lot of normal jobs, such as selling life insurance.

Viktor Farcic: Wasn't that also the era when software vendors started being aggressive with the UI approach to things? I mean, you've got Adobe Dreamweaver, where you can drag and drop things and suddenly you've created a web page. You also have VSB, and Oracle ESB where you can also drag, drop, and create all the iterations. I hear that it's part of the "anybody can do this" marketing idea.

Julian Simpson: That was the point I was making about Microsoft's marketing around branding everything visually. I worked at one company where there were a lot of dominant developers, and we were using Perforce. It was quite complicated to roll back and commit in Perforce, and in the end, the best thing to do would have been to write a script. I would then put the script together for you, which you could just run and revert that commit.

The person I was working for said no because he believed everything should be visual. This was a firm belief. If he couldn't click on a button and drop down a bit of text then it was too much and went against their beliefs. Microsoft wanted to encourage that; they wanted to differentiate against Unix. This all took place during the GPL-is-viral days, so I believe that selling products with GUIs didn't help one bit.

I have found that's the litmus test for somebody if you're trying to work out where their skills lie. If they don't have a GUI to nudge them in the right place, it's very interesting to see how they solve a problem.

> *"I think there is a realization that the GUI phase was a bit wrong, and I think that encourages developers to explore the command line more."*
>
> —*Julian Simpson*

Viktor Farcic: Do you think that's still a thing? I have the impression that the industry, especially from 2017, is moving away from all UI-based things. If you look at Docker and Kubernetes, it's completely command line. Everything is moving back toward Unix basics.

Julian Simpson: I haven't spent any time playing with the new version of Windows, but the fact that they have Windows PowerShell Core shows they've changed. I was really, really surprised when I saw Scott Hanselman deploy to Azure with a git push a few years ago. I think there is a realization that the GUI phase was a bit wrong, and I think that encourages developers to explore the command line more, which has changed my job. My job used to be understanding how build scripts worked and how the Unix or Linux production environment worked, which I think a lot of people are just getting now.

Viktor Farcic: When you mentioned Unix and Linux environments, do you think that we're finally seeing some changes there? It's one of the areas that hasn't changed in a while, for better or worse.

The evolution of containers

Julian Simpson: I think containers have changed a lot because you have this constant migration of value up the stack.

Viktor Farcic: What do you mean by that?

Julian Simpson: We used to keep this business logic and store procedures in the database, but it moved into code running above the database. I think we're a long way from seeing where the container thing is going to end up, but it seems like that's the biggest change. No one's interested in the host OS anymore.

Viktor Farcic: You mean as if it's not the lowest denominator anymore?

Julian Simpson: Yeah, I think in some ways it's incredibly helpful that whether you're looking at containers or platform as a service, people can deliver code using them. I haven't been that interested in the gory details of container runtimes; I'm just happy that if I want to roll out something, I can deploy it on ECS, or whatever container runtime as a service exists.

Viktor Farcic: I think CloudBees have one, don't they?

Julian Simpson: Yes, at CloudBees, it's mostly Jenkins-related, but we are now kind of going 100% Kubernetes.

I think in a way, containers are fulfilling the promise Java gave a long time ago: run anywhere. Microsoft Windows is still shaky in this regard, but it's getting there as well.

I also think it helps that no container vendor told anybody that they would be able to run containers on silicon in the way they promised in the 1990s. As you said, they didn't come through with those. I think you're right that my job used not just to be running Jenkins or whatever other CI server the project had chosen to use, but also configuring the environments for that. Now you can say that every build runs in a container. Well, yes, a lot of those problems have just vanished. If you can build a container to represent a production runtime with a blank wall, well, perfect.

Looking into the future

Viktor Farcic: Exactly. I hate this next question because I get asked it all the time, but I'm going to ask you anyway: where do you see the future?

Julian Simpson: I honestly don't have an answer for that. I think the public cloud is one area to keep an eye on. The benefit of such a massive arms race taking place between Amazon, Microsoft, Ali Cloud, IBM, and Google Cloud, is that for us developers who just want to deliver stuff, our choices are going to be amazing.

> *"We all know people who show up to their IT job and do what they're asked to do and then go home again. I think there is a huge risk to their careers when the inevitable automation takes place."*
>
> *—Julian Simpson*

I think the way that Amazon, in particular, is doing a lot around networking, so that I can extend an Amazon VPC bridge with my local network if I need to, will be interesting. I should probably be able to outsource an awful lot of IT stuff to Amazon and just focus on writing things that matter, and then obviously competing with Amazon when they write it too.

Viktor Farcic: When I asked a friend of mine a similar question, he also started with the cloud. His theory is that having incompetent people that do the same thing every single day will mean that they'll eventually lose their jobs because of Amazon and Azure. It will be kind of a great filter of people who do valuable jobs and people who just do "something."

Julian Simpson: I can see that quite easily. We all know people who show up to their IT job and do what they're asked to do and then go home again. I think there is a huge risk to their careers when the inevitable automation takes place. Some people will literally have their careers automated away. The adage "go away, or we'll replace you with a very small shell script" will never be truer.

Viktor Farcic: Exactly. The other thing that confuses me is that I heard the same theory about how people will be replaced with shell script 15 years ago, and it's still somehow not happening.

Julian Simpson: I think what's different now is that the shell script will just be calling the AWS CLI.

Addressing vendor lock-in

Viktor Farcic: Are you concerned at all with vendor lock-in? The idea that companies can basically take over and lock you in forever and ever?

Julian Simpson: I think I'm concerned. I guess as these companies try to differentiate all their services, there will be an inevitable kind of lock-in effect from that. It's obviously in everybody's interest to keep you locked into their platforms. But if they try to sell the same vanilla product, then it's a race to the bottom.

As a result, these companies will try to differentiate things. I mean, if I were a CTO of a company that relied heavily on one cloud platform, I'd be looking to mitigate against that risk; for example, possibly by just running a percentage of my workload elsewhere so that I have the skills to manage a different platform. I think the problem with being able to outsource everything is that you also outsource your skills atrophy, as a person and as an organization.

Viktor Farcic: That shouldn't be much different than the problems we've had with mainframes or the problems we had when everybody was outsourcing everything.

But as I was saying, on the one hand, I hear a lot of concerns about vendor lock-in, but on the other hand, I'm not sure that it's any different than when companies were outsourcing everything before, or when they were running mainframes, which were all vendor lock-ins. Somehow we, or at least some of us, still managed to get through those issues.

Julian Simpson: I don't think it's going to be as bad as one of the historical vendor lock-ins of the past, such as the Bell Telephone Company, something that had to be broken up as a monopoly. I think it's going to be the price you pay for taking the convenience of a vendor's offerings.

Viktor Farcic: That's very interesting.

Julian Simpson: If you just say that it's most convenient to run on Azure and then you only develop those skills in-house, then yes, I think it'll be very easy to just default to lock-in, and that could lead to an expensive exit. I think it's probably a net positive that you don't have to build platforms anymore.

> *"If I were a CTO of a company that relied heavily on one cloud platform, I'd be looking to mitigate against that risk."*
>
> *—Julian Simpson*

I've worked in several jobs where I had to install SPARC systems in offices, and it's annoying. I think for anyone who wants to deliver software or services, it's probably better that they don't have to employ someone to move servers around the office, rack them, then install them and try to make them work. That was the thing I did in the 1990s, and I think that what we have now is certainly much better. I think there's incredible value in being able to rent your IT services by the minute.

Viktor Farcic: If you exclude the big companies such as Netflix, Google, and Apple, what do you think about building a private cloud? Does it make sense and is it a viable option?

Julian Simpson: I would probably bet against my own ability to deliver a private cloud. I'm sure I could do that, but trying to keep that secure in this kind of security threat environment is probably a much harder challenge than it ever was. I am amazed at some of the security issues we've seen over the last few years.

Viktor Farcic: Do you think we have more security problems or are those problems just more visible now?

Julian Simpson: I think they're more visible today, and I think that security research seems to follow the trends as well. Once someone discovers one vulnerability, then there are more eyeballs looking for similar vulnerabilities. They seem to come out in waves. But I think as things become more connected, then security is a concern that wasn't as visible as before. The idea that your corporate network isn't a safe place wasn't an assumption we had 15 years ago.

Culture and collaboration

Viktor Farcic: That's a valid point. In closing, do you have any parting ideas and words, or is there anything that comes to mind that I forgot to ask?

Julian Simpson: No, I think we've covered what I think is most important, which is the culture. I'm super pleased that we haven't really discussed automation or any of the tools, except as examples of something else. To me, DevOps is all about culture and collaboration.

Viktor Farcic: Does that mean the culture shapes the tools or do tools shape the culture, or both? I mean, can you adopt one without the other?

Julian Simpson: My guess is no, because people's expectations must change. I think the tools they use and the culture in which those tools are used are tightly linked. If you could change the culture, then the tools might change consequently, or vice versa. But I think it's more than that.

Lindsay Holmwood did a talk at DevOpsDays 2016 in Wellington, New Zealand, where he pointed out that culture is kind of invisible and what you really have are artifacts that kind of tell you about culture. Archaeologists would dig something up and then make some assumption, and it's the same here. I think we see things every day that tell us what our company culture is, and maybe the tool is just an artifact of the culture.

> *"To me, DevOps is all about culture and collaboration."*
>
> —*Julian Simpson*

Viktor Farcic: I haven't heard that one before, but I love it.

Julian Simpson: Yeah. This is entirely stolen from Lindsay, so it'll be great if you talk to him. If your company has a need for massive amounts of control, then you're probably not going to go with distributed version control systems, or you probably want to use some rational product for capturing requirements. Even the phrase "capturing requirements" probably has some kind of cultural impact. I guess my parting words would be that I think tools possibly tell you what your culture is.

Viktor Farcic: I love it. I really love it.

8

Andy Clemenko

Senior Solutions Engineer at Docker

Introducing Andy Clemenko

Andy Clemenko is a senior solutions engineer and architect at Docker, Inc. He's also a technologist and DevOps analyst, with a focus on helping organizations make the transition from traditional development practices to a modern set of culture, tooling, and processes that increase the release frequency and quality of software. You can follow him on Twitter at @clemenko.

Viktor Farcic: I want to jump right into our discussion with the one question I'm asking everyone: what is DevOps?

What is DevOps?

Andy Clemenko: DevOps is a lifestyle. It's all about being able to adapt to new technologies, not only from a developer point of view, but also an operations point of view, while still being nimble. That's not to say DevOps is only that. There are a lot of other concepts built into it, which is why I call it a lifestyle. Beyond being able just to adapt, you've also got containers, twelve-factor apps, declarative infrastructure, and infrastructure as code. Yes, you've got all of these buzzwords around it, but at the end of the day, it's just a lifestyle. It's about being nimble, retooling, and moving forward.

Viktor Farcic: So, how does Andy Clemenko fit tools into that picture? Because, in today's field, I'm finding that every tool is a DevOps tool.

Andy Clemenko: To a certain extent, the tools almost don't matter, because you can hand a carpenter any hammer and they'll still be successful. Within DevOps, you give any DevOps or SRE engineer (whatever you want to call it these days) a tool—whether it's OCI, Rocket, Docker, Kube, Swarm, Jenkins, or GitLab, it doesn't matter—and they should be able to work with it. But again, it's about being nimble and open-minded enough to embrace the next thing, which will look entirely different.

> *"DevOps is a lifestyle. It's all about being able to adapt to new technologies, not only from a developer point of view, but also an operations point of view."*
>
> —*Andy Clemenko*

Viktor Farcic: Speaking of tools, I'm fascinated by containers. Do you think it's a coincidence that, as an industry, we've started talking about containers, microservices, and DevOps all at the same time? Is that pure luck or is there some relation behind it?

Andy Clemenko: I would say that it's a coincidence. Containers helped to accelerate that DevOps lifestyle adoption but, having worked on large Hadoop clusters, and having seen the DevOps methodologies with Puppet, Chef, Salt, and Ansible, what we've just done is effectively retooled and brought our tools up in abstraction layers. We're no longer orchestrating at the operating system layer. Instead, we're orchestrating at the cluster level.

But that correlation helped accelerate the move up. It's still the same now, regardless of whether you're working in industry, government, or anywhere really. There's this idea that when you have a development team and an operations team, they throw shit over fences. That DevOps lifestyle is about bringing those two teams and their functions together. Forget teams, because one team with the ability to effect change is quicker than two teams trying to do the same thing. It's in this acceleration that I think containers play a part. Honestly, what I'm trying to say is that it's about soft skills. It's about the people, it's about the teams, and it has nothing to do with the tooling, just like how Docker, DevSecOps, and GitOps are all just buzzwords. We're going to get to a point where whatever object you're creating—whether it's a container, a VM, or a JAR, it doesn't matter—has the metadata within it that says how it should be shipped, and who should approve its life cycle.

Viktor Farcic: That makes sense.

Andy Clemenko: But I remember last year, during a demo at KubeCon, a practitioner-driven conference, Brendan Burns did a presentation on self-deploying images, where your object understands not only what it needs to be in order to be healthy, but where it needs to go and, who needs to approve its use and security provenance. So, now you've got an audit trail built in, and you're wrapping that object with as much embedded metadata as possible.

Viktor Farcic: So, it's almost as if we are switching toward communication through code and metadata? I don't need to tell you what I want, as it's all self-contained in my artifact.

Andy Clemenko: Exactly, and as a builder, or as a team building those objects, you can describe what it should do, while having the opportunity to divert it. But today, if I give you a Docker image, you can do whatever you want with it. I love the idea that, in the future, I could give you a Docker image that I could lock so that only you could run it, and thus you can't execute into it, and you can't do funny things with it. But it's also got a security provenance, so you know that somebody gave it to me and then I gave it to you—through cryptography—so there's at least an audit trail.

The next phase, at least in the way I see it, is having these objects really be, I'm not going to say self-aware, but at least have more meaningful metadata around security, provenance, and deployment. What if, instead of having a `docker run` command that was word wrapped three times with passing in volumes and stuff, you just did `docker run`, and the container itself goes, "Hey, I should have this, where is it? I should have this variable, and you haven't given it to me. Can I have it?" A more self-aware state is kind of a weird way to describe it.

Describing the company of today

Viktor Farcic: Switching gears a little, if you were to start a company today, what would it look like? How would people behave and interact with it?

Andy Clemenko: I'm a big fan of smaller companies, where the lines between teams are blurred. So, if I'm starting a start-up, I want to make sure that our internal IT understands our product, and that everybody can work collaboratively. I think once you start getting over a couple of hundred people in size, that's when the fences immediately go up.

Something I hear time and time again from customer interaction is, "Oh, that's the networking team. They'll get to it when they can." With these fences, you have different North Stars, different goals, or you have different strategies or managers. I'm a fan of a flat organization with cross-functional teams. Like today, you might be interested in monitoring and helping with a customer solution, but that doesn't mean that internal IT can't take advantage of it.

Viktor Farcic: But are these fences inevitable, then, or are they just more familiar? I wonder myself because I'm yet to see a big company that works like that, which is something I would love to see.

Andy Clemenko: I think you get pockets, but unfortunately the counter to that cross-functional team is organizational stability. Because, if you've got a team, you'll find that, as your company grows, you're going to have pockets of these teams. So, the question arises about how you organize them? For lack of a better term, how do you *control* them, and how do you make sure that they're all moving together? The way you do that is you basically give each team a North Star, which starts to create those vertical fences.

The thing with that is that it's just organizationally tough, and the problem is a lot of people end up in middle management. Because of that, there's a vested interest in keeping middle management alive. Look at it from the perspective of a 300-employee company threshold. One threshold is 100, the second is 300, and then it's about 500 to 600 or possibly even closer to 1,000. But for me, in my ideal company, I like staying in the range of a couple of hundred employees.

Case in point is that I got an email last night saying, "Hey, I know you're in Raleigh next Wednesday. Can you be in Houston on Thursday?" I replied saying that I'm up for it; as long as they approved my travel requests, I'd be there, and I'd get it done. It's not my team, not my region, but they need help, so let's go.

Viktor Farcic: That's dedication!

Personalities, honesty, and breathing the environment

Andy Clemenko: The other thing is that right now there are two types of personalities in all industries. It's either type A or type B, quite literally. Those As are going to go in and do what it takes to get the job done. To use an overused term, for As, it's "mission, mission, mission." Meanwhile, type Bs are, to a certain extent, going to sit back and just push the button. I see it in all walks of life.

I'm a volunteer firefighter on the side, and I see it in the fire service; I see it in corporate, and I see it in government. In fact, I see it everywhere. The trick is that if you really want to keep that cross-functional team and culture going, you need to find those people that are willing to go the extra mile. Not every day, because that gets out of control. But find those people that are willing to do it, that show gumption and go do it, and then worry about complaining about it or getting compensation later.

> *"Those As are going to go in and do what it takes to get the job done. To use an overused term, for As, it's 'mission, mission, mission.' Meanwhile, type Bs are, to a certain extent, going to sit back and just push the button. I see it in all walks of life."*
>
> *—Andy Clemenko*

Viktor Farcic: That's very interesting, because I've had conversations with people who have said, "Oh, the company where I work is growing, and as we're growing, I'm starting to question whether I'm going to move on to something else, for the same precise reasons." I then often get a follow-up question along the lines of, "Oh, but if you grow to 1,000, that's great because more people will equate that growth with better business and stuff like that." I never really understood that because then you have to ask, what's in it for me? It's not my company. Why is it better if we are 1,000 rather than 200?

Andy Clemenko: If you're looking at it from a purely financial point of view, if there are two companies, one with 10 employees and another with 1,000 employees, who is making the most money? The answer is the person at the top. So, the bigger the company, the more revenue there is, and the more the stock's worth.

Are you directly incentivized to do it? At the end of the day, is money really your incentive? I wear a hoodie, and I'm an engineer with a degree in engineering who wants to solve problems and build some cool stuff; that's literally it. I'm in a place now where I help customers to solve problems and build cool stuff—I'm helping, and I love it. Do I see an extra dime if we sell an extra widget? Not directly. Maybe indirectly, at the end of the year. But that's not my personal North Star. I think it takes a certain kind of CEO to pump the brakes and not assume that massive expansion is going to solve all of the problems. Because, in my mind, not all growth is good.

Viktor Farcic: I guess it depends on what you're after. I feel the same in that I'm definitely after money, up to a point. I cannot live on 100 bucks a month; but there is a limit that I reach where I'm kind of like, "OK, it doesn't really make a difference anymore," unless I've got ambitions to buy a chopper or something like that.

Finding your North Star

Andy Clemenko: It's your North Star! Putting the brakes on this interview, I want to ask what do *you* see? I know our discussion has focused on me, but what do you see in terms of company size and embracing DevOps?

Viktor Farcic: In regard to company size, I feel similar to you in that the bigger the company gets, the less fun I have working in it.

Andy Clemenko: It's great that you see things the same way as me.

Viktor Farcic: I think that's kind of my definition. I feel that being in software engineering is, in a way, a privilege. My feeling for that is because we are one of the very few professions that we usually join for fun and can continue having fun.

At the end of the day, as long as I'm having fun, it's excellent. It's just that I feel that the bigger we are, the less fun I have.

I visit a lot of companies where I feel there's no hope. I work with them for a short period of time and show them how to do this and that. But then, I'll come back a year later and ask them what they're doing, and then they ask me, "What do you mean, 'Tell you what we're doing?' You were here last year; you know what we're doing!"

Andy Clemenko: That's the thing—nothing's changed. In terms of buzz phrases or buzzwords, bureaucracy is the anti-pattern to both DevOps and the DevOps lifestyle. I just want to do the DevOps lifestyle equation, but there's really a need for bureaucracy in these big organizations because you have to be able to organize that many people at some level. Otherwise, it's going to be the Wild West. You've got to be a better start-up. I really think we need to break up those big companies and keep them small. A CEO would have to have the courage not to grow to 10,000 employees because when you do, you're going to lose nimbleness, and the ability to adapt not only to this lifestyle but also, as the wind changes, to any new North Star that comes out.

But, unfortunately, money is power. What we need is the money that the big companies have in order to fund the little guys. It's like this weird symbiotic relationship that's not mutually beneficial; there's a gap somewhere. I'm on a contract right now that's 1,200 hours in, or 50 days, and our team has literally spent 500 hours of that time over the last two months getting our laptops and saying, "Hey, we need an NFS share; we need Windows VMs." We're very much in a state of saying we need this and that. The issue is that the company's response is, "Yeah; it's coming, man. Let's investigate." I've got a laptop here for them, which is always on VPN. Cool, that works great, but all of a sudden, I can't SSH into Linux boxes, and then they're blaming us for turning stuff off.

I mean, I can bounce and jump through—I'm a geek—but this is clearly a firewall issue. So, then the natural response is, "Well, we'll open a ticket." Fine, but now you've got to wait six weeks for the networking team to get around to it. I'd be there saying to the networking team, "Hey, guys, do you want this project to be successful?" To which the company responds, "OK, we'll accept your million-dollar check, but now our employees are getting frustrated and annoyed because we're not doing anything."

Viktor Farcic: But before I had a feeling that when I'm in those situations, it's like, you're not wasting my time because I'm getting paid for this, but you're completely wasting your money. At the end of the day, I get paid, so I don't care. But then I came to realize that maybe the perspectives are different. Actually, what I consider completely irrelevant—zero improvement—is a big deal.

Andy Clemenko: I guess it's about the DevOps lifestyle, and I think it's also about moving forward. It's about taking a step, and even if it's a tiny step that went from three months to two months, that's still a step forward. Spiritually, I feel frustrated when I'm not moving forward, whether it's with a company, life, financials, or whatever. I like that forward movement. I do believe that there's a certain extent where companies feel good about at least moving forward, even though it's not where you and I ideally would like to get them.

> *"The issue is that, some of these companies just say, 'We want DevOps.' That's their goal, but you're there thinking about how they don't understand what DevOps actually is."*
>
> —*Andy Clemenko*

One of the things I do when I start an engagement is try to establish a North Star, whether it's a short-term, mid-term, or long-term project. It could be a bunch of North Stars, or it could be a series, but at least you know where you ultimately want to go. Because, that way, at any point in time, you can ask yourself, "Am I in line or am I perpendicular? If I'm perpendicular, what's the cause of that?" Because sometimes you have to go back to find a new path, and that's fine, but you have to understand at least that you are going backward, away from your ultimate goal.

Unfortunately, the issue is that some of these companies just say, "We want DevOps." That's their goal, but you're there thinking about how they don't understand what DevOps actually is. My favorite is when companies say that they want Docker, which is something they say all the time. But the question is what does Docker mean to them?

I joke about the Docker lifestyle because Docker is not just containers. It's CI/CD. It's version control. Some of these places don't have sustained version control either through monitoring or logging. It's ELK and Splunk and Prometheus and Grafana.

It's all about these aggregate systems that you bolt on to your infrastructure. In fact, it's even a little bit of Puppet or Ansible. It's understanding Kubernetes YAMLs, to which all I'll say is, "Lord, help us!"

Viktor Farcic: Exactly!

Understanding what you're buying

Andy Clemenko: But it's also Jenkins, GitLab, and all of these things. Take the project I'm on now, for example. We need version control, and we need a CI system. So, I asked the client, "What have you got?" They're like, "Well, this team over there has—" I ask, "Do you have a central?" They respond by saying, "No, we don't have a central." They may then ask, "But can we stand up on our own?" But that's not really their job. What's going to end up happening then is you'll need to go to another team and ask them, "Do you understand what you're buying?"

A classic example is that you buy a car and drive it off a lot, but 200 miles later, you scratch your head because the vehicle's stopped working. You didn't realize you have to put gas into it, or that you have to change the tires, put oil into it, and clean the car, along with the rest of the maintenance. You may think of just going back and getting another car. But no, you've got to understand what you're buying.

Viktor Farcic: Exactly. I feel like one of the significant difficulties I have is that when I'm with a customer—let's say their goal is a continuous delivery pipeline—I feel that I shouldn't cheat them and that maybe I should tell them that they should not pursue, in this case, continuous delivery.

Andy Clemenko: I've had specific conversations with customers and have said something along those lines, that maybe containers aren't the right thing for them. If they're not willing to build a CI system or version control, and subsequently they're not willing to understand all of these things that make up the DevOps lifestyle, then maybe it's not the right thing for them.

It comes off sometimes the wrong way, but I pride myself on being honest to my customers and saying, "Look. You're going to need this, this, this, and this." In fact, I did it yesterday at an integrator. I wrote a laundry list on the board of what they need to provide because they're building a reference architecture—infrastructure, monitoring, logging, and CI/CD—and they're coming at it from a dev angle, so they're more worried about CI/CD, but I'm telling them that providing CI/CD is only one thing, because, hey, you're building awesome widgets, but where do they go? How are they executed? It's not useful if you can't deploy it efficiently.

Viktor Farcic: But sometimes, I don't think it's only to do with willingness or even ability.

Andy Clemenko: If your goal is to do the bare minimum, then keep doing that. Likewise, if that's working for you, great. But just don't get in the way of those who want to make a change and move forward.

You've got to be brave enough to say to those people that maybe you should just stay in the past. Perhaps you should just stick with Windows Server 2003 and not worry about containers, DevOps, and CI/CD, because these are lifestyles. Customers don't necessarily like the truth all of the time, but I would rather be honest with my customers up front and not try to manipulate them. I think honesty creates a healthier relationship because it establishes long-term trust, and sometimes, it has facilitated change within a customer. Every once in a while, a slap in the face might not be a bad idea.

Viktor Farcic: Absolutely, at least for an academic or salesperson.

Andy Clemenko: I was on a sales call yesterday, and it was just "sell, sell, sell." All this company cared about was moving forward. So, the question is, which Docker engine should they use for their Jenkins server? I feel it comes down to the fact of asking yourself whether you absolutely need the support. Is your corporate policy such that you absolutely have to have support? Because if it is, then we can just sell you two licenses for nodes and that's $1,500 a node per year. It's so tiny that it's like a rounding error for most of their budgets.

My response is you could run CE, and the amount of support you're actually going to need is going to be pretty much zero because I build CE with CI systems all of the time. The company's response was for us to send them a quote. The downside is we couldn't sell professional services, including the full product suite. But you know what? At the end of the day, at least the customer feels they've gotten an honest answer from the sales guy and me.

> *"Customers don't necessarily like the truth all of the time, but I would rather be honest with my customers up front and not try to manipulate them. I think honesty creates a healthier relationship because it establishes long-term trust, and sometimes, it has facilitated change within a customer."*
>
> —*Andy Clemenko*

Viktor Farcic: Earlier, you mentioned Kubernetes YAML. In fact, I believe you said, "Lord, help us!" Why do you say that exactly?

On Kubernetes, Docker, and lowering the barrier to entry

Andy Clemenko: Any time there's a new technology, developers have to lower the barrier to entry, especially for changing. For changing abstraction views and for changing tooling, you've got to make it easy. Rancher did a fantastic job of making orchestration easy. They had to catalog, and my God, it was great.

I had a company director once who wasn't a computer geek at all. To be able to deploy a ghost blog server by clicking two buttons blew his mind. You just have to make that barrier to entry really low. The problem I see with Kubernetes right now is that the YAML in itself uses spec four times in a single object type. YAML format is fine, and everyone can do the vertical lines and, in their code, get the spacing right.

But its overall structure? Well, a customer yesterday was talking about Swarm versus Kubernetes, and how you can take a single object in Swarm, and it describes the ingress URL-FQDN, it represents the number of replicas, and it represents the number of ports and the volumes in it and one object— in Kubernetes speak, that's seven. That gets a little frustrating; not to mention that right now there are 37 top-level objects in Kubernetes. And then there's my favorite one known as the CRD, the custom one. If our theories are good enough for you, you can make one of your own, and we'll just work with it. Kelsey Hightower said that Kubernetes is not the endgame. Somebody needs to come along, and I'll tip the hat to IBM and Red Hat that OpenShift became an opinionated Kubernetes. That's cool, but that's not Kubernetes, and I think it's unfair for them to sell it as Kubernetes.

Viktor Farcic: Right, so, in your opinion, what needs to come along to address that?

Andy Clemenko: Someone needs to come along and really say that we're all going to use Kubernetes underneath. We understand the Kubernetes YAML, but we're going to simplify it and make our own converter app to format on top of it.

That'll translate to the lower-level primitives, to the 37 top-level objects, such that the developer just says, "Here's my image," or better than that, "We talked about the metadata being transient with the image, but here's my image. Here's the number of replicas, here's the network it should be on, and here are the ports it's listening on—the number, and very simply, within 5-20 lines, it's minimal."

Look at Helm: they've been trying to do that, but Helm in itself is complicated. You've got to it pull charts. I'm not even looking at Helm, and people are saying that Helm's easy. But, no, it's not. You see it time and time again as you help these companies to understand the DevOps lifestyle—these tools are wicked hard.

Viktor Farcic: It's easy until it doesn't do exactly what you want, and then it becomes a nightmare.

Andy Clemenko: Look at the hype cycle around Kubernetes. I've got customers that are saying, "We want Kubernetes!" To which I say, "Are you doing something specific? Are you pulling? Why specifically do you need Kubernetes?" This is a question they can't answer because they don't have an answer to it. It really comes down to somebody up high having seen it in CIO Weekly, or it's the buzzword right now, and they've got to have it. Then you actually start showing them that YAML, or the fact that in order to tie an ingress controller to a service that sits in front of a deployment, you have to have an ingress object. That's four objects now.

Viktor Farcic: The reason why I'm asking is that when I jumped into Docker, I felt that it was one of the very few technology tools that I can use for everybody in a company. If you're a tester, then it's useful for you, and if you're a developer, then it's also useful for you, just as if you're an operator. At that time, Docker was almost a communication tool. It's useful for everybody, and the entry point is easy. I can explain it to my mother. But then along comes Kubernetes, which I admire because Kubernetes is extremely powerful and extensible, and it allows you to do anything, including make coffee. But now, I'm not actually able to explain what Kubernetes is anymore unless a person decides to dedicate their life to Kubernetes.

Andy Clemenko: It's a religion.

Viktor Farcic: Because of the complexity associated with it, I feel Kubernetes cannot be just another tool in your tool-belt. You need to be dedicated to it. So, in my book, it's useless for developers because they're never going to learn whatever they need to learn for Kubernetes. Though maybe I'm a bit pessimistic.

> *"Solomon Hykes didn't invent containers; let's be honest. [...] All that he and his team were able to do was merely make Docker run in a simpler form, and that, to me, was the pivotal moment."*
>
> —*Andy Clemenko*

Andy Clemenko: No, I agree with you, because that's something I see too. The exciting thing for us at Docker is the fact that Solomon Hykes didn't invent containers; let's be honest. We've had zones, we've had attributed, and we've had encapsulation technologies in the past. All that he and his team were able to do was merely make Docker run in a simpler form, and that, to me, was the pivotal moment. I really think what we need is an operational platform—a framework—to be simple, and that's why I'm excited about Kubernetes being implemented into Docker Enterprise.

If only we could take an Apple-like approach to it: let's make it simple; let's make it work, and let's lower that barrier to entry and move forward, then, hopefully, we can abstract on top of Kube just enough. Leave the door open if somebody wants to look behind and use kubectl all day long, but abstract it just a little bit to make it simple enough to work. When we talked about lifers versus go-getters and big companies, I think that the minute you have a barrier to entry slightly higher than an inch, it's enough to cause a lot of resistance. If you want to effect change at a company, you've got to make that resistance—the possibility of resistance—zero. I guess that's almost like a mathematical function. The closer to a zero amount of resistance you get, the higher the probability of change within the organization. Because I know when I first started looking at Docker, I saw it as a threat, at least from a sysadmin's point of view.

Viktor Farcic: You really saw it as a threat? What's changed since then? Because you're now a senior solution engineer at Docker, so your initial perception must have been wrong.

Andy Clemenko: At the time, I saw Docker as a threat because developers could just do things that required sysadmins. Thus, my knee-jerk reaction was that Docker is just anti-sysadmin. But that was until my first docker run. Then a lightbulb went off, and I had the epiphany of, "Holy shit! I need to go and work for this excellent company. I'm in!" But again, you've got to make the barrier to entry as low as possible.

Have you ever seen a new developer's eyes when you show them that 1,700-line Kubernetes YAML to deploy Prometheus and Grafana? I did it yesterday, and their jaw hit the floor.

Viktor Farcic: I know what you mean; that's a face I see all the time. People will often call me and say, "Viktor, can you help us with this and that?," or they tell me that they want to jump into Kubernetes, and after the first half an hour it's all excitement, but then the reality sets in.

I think it's interesting in the context of this discussion we're having about DevOps. But I think Kubernetes fosters the creation of those roles, and sysadmins will be able to use it.

What I would like to see in the future is for us, as an industry, to stop talking about Kubernetes and see that there is something on top of it that only a few people know about. I guess it's more or less what you described for Docker E.

Andy Clemenko: There is a thing with kernel developers today; there will always be extreme experts at each layer, but the number of people directly interacting with that layer becomes very small.

Viktor Farcic: Because you're not working with it.

Andy Clemenko: Exactly, there's no need.

Viktor Farcic: I'm running Mac right now while I speak to you. I don't know what's behind it, because I don't care.

> *"I honestly don't even care whether this container is OCI-compliant. At the end of the day, I just want it to work. I want it to be portable. I want it to be secure. And I want it to be easy."*
>
> —*Andy Clemenko*

Andy Clemenko: That's a good point. I believe it was Scott McNealy from Sun, who talked years ago about Sun Grid deploying and debuting SAS Grid effectively. He said that, when you plug in your hairdryer, you don't need to know about nuclear energy. You just want to plug in your hairdryer, and you just want it to work. So, apply the same thing today, because I don't care what orchestrator is underneath—I honestly don't even care whether this container is OCI-compliant. At the end of the day, I just want it to work. I want it to be portable. I want it to be secure. And I want it to be easy.

Viktor Farcic: So, what's next, then?

Looking to the future

Andy Clemenko: In the near future, I see serverless picking up some momentum, but I'm still waiting for serverless to be actually written into the lower-level orchestrator directly, and not as it currently is, which is as an extra layer on top. To me, serverless is just a rapid reaction scheduler, to some extent.

Elias Pereira has done some really awesome stuff with OpenVAS, to the point where it's got self-autoscaling of containers because it's deploying its own Prometheus. To me, conceptually, having similar functions at multiple layers seems redundant. So, let me ask this: if we can take OpenVAS and build it into the lower orchestrator, why don't we build into right into Kube or right into Swarm?

At least that way I'm advocating for a 38 top-level object. But the idea, though, is that if you have more batch processes like serverless, they can still use the same schedule. You don't need to build on top of them and add all of this extra stuff to do the same thing. My point is, I would love to see an orchestrator just be able to say, "OK. 1 through 5 are long-running; 6 and 7 are serverless." And again, we talked about that self-aware nature. What if you had a container that says, "If I haven't been used in 10 minutes, turn me off"?

In that case, you don't even have to have a separate object for serverless or daemons. The thing is self-aware, and it says, "Hey, I haven't been used. Spin me down." It tells the orchestrator, "I'm not busy, so turn me off," and then when the next request comes in, the orchestrator says, "Wake up." There you go. Why not? I say let's blur those lines. Wouldn't you say that makes it simple? Let me ask you, Viktor, do you remember the moment when you did your first `docker run`?

Viktor Farcic: That's what I'm saying. My first reaction when I was running Docker was, "OK, I started 10 minutes ago, and I already understand how it works. I don't know what's behind the scenes, but it works."

Andy Clemenko: And you were able to do a `docker run` and see your web page, resulting in you having that lightbulb moment, which is what we need for all of the DevOps tools. That's how change is really going to happen—with these lightbulb moments.

Viktor Farcic: Exactly, but going back to serverless, would you place your bets on something along the lines of what you've explained, or something similar to Lambdas with cloud proprietaries and all of those things?

Andy Clemenko: I wouldn't place any bet because computing today happens everywhere. It happens on your watch, it happens in your datacenter, and it also happens in someone else's data center. There'll always be this balance between on-premises and the cloud, and serverless and full daemon, or whatever you want to call it—server/serverless. It might not be 50/50; they'll flow. I think there'll always be both because of security and financial reasons. Too many times I hear customers saying that corporate policy says we can't touch the internet, so they're fully air-gapped. You can't use Amazon, you can't use Azure, or there's a project team building a VPN to the VPC, who'll dedicate a link, and all of that good stuff. But there'll always be this balance, and, indeed, all we're doing is just shifting responsibilities.

So, do I think serverless is going to take over? No, but I think it's going to consume anywhere up to 20% of the container space today. But guess what? What format on the backend is serverless?

Viktor Farcic: Kubernetes?

Andy Clemenko: So, it's the same underlying fundamental object, and the same construct. So, why can't we just make the construct more self-aware, whether it's a batch job—which serverless technically is—or a long-running daemon that's constantly serving traffic?

Viktor Farcic: Because my current concern with serverless is that I need to choose which platform to use and then almost stick with it forever. I would technically have liked what you just described—tell me how to explain something and then tell me whether it will run as Lambda, Azure function, or VAS. But that shouldn't be my concern.

> *"My current concern with serverless is that I need to choose which platform to use and then almost stick with it forever."*
>
> *—Viktor Farcic*

Andy Clemenko: It shouldn't be, but for me, it's a process. Fundamentally, inside the container, it's just a process executing whatever—whether it's wrapped in a Lambda function, Azure, an OpenVAS container, or a long-running Kube container, it's still just a process. The process doesn't care what it's encapsulated in. It doesn't know that it's not a conscious being where it spins up and it goes, "I'm alive! I'm dead. I'm alive! I'm dead." It just runs.

Having to build separate frameworks is creating, in my mind, more confusion. Granted, there's job security. But again, it's not a low barrier to entry; although, having played with it, OpenVAS is pretty darn slick. It's straightforward to create a function, it's straightforward to integrate it, and it's effortless to execute it, not to mention it's got autoscaling and all of these fun things. But again, I'd love to see that completely integrated with a single orchestrator.

I'll give Amazon a lot of credit. I don't like what they're building, so to speak, but I'll give them a lot of credit for lowering the barrier to entry. They've made it too easy to consume databases in VMs and object stores. But if you actually dig into it, it's incredibly complicated, with CloudFormation templates and all of the IM policies and security groups. I personally don't use AWS or any of that stuff because it's too complicated and annoying.

Viktor Farcic: But when you said they made it too easy, my first thought was that it used to be, but nowadays it's not.

Andy Clemenko: Actually, you're right.

Viktor Farcic: I prefer DigitalOcean now, because it has what I need, and it doesn't have 50,000 other things that I don't need but am encumbered with anyway.

Andy Clemenko: I'm a huge DigitalOcean fan.

Viktor Farcic: To be honest, I've worked a lot with AWS, and I still don't fully understand how it works. But now that I think about it, nobody does; it's just madness. I have a feeling that they went in the same trajectory as we described earlier for Kubernetes stuff, but it's becoming heavier and heavier.

Andy Clemenko: Exactly, and I think one of the disservices or discredits to Amazon is that they've made AWS very sticky because of how complicated it is, and to a certain extent, Kubernetes is going down that same path. It's very sticky because once you get it, you don't want to use anything else. Just look at the fact that if you put "AWS architect" on your resume or "certified Kubernetes" on your resume, your phone will not stop ringing. That's good for the person whose resume that is, but, you know, I think it leaves a lot of the little guys out of the market to a certain extent.

Viktor Farcic: But, you know, if being AWS-certified is in high demand, that means that it's actually too complicated, because I don't think that anybody says, unlike with Kubernetes, that they're a container-certified person.

Andy Clemenko: Or that I'm certified in Docker and Kube.

Viktor Farcic: But what do you get certified for in Docker? It only takes two days to get certified.

Andy Clemenko: Our certification is at a basic understanding of registry, and push and pull, and things like that. But you can absolutely learn it and pass the exam in a week or two; it's not hard.

Viktor Farcic: Exactly. Anyway, I know we're out of time now. It's been great talking to you, Andy. Thank you so much for your time.

9

Chris Riley

Author and
DevOps Analyst

Introducing Chris Riley

Based in the Greater Denver Area, Chris Riley is a self-proclaimed bad coder turned editor of Sweetcode.io at Fixate IO, a content marketing firm for those who sell to technical audiences. Through this, he's involved with DevOps, SecOps, big data, machine learning, and blockchain. He's a member of the DevOps Institute Board of Regents, a position he's held for over four years. You can follow him on Twitter at @HoardingInfo.

Viktor Farcic: I know your career has mainly revolved around your work as an analyst. But you're also the editor of Sweetcode. How did you get to where you are?

A bad coder turned industry analyst

Chris Riley: My answer can best be summed up by the fact that I'm a bad coder turned industry analyst. While I couldn't make it as a coder, I had a big passion for software development practices, building applications, and the processes around that. So, instead of trying to transform my skill set and become a better coder, what I decided to do was really focus on understanding the industry. So, I became a DevOps analyst in addition to being the editor of Sweetcode.

Career-wise, my last employer was a company called CloudShare, which was a DevTest environment specifically for large line-of-business application development; in other words, a SharePoint-, SAP-, or Oracle-type application. At CloudShare, I worked in product management, so I was essentially driving the direction of the product and keeping tabs on the market.

I'm also doing a lot of write-ups for DevOps.com, O'Reilly, and TechTarget. My content focuses on how organizations assimilate modern development practices and a lot of cheer-leading to enterprises to encourage them to make a move. I became very familiar with the market, which included playing with a lot of the tools myself. But after that, I started Sweetcode, which is now a more developer-focused site with a lot of really strong tactical content.

What is DevOps?

Viktor Farcic: I'd like to start with a question that will probably sound very silly to you: what is DevOps?

Chris Riley: I believe very passionately that DevOps is not a thing that you can simply do. You don't just say that, on a specific time and date, you "did" DevOps. "Doing DevOps" should never be a phrase anybody ever utters because you're never "done" with DevOps.

> *"You don't just say that, on a specific time and date, you 'did' DevOps. 'Doing DevOps' should never be a phrase anybody ever utters because you're never 'done' with DevOps."*
>
> —Chris Riley

DevOps is not a thing; it's a principle, it's a practice, and it's what you use to drive all of your decisions on how you build your delivery chain. That means it encompasses everything from the dreaded word "culture" to implementation. A great example is if you walk into the door of Slack and take a look at their development environment. You might say, "Wow, look at you guys: your developers are supporting their own code. If they build it, they support it, and you're releasing hundreds of times a day. You guys have continuous delivery—this is amazing! You guys have done it, you have hit the jackpot—you are DevOps."

You can't say that because the "you are DevOps" element is not actually a thing. As we saw with Slack, they have been and always will be trying to figure out how to do a better job. That's what DevOps is. They're always thinking how they can do something better, even though, from an outsider's point of view, it might look like they have the best development environment and delivery chain in the world. They're still thinking, "How can we do this better? What can we automate more? What can we make go faster? How can we do more releases?" If you're concerned about better-quality software and releasing it faster and more frequently, then you're "doing DevOps," and you don't even need to call it DevOps. That's what I think DevOps is.

Viktor Farcic: I feel as if you're describing an extended version of Agile, or at least something similar to that.

Chris Riley: I disagree. While Agile was more cut and dried, with clearly a more defined system of operations, DevOps is a bit more ethereal and philosophical. The reason that's so important is because of Agile, or even before that, what we learned with Waterfall development practices.

If you're an organization that thinks you're going to take on a project to implement DevOps, and that, by the end of the day, you're going to be doing workable DevOps, what you're actually going to have is a *DevOps shop*. What happens is, as soon as you've done that, the *DevOps shop* is no longer DevOps. It's dead, because, for instance, CloudBees has acquired Codeship and suddenly you need to reconsider how you're doing continuous integration because, possibly, you're using a different release automation tool, and now you need to consider, "Is my release automation tool different, or is there a new generation out?"

If you architect your delivery chain too rigidly and say, "This is our DevOps delivery chain," to the point that you can't adapt the next thing that comes out, you're not practicing DevOps. In DevOps, you're always looking forward. You're always looking at what's next, with the idea being that we don't end up in a cycle where six months down the road, after building something, we're then saying, "Oh, man, this is old. We need to retool again because so much is changing, and it's better, and we weren't prepared for that, and we didn't know things were going to change," which would be the most ridiculous statement in the tech field, period.

> *"You really can't get a certification in the principles and the philosophy of DevOps. As soon as you think you can, you have already alienated the environment."*
>
> —*Chris Riley*

That's where I'm uncomfortable about DevOps being a principle and philosophy, because it makes it much harder to manage and build a DevOps environment. It becomes a very large people problem, and people problems are the hardest problems to solve. You can't ignore that fact.

Viktor Farcic: I completely agree. That's why I get a bit disappointed when I go to conventions, as you do, and I see all of those commercials advertising every tool that I knew from three years ago as being DevOps-certified. It's very much, "Buy this, and you become DevOps." I don't know if you have the same feeling, but I'm freaking out because it's too commercialized.

Chris Riley: I'm a regent of the DevOps Institute. They started by offering courses on the high-level aspects of DevOps and culture, but they have since adapted and are now focusing a lot on tactics. You really can't get a certification in the principles and the philosophy of DevOps. As soon as you think you can, you have already alienated the environment. What you can get certified in are the specific processes and implementations.

Even in release automation, things are changing. It's not a static environment.

The speed of change

Viktor Farcic: You're right about the speed of change being tremendous. In today's world, it's impossible to follow. If we stick with your Jenkins examples, in a couple of years' time, it moved from one container scheduler to another, it got a few hundred new plugins, new UIs, ditched the *old way* of defining jobs in favor of the everything-as-code philosophy, and so on. Jenkins is only one of many examples. I'm lucky that my job allows me to spend more time learning new tech than most other people, and yet I have a constant feeling of falling behind.

Moving on, though, I saw that you're very focused on transitions from one culture to another. You've spoken with a range of people, from those in big enterprises to those in small start-ups. Have you seen any patterns or differences between the approaches?

Chris Riley: It's changed a lot in the last four years from when I had the initial conversations with an enterprise, when most people were opportunistic and saying, "Oh, yeah, we're considering DevOps. That's good. We know something new is coming." Then, you had this bifurcation of the small start-ups building bottom-up DevOps shops or principles.

I shouldn't say that because I just said DevOps is not a thing. In the early days of DevOps, it was almost as if you had this exclusive members-only DevOps club where enterprises need not apply. The mindset was, "Hey, let's leave this to the secret club of people who know how to release software really fast." But then it changed very, very quickly, and enterprises very quickly jumped on board. However, the huge wave of adoption didn't actually come until Docker. When Docker came out, it felt like Docker was already behind, so enterprises picked up the pace a little bit, and you saw a lot more adoption because Docker was so pervasive.

What I should say is *containers* were so pervasive that enterprises accepted and bought into DevOps immediately. So, it happened very quickly. The bifurcation was not as big. What's big is that enterprises don't have the luxury of just ripping out everything and starting over, whereas start-ups can tool their entire delivery chain to be in line with the DevOps methodology.

DevOps in the tech industry

Viktor Farcic: Sometimes there is an advantage in starting late. Start-ups created now don't have the baggage that bigger and older companies have. Not being able to erase history often slows us down, and in an industry like ours, where everything can change from one day to another, being a start-up without legacy applications can be a huge advantage.

With that frame of mind, how do you promote new values, processes, and tools? I guess it doesn't matter whether it is DevOps or something else; there should be a mechanism that a company can use to propagate change.

> *"Application development will generally buy into DevOps, as will most organizations. If they don't, then you have an HR problem."*
>
> *—Chris Riley*

Chris Riley: The coolest thing I've seen in enterprises, and it works really well, is adoption via stewardship. These companies have built—and I hate this term—Centers of Excellence, where they will build an awesome DevOps environment and culture somewhere within the organization. It will do a great job of cranking out the code for maybe a very small, not super-critical mission application, and they will use that, and they will steward it across the organization.

Some organizations use it as a political thing, and they will steward more naturally, such as promoting internally, whereas other organizations make a structure out of it. In fact, there's a very large media company in the US where that's exactly what they do.

They have this small DevOps environment that invests in tools and the processes. They say, "Hey, development teams! We have a thousand small development teams (I don't know if it's a thousand, but it's a lot of small 10- and 20-person development teams). All of you out there are doing your thing, and you're doing it your way and that's fine. However, if you want us to support you, which means both budget and technical support, then you're going to have to use one of the tools that the DevOps team created." That's a very natural driver rather than having to say, "Oh, we probably should get on board with it," and they do.

With this particular media company, it's a little bit easier because their development teams are so separate from each other. They have a development team for each media site that they own. There's a lot of them, so it's a little bit easier because they're already structured with the two teams, versus, say, a bank that is structured with one monolithic team. Even in large banks, what they have is called the shared services division, and that's a buttered layer between IT and application development and the shared services that will buy into DevOps.

Application development will generally buy into DevOps, as will most organizations. If they don't, then you have an HR problem. The hard part is integrating with the IT team. What shared services do is approve processes and tools. They negotiate with IT on what could be used and what can't be used on behalf of the developers, and it works. It's a big effort, but it all works at the end of the day.

And I think that's really cool because enterprise adoption is always an excuse, but I don't think it is anymore because a lot of people will just say, "Yes, DevOps is really cool, but we're too big." The whole "We're too big" response isn't adequate, but I think a lot of enterprises have tuned into that.

Viktor Farcic: When I hear companies use "We're too big" as an excuse—and I hear it quite often—my first thought is always, "No, your culture isn't ready. The type of organization structure or the communication within your company is not aligned."

Chris Riley: Yes, and unless these companies initiate a DevOps strategy, they're going to fall behind the competition. Eventually, they're just not going to have a choice, because somebody's application is going to be better. For instance, Amazon is going to come and enter healthcare, which is now what Amazon is talking about doing. So, now hospitals have to worry about having ease of use and quality applications.

Viktor Farcic: When those things happen, when somebody truly disrupts the industry, that results in the industry's need to suddenly change for the better. It leaves me wondering whether it's already too late when that happens.

Chris Riley: It is, and it isn't. This isn't related to DevOps, but before Satya Nadella came on board as the current CEO at Microsoft, it felt as though Microsoft was too late. And then they did it, but they could do it because they had the money. It's the sheer power of cash behind them.

You know, what's funny to me is that there's a very large

financial institution that's famous in the DevOps space for building its own open source DevOps tool. But a small division within this organization already reaches out to the DevOps community on a regular basis—and they're not even connected to the group who are developing this tool—asking consultants to come in and explain to them what DevOps is. It's absolutely baffling. You have an entire team that's going around talking about how amazing the DevOps is, who have built their own tool, and it's great, but the team developing the tool doesn't even know this other division exists! But back to your point. It's like your structure is broken; you have a communication problem that means something is seriously wrong.

Viktor Farcic: Exactly. Have you ever been in a situation where somebody says, "Oh we tried it and we failed. This does not work, and this was all a waste of effort?"

Chris Riley: Oh, yeah, the partial-attempt-and-failure response. It's akin to saying you're too big.

What I do is ask, "What aspect of the DevOps methodology did you try to input? Did you try to go directly to continuous delivery? Because that's not a good idea. Why don't you automate testing first? Let's automate something smaller. Don't go to canary releases tomorrow and tell me, "Oh, we did the canary release thing; it released some software too fast and people were pissed." If you say that, then my response would simply be, "Why did you pick that? Automate something else."

Viktor Farcic: I've heard the story that nobody can skip through time if you don't know what automation is. They say that you're going to fail to implement containers because your gap is going to be too big to jump into something.

Chris Riley: I don't think you can jump in there, and more widely, that mentality has been a problem all along, where people think that a tool is going to solve the problem. They think Jenkins is a release automation tool in the DevOps market, and that if they buy into it then they've done DevOps right, because Jenkins is going to bring DevOps to their organization, and then they're done. That mentality never works. If you expect the tool to do it for you, then you're wrong.

Bottom-up or top-down?

Viktor Farcic: That's why I think it's very dangerous when you buy into tools that promise certain cultural changes just by existing. In your view, then, what works better: bottom-up or top-down? And more specifically, when there's an initiative, where should it come from?

Chris Riley: I'm going to answer that a little bit differently because I think both questions, in their own ways, are critical. But that being said, if I had to pick one, I would say bottom-up. If you have an issue with bottom-up development, as in you have a developer who's telling you they don't want to focus on building the application and they don't want to get it out the door faster, then you have the wrong developer. If that's your problem, then that presents you with a bigger challenge, because you shouldn't have to explain to a developer why building an application and speed to market are good.

For that reason, when looking at bottom-up versus top-down, I think 90% of the effort is top-down because that's where the biggest hurdle is. This is something that's very common in quality assurance teams, or Quality Engineering (QE) teams, who are driven to do something new because they believe in automation. They have this holistic point of view of the entire delivery chain. They see everything. But QE teams never have a budget, ever, and they have to justify to research and development teams (R&D), who may have to then justify to somebody else in order to gain the budgets to get functional testing tools for Selenium, for instance.

That's the hardest part. And when these people go to those decision makers, if those decision makers don't understand the value of DevOps, they may not say it's dumb; but they may say you can't do that, or they may just be dismissive because they don't understand how it's going to impact the bottom line. It's becoming easier to explain, because you can very easily see a lot of industries now point to very high-quality applications that are getting better customer satisfaction, more customer engagement, and actually impacting the bottom line.

> *"A lot of industries now point to very high-quality applications that are getting better customer satisfaction, more customer engagement, and actually impacting the bottom line."*
>
> —*Chris Riley*

That's changing minds, and sometimes, changing minds is impossible. But you also have the problem of compensation structures. If the operations teams are compensated for making sure stuff never breaks, then they're in a direct conflict of interest with the developers who are compensated for making sure that they get the application out of the door. Operations don't want anything to change, ever, because when things change, things can break.

When IT operations are focused on the fact that they don't want developers to release anything, they're naturally going to become a bottleneck. So, compensation and organizational structures can only be changed from the top down. Going from 100-person development teams to 5- to 10-person development teams is just another big structural change that can only happen top-down. I just think that's where the effort goes, and the effort has to be spent.

Viktor Farcic: When you mentioned developer teams, do you refer to self-sufficient teams that can develop and operate?

Chris Riley: I know there are different ways of approaching this, but the cool thing about containers and microservices is that they're not just infrastructure tools; they're also application architecture tools. If you start to consider building and breaking your application down into services, you naturally run into the fact that we need smaller development teams because, for example, you don't need 100 people writing a login service. You only need two. I think this new architecture naturally takes organizations that way, which is cool, but they have to be ready for that change. That being said, I still gravitate toward the small teams that have a DevOps engineer, developers, and quality assurance folk.

I have not, with the exception of some very rare environments, bought into the idea that if you build it, then you also test it and support it. I do think if you test it, you need to test your own code, but somebody else is creating the automation. I don't think that it's appropriate to go to a developer and say, "You need to write Selenium scripts for your code," because it will never get done. Somebody else has to be doing that. I still think that there is a need for that QE unit, either a team that butters across all developers or individuals within smaller teams.

DevOps departments

Viktor Farcic: What do you think about DevOps departments then? I'm seeing quite a lot of them today, especially in enterprises. When I take a closer look at these enterprises, I'm told they're going to form this DevOps department that will be in charge of doing DevOps for the whole company.

Chris Riley: Going back to that large media company I referenced earlier, that's what they do. They implement but they're not responsible for implementing organization-wise. They're more responsible for knowing both what the best practices and the best tools are. What they do implement organization-wise are things such as chatbots, integrations with AWS or whatever the cloud provider is, and things that truly are tools that you would use because what they're integrating with is global.

Everybody uses Slack, so they can create things for Slack. Everybody is using the same cloud, so they can create things for this cloud. That's where I think you have a DevOps department. I don't think it's necessarily true that you go into any organization and say, "We need to form a DevOps department," and then that's the answer to the problem.

"DevOps engineer," as a title, makes sense to me, but I don't think you necessarily have DevOps *departments*, nor do you seek that out. Instead, I think DevOps is a principle that you spread throughout your entire development organization. You should look to reform your organization in a way that supports those initiatives versus just saying that you need to build this DevOps unit, and there you go, you're done—you're DevOps. Because by doing that, you really have to empower that unit, and most organizations aren't willing to do that. You can't just set people off on a race to build DevOps and then not give them the tools to actually do it. I think that's normally what happens next if you just build a DevOps organization.

> *"'DevOps engineer,' as a title, makes sense to me, but I don't think you necessarily have DevOps departments, nor do you seek that out."*
>
> —*Chris Riley*

Viktor Farcic: In my view, having a DevOps department creates another silo. I heard once—and it's a description that I really like—that DevOps is all about empathy, and that by joining different people together in the same team, you develop empathy in people, and they finally understand each other's pain.

Chris Riley: The only problem with saying things like that is the CFO doesn't give a shit about empathy, and the person with the money may not care about that at all. The HR department might, but that's the problem with selling anything. You have to speak their language, and the CFO is going to respond to money. Either you're saving us money, or you're making us more money, and I think DevOps is doing both, which is cool. I think what's nice about that explanation is the fact it doesn't seem insurmountable. It's kind of like how Pixar was structured.

After Steve Jobs started at Pixar, he structured all of the work environments where the idea was to create chance encounters among the employees, so that the graphic designer of one movie would talk to the application developer of another, even when they don't even have any real reason to interact with each other. The way they did it at Pixar was that, as everybody has to go to the bathroom, they put the bathrooms in a large communal area where these people are going to run into each other—that's what created that empathy. They understand what each other's job is. They're excited about each other's movies. They're excited about what they're working on, and they're aware of that in everything they do. It's a really good explanation.

Viktor Farcic: I agree that CFOs and the young people very high up on the corporate ladder mostly understand money. How do you translate that? What do you say and what will you earn if you do DevOps? How is it translated into money and how do you measure it?

Chris Riley: Sometimes it seems like it doesn't measure directly. When I talk to organizations who are building line-of-business applications and the internal applications they use to do their job, I explain things differently because, in that context, user satisfaction doesn't matter as much. Their users aren't paying them, and they're not going to up and leave.

They're going to do what they're told.

There is something to be said for customer satisfaction. Coming from the SharePoint space, this is something I know very well. If people inside the organization don't like SharePoint, they won't use SharePoint. By virtue of not using SharePoint, you're not hitting your initiative. So, users do matter, as does user experience, which is both look and feel as well as keeping things up to date and addressing issues when they come up. If somebody has a bug, it gets fixed.

Typically, in the line-of-business scenario, it's going to take you at least three months to fix that bug, by which point your customers—who are typically internal users who hate their jobs—are less productive. That effect then snowballs. So, that's the line-of-business case.

If you're a bank, you're trying to not lose customers, because it's a highly competitive market, and by default, everybody hates banks. Firstly, you'll want to create a customer experience that reduces costs because people are not engaging with your branches and calling your customer support line as much. Secondly, you can release new offerings—the new checking account, whatever it is—faster, which means that you can get customers of those offerings faster and engage more of them. All of these things are not going to be deliverable unless you have a really powerful application, and that powerful application is going to have bugs because bugs happen. You need to be able to respond to those bugs because the customer today is highly critical, and you can't change the customer.

You're also going to have to adapt to how your customer uses applications and what they expect. What they expect is an app that works. They want to see you making frequent changes, resolving problems faster, and being responsive to their usage behavior. All of this is an expectation now, and unless you're an organization that thinks you're powerful enough to change the world's user behavior, you need to be able to respond to that because, if you don't, you'll lose customers no matter what you do; or at the very least, you're just going to have angry customers who are going to need more support, which, in turn, is going to be more expensive for you to work with your customer base, and it's going to be harder to sell them new things.

Viktor Farcic: That's a valid point and one I find quite interesting.

Chris Riley: Really, any organization can relate to the bottom line of either losing customers and not being able to compete, or not being able to execute on new initiatives fast enough. It's all boiling down to that day. To me, it seems like a no-brainer. If you're in a room with somebody who's really going to fight against this, then all I can think is, "OK, it's going to happen to you whether you know it or not."

Take Apple, for instance. Apple is going into banking in a very sneaky way. It's going to creep up on these banks with Apple Pay because now, with Apple Pay, I can send you a text message with money. If you don't have a linked card, you now have credit with Apple and an account with Apple, and they're just doing that because they can. It should scare the banks.

I think it's exactly like, "OK, it'll happen to you, and you're going to regret it." You'll lose your job, but then, at the next company you go into, you're going to be the biggest DevOps champion in that company because of the experience you had in your previous job.

Viktor Farcic: While I agree with you on many of the things we've spoken about, I have the impression that you are mostly referring to in-house development. Do you have any thoughts about what happens to companies that externalize their software, making it a commodity?

Outsourcing and the commoditization of software

Chris Riley: That's an interesting point, and I'm going to be bold. I don't want to alienate an industry, but I think that these outsourced companies have hopefully embraced DevOps because they have to support their customers, as well as because they want to build applications faster and better.

That being said, I believe that technology is becoming such a core component of business these days that it's a huge mistake to outsource your application development. I just don't think it's something that companies should be doing. Having experienced something like that before, I know how it works and I know the negotiations that happen because you have to succumb to the development firm's limitations, skill sets, or whatever it is. Making changes and the complexity around that is difficult. I just don't think that any organization should consider outsourcing unless something is just not financially feasible. But you have to be honest with yourself when you say that you're building a mediocre application if it's an issue of money, and you have to be OK with that, and you have to know that, at some point in time, you're going to have to make the switch back from outsourcing.

For example, there's a company that builds an influencer marketing platform, and the first three versions of it were not great, mainly because it was super buggy. But the platform solved a problem, people were interested, it worked, and they got customers—but it wasn't great. This company then decided to go in-house, and when they went in house, they focused on hiring a development manager that understood DevOps and everything changed. Because of that switch, their application quality went through the roof. It just was awesome, and this is a very small company, and now their platform is very cool.

> *"I think that these outsourced companies have hopefully embraced DevOps because they have to support their customers, as well as because they want to build applications faster and better."*
>
> —*Chris Riley*

Viktor Farcic: I think it's only a question of whether a company has already realized that they're a software company. If they are, then software development is a core business, and nobody disputes that you do not externalize core business. It's all about whether a company is aware that every company is a software company today.

With that being said, I'm curious about trust. How do you trust an external company will do such important work well? Can you outsource development and yet maintain control and quality?

Chris Riley: You see the same on a dating site, which is typically fully outsourced. I think this is interesting from a SecOps and application development perspective. AshleyMadison.com is a great example. All of their development was outsourced, and we've all seen how that worked out for them. They blindly accepted what was being developed, and it turned out to be a massive exploit and just really dumb. I believe it should be illegal for organizations not to encrypt passwords in their database. If you do that, then you should be breaking some sort of law, because it's not fair to any of your users, because you don't have control over that data when you outsource, really.

I just believe that organizations need to have their development in-house and the only reason to outsource is if it's just not financially possible. If it's not financially possible, you have to realize you're only going to outsource for a short amount of time.

Viktor Farcic: To be honest, you have to question the concept of financial feasibility when you've seen how much work a single good developer can do, even though they might be expensive.

Chris Riley: No doubt. We've experienced this at Sweetcode, and that's why I'm kind of impassioned about it. We have a platform internally that we use to streamline the process of doing research, deciding what we want to write about based on that research, finding one of our contributors to write it, and then writing it and publishing it.

We have a platform that streamlines the process, so it takes less manual effort to get it done. We have written this platform three times now. The first time I wrote it, it sucked really bad. The second time, we went to an outsourced company. I know enough about application development as I'm really good at architecture, so I was in a luxurious position where I could review their code because I knew what was going on. Most organizations don't have this. I realized the quality was horrible. The thing worked, but the quality was so bad that any new developer coming on board was not going to be able to take it on. In that situation, the best option was to rewrite.

The only thing I would say is that, for those who don't know anything about application development and have a great idea, they may have to turn to a firm for expertise, and that's a bad position to be in. I mean, if you're a founder, it's almost like every company has to have an application, just as every start-up has to have a technical founder.

> *"For those who don't know anything about application development and have a great idea, they may have to turn to a firm for expertise, and that's a bad position to be in."*
>
> —*Chris Riley*

Viktor Farcic: Does that mean if I externalize something, then that something is probably a thing that I don't consider within the realm of my core business? That sounds to me as if it translates into, "Oh, software is not really important for me. Let me put it in the same box as cleaning services," or something along those lines.

Chris Riley: You're right—I mean, what do we outsource at our company? We outsource our legal, which is actually pretty damn important, our bookkeeping, our CPA, and our HR. We are not in the business of law or accounting or HR.

You're absolutely right that they're all good quality services, but it's not important enough for us, for the product and the offering that we're building, to try to bring those in-house. I think you're right, though, that if you don't give it enough consideration, then you just don't care.

Viktor Farcic: To finish up, I was wondering whether you had any advice for those just starting their DevOps journey.

Starting your journey in DevOps

Chris Riley: The DevOps culture will come no matter what. It could come with a bloody mess or some kumbaya moment, but it will come on its own as long as organizations focus on automation and releasing better applications sooner.

For that reason, I don't recommend that organizations waste time talking about communication or culture. Instead, I think they should be putting quotas on the number of releases a day, response time to issues, and the percentage of automation. They should make these objectives tied to bonuses and job performance.

If the organization pushes the needle to have more frequent releases and better application quality, then they will figure out the culture, and they'll figure out how to communicate better, because these will all be major barriers.

Some will figure it out via employee attrition, and others after lots of arguments. But at the same time, that same organization would have distorted the lessons of culture to begin with, had it been taught top-down.

Viktor Farcic: That's brilliant. Thank you very much for your time.

10

Ádám Sándor

Cloud technology consultant

Introducing Ádám Sándor

Ádám works to improve software delivery rates in business by utilizing cloud technologies. A certified ScrumMaster and Certified Kubernetes Administrator, Ádám spends much of his time involved in the technologies of DevOps. You can follow him on Twitter at @adamsand0r.

Viktor Farcic: To start, could you tell us what, in your opinion, is DevOps, and how do you use DevOps in your career?

What is DevOps, and how is it used?

Ádám Sándor: I'm a Java developer turned cloud-native consultant currently working for Container Solutions, an Amsterdam-based consultancy company, where we help companies adapt to cloud-native technologies while exploring the best practices in DevOps.

I believe that DevOps is a way of developing software where you break down the barriers between the people who develop software and the people who run the software in production. Ideally, this would mean that a single team can be responsible for running their own software in production, which can improve the time it takes to fix problems. DevOps can also improve the design of software because developers get plenty of feedback—which allows them to design solutions in such a way that they will be able to run those solutions. I very much believe this is part of the "you build it, you run it" philosophy.

Viktor Farcic: But why would anyone want to do that?

Ádám Sándor: Because DevOps helps speed up the delivery of software, while reducing the risk of deploying it and breaking something. DevOps also helps meet a growing need to improve customer satisfaction by being able to quickly deliver new features and to fix any problems that customers are experiencing.

> *"DevOps is a way of developing software where you break down the barriers between the people who develop software and the people who run the software in production."*
>
> —*Ádám Sándor*

Viktor Farcic: So, how do you start implementing the DevOps process?

Ádám Sándor: At Container Solutions, where I'm a cloud technology consultant, we begin by conducting a discovery process: two of us go to a company that is already working with an idea. We enter the discovery process after some pre-sales meetings, and so as a result, we already have an idea of what their problems are, and what they would like to solve. The issue is usually focused on their software delivery process. Over the course of a couple of days, we conduct workshops that explore the company's software landscape, their delivery processes, and their overall architecture. This lets us learn about what's going on in the company and verify whether the problems that the client has identified are the *actual* problems that they need to deal with. It's important to make sure that we're out to solve their actual problems, rather than provide some quick reactions to some bad things that might have happened to our client.

A good comparison here would be a doctor who sees a patient with a headache but doesn't just give the patient some aspirin because their head hurts—instead, they listen to the patient and they might discover that the patient needs to change their diet. In the context of the companies I work with, one company might invite us to install Kubernetes so their software development becomes more efficient. But we look carefully and we see that the delivery of their software passes through three departments. First, the developers develop the software. Then it goes to the testing department, before it's finally transferred to the operations department. Now, that process right there is the real problem! Kubernetes won't improve that company's software delivery. The company's problem, in this case, is not software based, and so we try to convince them to break down these barriers and make teams responsible for their production environment. Once that problem is solved, we might still bring in Kubernetes to more efficiently implement the new processes.

Viktor Farcic: How often do you find people go to the doctor with the wrong symptoms? Do people even know what's wrong with their technology processes to begin with?

Ádám Sándor: It's hard for me to put a number on how many times people come to us with the wrong symptoms, but it happens both ways, and sometimes the customer can be very right. Sometimes they've done their homework and they come to us with a good idea of what their problems are and how to solve them. They can still be struggling to reach the next step of actually implementing solutions though, and in those cases it's usually because they don't have all the knowledge they need in-house. That's where we can help in those situations.

At other times, clients can be very wrong about their symptoms, even to the level where we can't help them because they're simply not ready to change. In those extreme scenarios, a company can be grasping at straws for new technology to solve their problems without actually identifying the real issues at hand.

Kubernetes – the solution to all of our problems?

Viktor Farcic: My understanding is that you mostly work with Kubernetes, which means you're into the latest and greatest. Is that a concern for you?

Ádám Sándor: We've never had experience with this technology failing, so in that sense, it's not an issue in that it's the latest and greatest. We never advise customers to jump into something, even though we are surfing on the edge of new technology and watching out for everything that's coming our way. Usually, we recommend technologies that have already proven themselves for at least a year and that we know will work for the customer.

Viktor Farcic: Does that mean everybody should move to Kubernetes? What does it involve? I imagine it's not only creating new Docker images and YAML files. Let's say that I'm a company that has existed for a long time and I have everything, how does it look for me?

Ádám Sándor: For such a company it will start with a proof of concept to prove internally whether Kubernetes works for you. Depending on your short term plans this will either focus on moving a legacy application to Kubernetes or creating something new using technologies the company plans to move towards. Whether a company wants to move some or all of it's legacy applications to Kubernetes can depend on many factors. What I would point out is that it's not impossible or even undesirable to do so.

Kubernetes is actually a surprisingly good system for supporting legacy applications, for example, with simple things like being able to inject configuration into a pod using files. You can very easily simulate a configuration files-based environment to old-school services that require huge config files, and so containers are a pretty backward-compatible technology.

> *"Kubernetes is actually a surprisingly good system for supporting legacy applications, for example, with simple things like being able to inject configuration into a pod using files."*
>
> —Ádám Sándor

Viktor Farcic: Another thing I'm curious about is if your site has a horribly managed legacy infrastructure with poorly designed applications, and you want to move them to containers and the cloud, would you first move them to Kubernetes on site and then switch to the cloud, or first move into the cloud without Kubernetes, or both?

Ádám Sándor: If possible use a cloud provider. They will do the heavy lifting of managing Kubernetes and other services you use freeing up your resources to focus on more business-centric tasks. But there can be valid reasons not to do that—heavy investments into a new datacenter, regulations about data storage, and so on.

Viktor Farcic: Wouldn't that create a defensive politic? Because if you have an army of engineers in charge of infrastructure on site, what do we do with them if we move everything? Will there be space for all of them?

Ádám Sándor: I don't know if there will be space for all of them, but I've never seen a project where people would have to be fired because there's simply no need for them anymore. Yes, with a cloud provider you don't need to run Kubernetes. But actually, there is plenty of work in setting up development and deployment tooling, and systems to track what's deployed where. This is the more business centric work I mentioned - ditch low value add work for stuff that will bring more direct value to your business.

Exploring the motivations for change

Viktor Farcic: What do you think is driving all of these requests for improvement? Are they driven by the competition or by a genuine interest in new technology?

Ádám Sándor: I think the biggest motivation we see—and what most companies are missing—is the ability to release software fast. They realize that they should release new software every half year, but they need to come to this realization before the competition is already gaining on them and put the proper processes in place early enough so the production pipeline is filled. It's this big pressure in today's market that ends up making engineers leave because, frankly, it's just a horrible environment to work in.

There is also an excitement for new technologies because when companies in the market are looking for engineers, their HR department feels that new recruits will ask, "OK, what technologies are you using?" And when they hear that what's being used isn't the very latest iteration, these new recruits won't be interested in working for the company. What management still feels most acutely is that when they have a new idea, by the time they get it into production, it's already way too late.

> *"What management still feels most acutely is that when they have a new idea, by the time they get it into production, it's already way too late."*
>
> —*Ádám Sándor*

Viktor Farcic: I've heard before that one of the motivations is not management's motivation for improvement, but actually attracting and keeping talent.

Ádám Sándor: Definitely!

Viktor Farcic: Does this mean that engineers are getting picky?

Ádám Sándor: Engineers are getting picky. If they're any good at their job, they won't join a company where they will be manually installing Linux servers.

Viktor Farcic: I'm just thinking that it's kind of contradictory with the politics of externalizing development to a third party because you can get on one site and then decide to ship everything to someone else.

Ádám Sándor: I think the "let's ship everything" mindset exists because the outsourcing trend isn't as strong as it was before. I'm no expert on this, because I've worked in only a small part of the market, but I have seen companies insourcing, as well as those who outsource but build up long-term development teams in cheaper countries. They don't think of those development teams as disposable labor, but know they are building them up for long-term use while attempting to integrate them into the company as first-class employees.

I think that companies and people are realizing that they need to attract people in order to keep people. Even if you don't have the challenge of hiring staff in another country, usually in Eastern Europe or India, there is just so much that needs to be known about the company, its products, and the current state of its applications and infrastructure. The process of hiring is expensive anyway. You want to retain employees for a long time, and you want to hire good people because people who are unskilled are even more expensive to train. You can hire someone on a cheap salary but then spend half a year getting them up to speed, which is going to cost a lot of money, and even more time.

Viktor Farcic: Is it the economy then that's driving companies away from outsourcing?

Ádám Sándor: I think it's also the new way of development for the whole DevOps culture: the idea that you build it, you run it, and that what the team owns is really a product. You marry the team to the product. The product owner, the designers, and the business analysts—everybody's a part of the product team. You want to keep them engaged with that product in the long-term because they really understand it. Companies really started valuing this long-term engagement, and that just doesn't work with outsourcing, or hiring disposable people.

Viktor Farcic: So, what's next? Is there anything coming next, or will we ride Kubernetes for a while to come?

A future beyond Kubernetes

Ádám Sándor: I'm quite surprised that the next thing is so slow to arrive, and that's probably because Kubernetes is not yet that widespread within the industry. But I do believe the next thing will be products built on top of Kubernetes, once Kubernetes becomes more widely used. But until then, Kubernetes is kind of at an impasse because it's a higher-level service than virtual machines and low-level networking.

I believe it's going to be either Kubernetes integrating more and more stuff, so it morphs into something that's somewhat different than it is now, or other products that will be built on top of it. But I don't see any of those products coming along any time soon. I think Helm is a good example, but that's not a commercial product.

> *"Kubernetes is not yet that widespread within the industry. But I do believe the next thing will be products built on top of Kubernetes...until then, Kubernetes is kind of at an impasse."*
>
> —Ádám Sándor

Viktor Farcic: If you want to run Kubernetes on site, would you recommend that I run it on top of a VM, or bare metal?

Ádám Sándor: I honestly don't have an informed opinion on that. Theoretically, it's much more efficient to run Kubernetes on bare metal, but the low-level networking stuff might just be too hard. Maybe it's best to let solutions like VMware take care of a lot of the really low-level hardware stuff; in which case, it's better that they speed up VMs. I don't think Kubernetes is mature in this environment, but again, I'm no expert.

Viktor Farcic: Do have any experience with or an opinion about unikernels?

Ádám Sándor: I don't have much experience. All I see is that they're a great idea. If you just look at it from a high level, they could totally beat containers because they feature the good parts of containers while running on hypervisors, which are basically what public clouds are—giant hypervisors.

But what I also see is that unikernels don't seem to mature fast enough to attract enough attention. The tooling is simply not there. Actually, cloud providers don't let you run whatever you want on their hypervisors, just their own VM images. So again, theoretically, it could go there, but practically, it's not really happening at the moment, and I don't have enough industry insight to know whether, secretly, Amazon is working on something or not.

Viktor Farcic: How about other cloud providers? This is something that I agree with, and correct me if I'm wrong, but for most of us, it doesn't make sense not to use cloud providers like AWS or Google because they're commoditized and know better than we what they do. What does that mean for the future of all the software and vendors built around capturing infrastructure and configuration management tools?

Ádám Sándor: I don't think configuration management tools will become obsolete because of cloud providers. You would totally provision your AWS infrastructure using Puppet, Chef, or Ansible.

Viktor Farcic: But should you, or even could you do that?

Ádám Sándor: As it stands, I don't think using Puppet, Chef, and Ansible makes a difference whether you use it with a cloud provider or with your on-site infrastructure. It's VMware who is on the spot with this; they are the competition to the cloud providers.

The problem with Puppet, Chef, and Ansible is that they don't really push you towards better infrastructure. They're just a nicer way of restricting the level of abstraction they provide on the operating system. That doesn't lead to a better way of deploying software; it's basically just nicer than writing a script that SSHs into machines and runs some other script there. But it's not that much nicer, so you don't get immutable infrastructure.

If you launch a thousand machines and want to run the same Puppet stuff on them, three will fail, and what do you do with that? You have no way to deal with this stuff, and it will take a really long time to speed up any machine, so basically, just these tools by their nature are the wrong thing. If we stay in the world of virtual machines, then the right solution is pre-baking images and then managing them.

That's where Docker comes in, because it's a hassle to install and to pre-bake virtual machines. There is nothing like a golden image and extending, so Docker comes in and solves that problem, but instead of doing it with virtual machines, they're doing it by building container images.

Viktor Farcic: Does that mean that their potential use from this would be building these images?

Ádám Sándor: It could be. But then, when you are building an image, nobody needs to use Ansible in a Docker file, even though they could, but I think nobody feels a great need to do that. Actually, we go back to scripting, because it's enough.

Viktor Farcic: From my understanding, I like those tools because no matter the state of my server, it would converge the image into the desired state.

Ádám Sándor: If I'm building images then I know the initial state, Vanilla Ubuntu...

Viktor Farcic: Exactly. I'm not sure I see why I wouldn't just run a shell script. I need apt-get to install this; I don't need to check whether this is installed because I know it's not.

Ádám Sándor: The funny thing is that, actually, these tools sort of work. Kubernetes does the same thing; it converges the state to where it should be. In that sense, it's not doing anything different from Ansible. Kubernetes actually works so much better because it does it on a whole different level of abstraction. When you already have pre-built images and you just need to orchestrate instances of those images, then you can do the dynamic state management, and you're okay.

Nobody's crying for immutable Kubernetes clusters, but all the crap that you do inside the operating system, the low-level things like putting a file here, copying another there, and setting a flag here, that's the stuff that you do want to pre-bake and get done with and never touch again, unless you build another new image.

Viktor Farcic: That means you follow that logic with immutability and pre-baking images. Does that then mean not always, but sometimes, actually using ConfigMaps in Kubernetes would be the wrong thing to do, if the idea is immutability?

Ádám Sándor: Yes, immutability needs to stop somewhere. Kubernetes itself is a super-dynamic system so, yes, it's absolutely contradicting immutability. But simply put, immutability makes sense up to a certain degree. I have seen super-configurable applications, and if you put those applications in a Docker container, you'll have 150 environment variables to configure that image, and that's not really where you want to be with your infrastructure.

Viktor Farcic: Do we need those things?

Ádám Sándor: You really want just to have a few very specific things that are different between environments. Get them, configure them, and don't touch the rest unless you are building something like a database image, which of course needs to be working in thousands of environments. But then, if that's the case, you can again lock down some parameters and build your own image from it that only changes those parameters for each environment you actually require. Ideally, all your environments would be exactly the same, and you should look at that state and then just drift away a little bit from that, just as little as possible.

Viktor Farcic: What would be a little? A number of replicas?

Ádám Sándor: Number of replicas, user passwords, whatever. Just these very basic things. Certificates, public hostnames, and so on.

Ubuntu and Red Hat in this new world

Viktor Farcic: I like discussing the question of what's becoming obsolete. That brings me back to operating systems. Do we need Ubuntu or Red Hat in this new world?

Ádám Sándor: Simply put, yes, we do. There are currently two places to use operating systems right now. One is on the server that is running the containers, and the other is inside a container. So, on the server that's running the containers, we already see a shift towards very minimalistic operating systems where they just do the bare minimum.

> *"[Do we need Ubuntu or Red Hat in this new world?]*
> *Simply put, yes, we do."*
>
> —*Ádám Sándor*

Viktor Farcic: I'm thinking of platforms like Rancher and CoreOS.

Ádám Sándor: Exactly. Take CoreOS, for example. It's very minimal and just launches containers, that's all. It runs Docker, and that's it, the OS inside the container.

Viktor Farcic: Is that even an OS?

Ádám Sándor: Well, we can call it an OS because it acts like one. But of course, it steals the kernel from the actual machine it's running on, while still pretending to be an OS. It's really an OS in the sense that all the tools are installed, and all the programs are in the Linux distribution. Do we need all that stuff? Often, we don't. Yes, they're nice to have for debugging reasons, and they're nice to have around for more legacy applications, but the legacy is in the very weakest sense because installing a JVM on a bare Linux where just the kernel lives is very difficult.

So, it's probably alright to have a bit of a Linux distribution around it. Maybe in the future somebody could produce a very minimal image that really only has what the JVM needs. That would be nice because it'd be more secure and smaller, but I really think that one of the main reasons why Docker has become so popular is that it's so backward-compatible in the sense that you are inside the image, you're just doing

Linux stuff. It's very easy to get there, so it provides the good stuff without sacrificing much. The fact that there are some programs in there that aren't really used is not such a big issue.

Viktor Farcic: I presume then that, in a way, it will be a threat to companies like Red Hat, because you just named Ansible and Red Hat as being less relevant.

Ádám Sándor: Red Hat knows that, and that's why they're building OpenShift, and then Red Hat Atomic Linux to run OpenShift.

> *"Red Hat was the smart one who recognized Kubernetes early on and jumped on board. Now they're at the point where they can practically get rid of their own Linux distribution because they have the new things on OpenShift."*
>
> —*Ádám Sándor*

Red Hat was the smart one who recognized Kubernetes early on and jumped on board. Now they're at the point where they can practically get rid of their own Linux distribution because they have the new things on OpenShift. Meanwhile, Ubuntu and Zeus are both trying to get on board, and the issue is that they are nowhere near the level where Red Hat is, and that's why Red Hat is already at the point where they can buy CoreOS, their biggest competition in this space.

Viktor Farcic: What do you prefer? Vanilla Kubernetes? Or do you prefer to layer on top of it?

Ádám Sándor: I do like OpenShift. If somebody is willing to pay for it, then both the support and security it provides are worth it. Kubernetes is like Linux. There are countless people committing to it and a lot going on, so nobody adheres to strict governance, which is completely fine. But let's say you want to build an internal cloud for your bank. You want to be sure of its security, though of course nobody can guarantee it absolutely. The features and security that Red Hat provides with OpenShift make sense.

Viktor Farcic: If I'm not willing to pay, should I go with OpenShift Origin or Kubernetes?

Ádám Sándor: I think you have to choose what you value more. If it's a fast pace with new features and completely open source, then you are going to want to go with Kubernetes, versus the slower pace, greater stability, and lack of openness that you get with OpenShift. OpenShift does, however, feature extra features like CI/CD pipelines and a nice GUI, which some might value. But then again, some might not. So that's your trade-off. OpenShift Origin is open source, of course, but you're not going to be fixing bugs in it.

Viktor Farcic: What comes to your mind?

Ádám Sándor: Cloud provider comparison.

Viktor Farcic: What do you think about the rest, outside of the three big guys? Microsoft Azure, for example.

Ádám Sándor: I don't know the rest of the pack very well—but currently with any cloud provider I would look at the quality of their managed Kubernetes and serverless offerings, because you will need those to build modern software. But Google Cloud doesn't seem to be able to capture a large market share even though their Kubernetes offering is the best out there.

Viktor Farcic: I think a lot of readers will be shocked by the fact that there is an area in which Google is considered a small player.

Ádám Sándor: It's weird, but true. Google really messed up in the public cloud space. A few years ago their strategy totally broke down. Funnily enough, Amazon's new thing is how they also tried to skip containers and to define the future, which is the whole idea of lambdas. It's a super-restricted programming model but has great scaling and is very cloud-native. Google actually kind of did the same with App Engine back in the day. They put all their bets on an attempt to go serverless, but it was simply too early. They were like, "we're not doing this primitive stuff where you just spin up virtual machines because networking is just like VMware." They provide a proper programming model and a special database where you'll be super-tied-into the cloud, but very cloud-native, very easy from the cloud providers' perspective to run your application in a cheap way.

It was a great idea, except people said, "I just want to go to a GUI, click and spin up a VM, and then do the exact same stuff I've been doing for 20-plus years." It's slowly changing now Docker containers are popular, because you can still do the same stuff you were doing before but in an ever-so-slightly different way.

> *"Docker containers are popular because you can still do the same stuff you were doing before but in an ever-so-slightly different way."*
>
> —*Ádám Sándor*

Viktor Farcic: Correct me if I'm wrong, but doesn't Kubernetes sit on top of a provider and abstract whatever the provider is doing? Theoretically, if it's stable, my Kubernetes is going to do the same things no matter if I'm running on Azure, AWS, or Google. But isn't that a threat to the business? What will be a differentiator? What prevents me as a user from going from one to another?

Ádám Sándor: Price. If Kubernetes becomes that much of a commodity, then it's just going to be the price. But there's more to it than that. It's also the services around it. How is the machine learning stuff? That's where they are really going to differentiate and try to hook you with things like lambda, where they can also lock you into their code execution.

Viktor Farcic: But would they really care about additional services outside Kubernetes?

Ádám Sándor: Of course—there is a lot of stuff Kubernetes just doesn't do. Databases, machine learning, DNS, and others. The ecosystem of the cloud provider absolutely matters. So does the depth of integration of that ecosystem with Kubernetes and the quality of the Kubernetes offering itself.

Viktor Farcic: The services offered are what differentiates or will differentiate one provider from another. I assume there will be no provider that's better at all the services than any other. One will be better at machine learning, another will be better at big data, and stuff like that. But does this mean that the future consists of us running our cluster or clusters spread across multiple platforms?

Does the future revolve around clusters?

Ádám Sándor: For a larger company that might make sense, but there is a pretty big cost involved because the whole management of the cloud itself varies. For example, there might be differences in the API or the UI.

If you're on Google Cloud and you're running your applications on Google Kubernetes Engine, just managing the stuff that is not inside Kubernetes is not rocket science because the APIs and everything are pretty nice, but you will have plenty of code, terraform, or whatever was written that is dealing with that part. It's not that easy to just import part of your application over to Azure or AWS and write some CloudFormation and deal with the pricing and the whatnot. You have to be sufficiently big to be able to utilize these kinds of synergies, as long as you understand that it's not going to be easy to just use multiple providers.

Viktor Farcic: That's a great point. I know that other contributors in this book have also raised the issue of vendor lock-in. But sadly, I know we're out of time now. I just wanted to thank you for taking the time to talk to me today.

Ádám Sándor: No problem at all, I've really enjoyed it. Thank you.

11

Júlia Biró

Site Reliability
Engineer at Contentful

Introducing Júlia Biró

Júlia is an experienced infrastructure and tooling engineer with interests in scalable systems, automation, and DevOps. Her experience at companies including Prezi, Ericsson, and currently Contentful give her a wealth of knowledge of how DevOps is integrated into modern IT practices. You can follow her on Twitter at @nellgwyn21.

Viktor Farcic: I know you've worked in DevOps for most of your career, Julia, so I was wondering if we could begin with an overview of your experiences with DevOps and how you got involved in it?

The lightbulb moment

Júlia Biró: I was born and raised in Hungary and trained as a mathematician. I wanted to see if I could take my favorite subject from school and turn it into a career. That turned out to be not such a smart idea. I was not cut out to do math as a career, and I found myself being more interested in the more practical problems. Because of that, in the end, someone suggested that I might want to learn programming, and this is how I gravitated towards the IT sector.

Once I was committed, I started training as a software engineer, and eventually, I was lucky enough to join a wonderful company called Prezi, where I was a very junior engineer placed on the infrastructure/DevOps team. It was as if a light bulb had switched on within me. I suddenly found myself knowing that this kind of engineering was what I wanted to do, and from that moment three and a half years ago, I would say I became a DevOps engineer.

The dictionary definition of DevOps

Viktor Farcic: Now imagine that we're looking up the word DevOps in the dictionary. What definition would we find?

Júlia Biró: In my dictionary, you would find that DevOps is an idea of the functions and responsibilities of teams running services in a company, and the corresponding set of tools to make that happen. There is this fancy name for it, the DevOps toolchain, but it's just a buzzword. It's really whatever anyone wants to understand it as.

> *"DevOps is an idea of the functions and responsibilities of teams running services in a company, and the corresponding set of tools to make that happen."*
>
> —*Júlia Biró*

Viktor Farcic: Could you expand on what you mean about it being a buzzword?

Júlia Biró: It's the idea that DevOps is a silver bullet that will make you successful, and that if you adopt DevOps, then everyone will be so much happier. But to really adapt to what DevOps is would be akin to changing three of your internal organs or becoming an animal. It's a really deep structural change that is hard to make unless you are starting very small and have this idea of going towards that ideal from the very beginning. You also must have the flexibility to do it from the start. So, unless you have all of that, then it's very hard to achieve, although there are examples of that happening.

Viktor Farcic: From what I understand, you worked at Ericsson, which is fairly big, before you worked in Prezi, which is comparatively relatively small. Did you see a difference?

Júlia Biró: Very much, though I don't consider Ericsson, at least the parts where I worked, to be DevOps in any sense of the word, partly because the product that I was working on was very different. I don't see how DevOps works with products that have 15-year life cycles and two-year release cycles, which is the case with software that runs on the kind of infrastructure Ericsson produces. I'm not saying it's impossible. It's just I haven't seen it.

What I have seen up close though is that leaders in DevOps practices seem to have adopted the DevOps mentality from the point when their company was very small, and as a result, they grew with determination. But it isn't that they decided to change a big thing into DevOps.

Viktor Farcic: Your profile says that you enable teams to take full ownership of their product. What do you mean by that?

> *"There's this concept in DevOps that the team should own their service, from writing and testing the code to running it, and to the point where they should actually react if something is not functioning well."*
>
> —*Júlia Biró*

Júlia Biró: There's this concept in DevOps that the team should own their service, from writing and testing the code to running it, and to the point where they should actually react if something is not functioning well. This is an idea of DevOps that I think is benefiting companies that are doing that.

The first prerequisite for that is that a service needs to be ownable, meaning in size and in complexity. It should be small enough for a reasonable team to own it, which is true for microservices. Then the idea is that one team should do everything, not that someone writes some code, and then separately someone else tests it, another person deploys and runs it, while a third team wakes up in the middle of the night when it breaks. I believe most companies will benefit if they move towards the full ownership model because then teams can be more active and creative in developing new things, and at the end of the day, they will have better quality products because there is less friction between the teams and a bunch of tools that can help them make that happen.

Viktor Farcic: I assume that you're not talking about a 100-person team.

Júlia Biró: To me, a team is a number of people who can reasonably cooperate in an organic way without someone telling them what to do. From my experience, I don't see how 100 people can do this together. Again, I'm not saying it is impossible, but I have no experience with teams this size.

Viktor Farcic: So, in that case, you have relatively small teams, but with a greatly increased amount of expertise they need to cover. Because that one small team needs to be capable of testing and deploying, along with all kinds of other things. How do those teams get that knowledge? When I speak with some teams, all I get from them is that "My people know how to write Java getters and setters."

Júlia Biró: Maybe you just give the team a piece of paper and tell them to build a Turing complete machine on that and go from there. Just joking! There's this idea of a full stack engineer, who can write both frontend code and backend code in a service client architecture. But the key here is to provide structured and well-documented tooling that people can actually use. It's the same way that you learn to use your washing machine and your coffee maker, or in our case, how you learn to use your CI, and your deployment tools. You need to make them easy, well documented, and well maintained.

What the DevOps or infrastructure team does is take away the complexity and provide DevOps as a service to the company, and to the other teams who are still doing the owning. The teams are still in ownership of what gets deployed when it gets deployed, and where it will be deployed, but they don't need a lot of access or knowledge to do that.

There are areas where it's easier to do this because the CI systems are very clickable and the UI is very good. Admittedly, creating tools with good user interfaces for other tasks take more effort. You can create a deployment system where you click a button and it's deployed, then you click another button and it's revoked. On the other hand, there are tasks where UI is not enough, and your team will need to acquire new knowledge. For example, in configuration management, if you want your teams to handle the environment that their service is running, they'll need to learn some kind of configuration management tool, which is usually, "Oh my god, I need to understand what an OS is*," which will definitely require a bit more knowledge than just writing JavaScript, unless you go serverless with Lambda (*Since the recording of this interview, the pressure for teams to understand and manage running environments have seriously decreased, owing to the spreading of container-ized platforms and serverless.).

Viktor Farcic: The thing is, when you go serverless with something like Lambda, there is no turning back.

Júlia Biró: But soon, serverless and Lambda will have their own complex management tooling. There is always this emerging layer of hiding complexity and the need to control that by building very, very complex things from that and then that itself becomes complex.

Viktor Farcic: Now that you're a site reliability engineer, do you find that there's a difference between a site reliability engineer and a DevOps engineer?

Site reliability engineering versus DevOps

Júlia Biró: In my understanding, site reliability engineering is a subset of DevOps engineering, a very specific subset with very different goals. A DevOps engineer's job is to make the other teams effective and to help this full ownership principle, while a site reliability engineer is a very simple metric that defines the success of my work, which is the uptime of the site.

> *"A DevOps engineer's job is to make the other teams effective and to help this full ownership principle."*
>
> —*Júlia Biró*

In my job, I provide the tools for the other teams so that they can operate their systems in a way that achieves high availability. My toolkit provides them with good tooling and good guidelines for testing, monitoring, alerting, easy deployment, and easy reversion. At the end of the day, I'm making sure that they themselves can run their services in a reliable way by owning that knowledge—from how to make good tests all the way to knowing how to handle incidents in an effective way.

Viktor Farcic: On the one hand, it would be managing tools, but on the other hand, it would be teaching.

Júlia Biró: That's exactly it! A DevOps engineer's job is to provide not only tools but also the best practices for teams. For example, it's within the DevOps realm to provide a good local development environment or a good testing environment for the organization.

As a site reliability engineer, I'm not that interested in the local development environments; that is not my realm. Where I am now, I haven't even seen our local development environment, and I've been there for five months now. But it is very much within my focus what kind of monitoring they should be doing. Monitoring should automatically be installed for a service. In fact, I have a constant barrage of questions that I should be answering, like how do I empower the other teams to create their own monitoring? How can they set up alerts very easily? How can they create good dashboards? What makes dashboards good? How is it going to be always available and providing the right information?

You can only expect teams to run their service responsibly if they have tools for that, while also having all the know-how and the concepts around it. It's very much my job to provide that. To give you an example, I am pushing right now for my company to adopt a new, more effective process for incident handling, because if we handle incidents better, then it means those incidents are going to be shorter, which is going to raise our availability and generally improve the company's uptime.

Viktor Farcic: Correct me if I'm wrong, but if the development teams have the ultimate responsibility for what they're doing, do they have a say or a choice in the sense of, for example, making the decision of whether or not to use Kubernetes? I mean it doesn't matter really if the team says no, it's my responsibility, I'm going to use something else. Is that their choice?

Júlia Biró: There are multiple points of view here. One is that the homogeneity of the stack and in the tools is usually beneficial in a company because it enables cross-pollination, mobility between teams, building and spreading of knowhow and expertise, and code writing. So, all of these are pointing towards it being better if we are all speaking the same language.

But on the other hand, with the heterogeneity of tasks we have, you might find that there is a better tool for the job. In general, the sense of freedom (and autonomy) is not to be underestimated. The approaches that I saw working well have one or two standard stacks that are supported. If you choose a different tool, then it's on you to get to the same level of quality, but if your team has the time for it, then why not? Right now, at Prezi, there are two standard stacks. There is tooling, monitoring, testing, whatever around it, and if you choose to do another stack for a user-facing service, then you need to build, for example, inter-service communication, client libraries, and so on.

The other thing that is important is to have a production-readiness checklist, with very specific acceptance criteria. You can help people by giving them an easy, simple choice: diverging from the standard has an expense. You have the teams pay for it and not the whole company, and the rest is just quality and process control in the classic sense of the word. Do whatever you want, just make sure you meet the criteria, and your tools are compatible, and then it's okay.

Viktor Farcic: So what would you say if I said that it's as if you could choose your responsibility, but it's in somebody else's interest to actually make it tempting and interesting for you to use, to the point where you don't really want to move away from it much?

Júlia Biró: It doesn't mean that you are not going to move away, because if it's very important for your user experience that you are actually going to provide tooling around the third stack, then other people will start to use it. It's just that the main goal you want to achieve is that people can very easily create a new service and own it, and so you want to spare them the work that they don't need to do.

This is what all the standard stacks and tooling are there for, but also the know-how for the same tool. You don't want people to solve the same problem of what is the best way to test or monitor a service 60 times independently of each other. What you want to do is give them good solutions and if they don't work, then they can look for their own solutions or they can raise the problem with you. But your end goal is to reduce friction and reuse knowledge wherever you can.

Viktor Farcic: I'm curious to know, where are the women in DevOps? I don't see them much in the field.

Women in DevOps... or the lack thereof

Júlia Biró: Well, you're talking to one! That being said, historically speaking since the mid-1980s, the ratio of women in STEM and tech fields has dropped. There's this great article (`https://www.npr.org/sections/money/2014/10/21/357629765/when-women-stopped-coding`) by the National Public Radio about why that's the case, and I would really recommend it to any of your readers.

But nowadays, we find that there is a rising tendency, partly owing to the attention of diversity gaps and partly owing to the will of the industry, for the other half of the population to try to become engineers too. They realized that the same ratio of women is going to be good at programming. But here's the thing: currently, the easiest way to get into tech and code learning is via the frontend. From my own experience, when I first tried to program it was just HTML and CSS, which is not even programming.

> *"The veterans in DevOps used to be real system administrators crawling between servers and configuring routers, which is not what they do anymore. But new people are coming from other areas of software engineering and IT."*
>
> —*Júlia Biró*

Most of the incentives that are inviting women into tech are starting in the frontend, where they'll be introduced to frontend or dynamic websites, and languages and frameworks like HTML+CSS, JavaScript, Python+Django, and Ruby on Rails. Why those languages? Probably because they're the easiest to try at home since you can become a very good frontend developer at your kitchen table. But infrastructure orchestration is not something you can do without some resources, and some problems only appear over a certain scale. It's a field that just needs some time for people to see into.

The veterans in DevOps used to be real system administrators crawling between servers and configuring routers, which is not what they do anymore. But new people are coming from other areas of software engineering and IT, and simply put, most of the women who are present in the field are predominantly at the beginning of their careers, so they are more on the frontend side, but they are seeping in slowly and steadily. Actually, it's not just me saying that. There's this great developer survey from Stack Overflow (`https://insights.stackoverflow.com/survey/2017#developer-profile-developer-role-and-gender`) which shows this.

Viktor Farcic: The reason I asked is that I know you're doing a lot of out-of-office activities with the likes of Rails Girls and Django Girls.

Júlia Biró: The various events I'm volunteering for are all aimed at inviting more women into tech. I'm working with organizations that are very emphatically extending this invitation, it's not about teaching skills to girls and girls only; it's more about letting the girls or women know that they should try tech because it's a fun thing to do.

I do this in all kinds of ways, such as participating in Rails Girls and Django Girls, which are open source workshops for women. These are one-day workshop events for building a dynamic web app from scratch attended by people who usually have zero previous knowledge of programming. The fun comes into it by the fact that at the end of the day they've created something that that they can actually show their families because it's deployed on the internet on real servers. The goal of these workshops is to give this feeling of how it works when you create something with technology. After attending these workshops, some women I know have actually changed their careers, and learned Python or Rails, and eventually became professional developers who now have totally legit careers in tech.

Another area where I'm working is taking the same concepts but aiming them at kids. It's said that by age 13, a girl realizes that math and technology aren't girly things. In fact, this article (https://www.theguardian.com/society/2017/sep/20/children-are-straitjacketed-into-gender-roles-in-early-adolescence-says-study) is a very important read about how we're straitjacketing gender roles in the early teenage years. What these programs are trying to do is get to these girls before that. We're trying to give them a very good experience with technology by creating stuff, where they learn that, *Wow, this can be for me.* If they happen to enjoy it, great, and if they don't, then no big deal; all they did was spend a day in a workshop with 15 other people and visited a cool office.

Viktor Farcic: Have you ever tried anything that aimed to get girls involved with tech from a high school age so that they could carry it through to a college degree?

Júlia Biró: Yes! There was a version of the kid's workshop where we did a 10-week course in Processing (`https://processing.org/`) for high school girls. I'm very proud that some of my former pupils from that course are already training as engineers.

But it's important to note that it's not just women who are not getting this invitation to join the tech world. I have also taught at art universities because I think that programming can be a creative tool in art, and I wanted to give this tool to artists. During this period, we were teaching introductory programming courses to artists, and some of them really liked it, and some of them even tried to use it in their work.

The organization that I'm working with in Hungary is Skool (`skool.org.hu`)—a project of the Technology Education Foundation—which works with young girls. They have a program where they are working with kids in children's homes, which is amazing because they're usually a group of young people who don't get an invitation into tech, but now they are getting 10-week courses in the children's home.

Viktor Farcic: That's really brilliant.

> *"Diversity does not just have to be about getting more women in the field. It's also about having more people from diverse backgrounds, like reaching out to underprivileged children."*
>
> —*Júlia Biró*

Júlia Biró: It really is, because diversity does not just have to be about getting more women in the field. It's also about having more people from diverse backgrounds, like reaching out to underprivileged children. Tech can be a social mobility fast elevator. Within a very small amount of time you can grow your earning potential a lot. All you need is a laptop and a connection to the internet, and you can become a wonderful engineer if you have the talent for it. But some people don't even have access to those basic tools. Trying to give access to those entry-level tools is part of the job. But it is also important to recognize that being underprivileged has serious negative impact on the skills necessary for learning, so it is not just a laptop that is missing.

Viktor Farcic: Moving on, what do you think will happen next in tech? If you were to predict the future, what are the bottlenecks of today that need to be solved, and what are the major obstacles you see us facing today?

The future of tech and the challenges we face

Júlia Biró: This might sound naive, but complexity is one of the biggest obstacles that we're going to face in the near future. Even when we are using standard tooling, our infrastructure is made up of so many different pieces, and we want to do it right. We want to document it all anyway, so we do it in Terraform. It's just complexity itself.

My gut feeling is that Terraform is a ticking bomb because it's hard to make and test modifications on it, and it's just as equally hard to find your way around it. Basically, Terraform is a new programming language that has multiple bugs.

You can also experience complexity when you want to make modifications to a service in a microservices environment. At Contentful, although we have a local development environment, I needed to start six surrounding services to run locally so the servers would start and I could test it. This complexity is related to what the human mind can hold, which is why I think this is now a bottleneck.

Scaling used to be a bottleneck 15 years ago, but not anymore. If you do it well then with reasonable limits and with infrastructure scaling, it's actually a very, very easy thing now; it's just the pace in which technologies change that is creating a bottleneck now. Once you become a certain size, changing technology is very, very difficult. But this is not a new problem. People will be stuck on Kubernetes the same way they were stuck on Java.

Viktor Farcic: You mentioned the pace of—I don't know whether to call it new stuff being developed or innovation—but the pace has increased. How do you follow that?

Júlia Biró: I actually feel bad about not following it.

Viktor Farcic: But if the pace is increasing, are we going to become superhumans?

Júlia Biró: I don't know, and that's why I'm saying it's a bottleneck. As new problems and technologies arise, technologies themselves become more quickly outdated. But at the same time the next and better tools are becoming available at a faster pace. Though this actually has a huge benefit, because no one has to have more than two years' experience with a given tool, and so it doesn't really matter whether you're in the field for two years or 20 years. It means that at the end of the day it's going to be increasingly easier to access this field.

For example, I don't need to have been a hands-on system administrator for 10 years to become an effective infrastructure or site reliability engineer. Unlike me, many of my colleagues, who have 10 more years' experience than me, half of that as systems administrators running the internet in the golden days. It'll probably be a psychological limit to how fast companies can adopt new technologies, and it will not be faster than that. But regarding your question about the learning, It's like everything else. If people put their lives to it and spend eight hours working and then another eight reading about the next thing, then they're going to be super good at it.

Viktor Farcic: Does that mean if a company is able to follow the trends, then people working there need to have free time for studying and learning?

Júlia Bíró: Of course! I always say that my job is to understand the new thing, and then automate it away. All the problems that I have ever solved should be automated or at least documented, so I don't need to figure the answer out again. Preferably, if I have the time, automated, so no one else has to think about them again. And of course there is time for things like conferences because the rest is just programming, which, of course, is not just programming but also a skill. It's always going to be another layer of abstraction and another set of complexity that we will need to handle and get the tools for.

The inevitability of increasing complexity

Viktor Farcic: Does that mean increasing complexity is unavoidable?

Júlia Bíró: Exactly, just evolution.

Viktor Farcic: I like that one.

Júlia Bíró: Here's the thing. Once you can do something, you put two of those together, and then by the time you have put five together, you feel like, "Oh, this is terrible," and you automate it. Then by the 22nd time you realize that you want that particular instance to be slightly different and that you want to put an if there. You basically want to control it with variables in a full programming language and then, bam! You have created another layer of complexity.

But once you have a programming language with it, there's nothing that's going to stop you from having 5,000, instead of 50. It's easy to say, "Here I have another layer." After that, all you need to do is teach everyone about that and put that into the code, and from there, code review and from there move onto testing and developing an entire environment for that.

Viktor Farcic: You mentioned the complexity of legacy applications. Is there a moment when it doesn't make sense to maintain something anymore? For instance, say you've got a legacy system written in COBOL or Java. If you want to reduce complexity at some point in time, you need to start over. But at the same time, nobody wants to throw away five years' worth of applications.

Júlia Biró: You could always refactor it into smaller pieces if you can factor it away, and that seems to be the DevOps idea right now. Not to throw away the monolith and replace it, but to actually break it down into smaller pieces. And, of course, the smaller pieces give complexity, but inside of them, they are more containable and accessible.

Viktor Farcic: So, we are replacing one complexity with another.

Júlia Biró: Yes, basically that's what is happening. But the advantage of this is that replacing it results in a more dividable and parallelizable complexity. If you have a monolith and you have 100 people working on it, then all 100 of them need to have the complexity of that monolith in their heads. If you can break it down to 10 pieces, then 90 people will have to know the complexity of one-tenth, and maybe some dependencies, and 10 people will need to have the complexity of the DevOps toolchain or running microservices.

Viktor Farcic: As we begin to wrap up this conversation, is there anything you would like to talk about that I've not asked you about yet?

Júlia Biró: In my career, I came from one company where I really experienced DevOps, infrastructure, and site reliability, along with all these new concepts. I then joined Contentful in May 2018 just after it experienced a big burst of growth, and it took some time (about a year) for it to adjust to its new size and for the necessary tools and processes to emerge. In the year since, it has really caught up.

Thinking pragmatically

What interests me right now is that these differences make me think really pragmatically about what is done, why it is done, and what it is that I should import from Prezi and initiate at Contentful. For example, what are the DevOps ideas that are obtainable and worth obtaining for my new company? I see that because, for example, my Contentful stack has younger and fresher technologies than the stack at Prezi. Yet, on the other hand, some of the toolings are much more mature, and the complexity is crushing.

What makes me tick in my daily work is my belief that Contentful will grow, and I chose to follow it because I want to be in there while it's growing, and I want to facilitate that growth.

Viktor Farcic: Would you say that it's easier to promote things when in one situation over another? Is it easier with a well-established stack or a young company with less?

Júlia Biró: It's quite different. For example, one of the signs of maturity is that by the time I left Prezi, there was a very well-defined process of how to promote ideas. A year ago, when I first started trying to promote ideas at Contentful, I didn't even know which was the right platform to start on. A year later, there is definitely a clear process. On the other hand, because there are only half as many engineers and layers at Contentful, I really only need to convince two or three people over lunch, and then something may get started.

> *"One of the signs of maturity is that by the time I left Prezi, there was a very well-defined process of how to promote ideas."*
>
> —*Júlia Biró*

I don't have a preference for this or that. With Prezi, I needed to learn a lot of tools. For example, as a member of the team who was responsible for the monitoring pipeline, which itself consisted of six different microservices. And that was just monitoring, and that was hard. Now at Contentful, I often feel that we don't have a real structured concept of working out where we are going.

The worst thing is that I'm constantly thinking we have no idea how we are doing this really. I say it not like we don't know what technology to use, but that we don't know how we want to use that technology. All these things are mushy and undefined, and that gives you a lot of uncertainty, which is hard for me to deal with because I don't deal with uncertainty very well. So, for me, this is the challenge. But on the other hand, if I set my mind to tidy up things, then it's very easy because all I need to do sometimes is just write down something and try to get the others to follow or agree on it. Just creating processes is almost as effective as creating tools, because it can already fix things.

Viktor Farcic: Here's a question. Every company thinks that they are special and they're doing things in a special way. Yet, there are some commonly proven things that work better than others. Our industry is so heterogeneous that actually we still don't know what works better than others. Or is it the case that companies are simply uninformed and incapable, or is it something else altogether?

Júlia Bíró: No, I don't think we are so heterogeneous actually. As I was looking to change jobs, it was very easy for me to find a company that uses 60 percent of the same tools as my previous company; the only difference was that they were used in slightly different ways. The beauty of the microservices architecture is actually that the diversity is contained inside the microservice and then, as an engineer, standard problems mean that you can have standard solutions, and it's an advantage.

There was an idea at Prezi, which I think makes sense, that you should focus your efforts on the specific problem domain in which your expertise and your service area lie. You should try to solve the other problems as easily and in as standard a way as possible. In Prezi, that meant that we have our very own special solutions for rendering visualizations and other things, but we don't want to reinvent the wheel when it comes to monitoring because we are a visual communications company and not a monitoring company.

At Contentful, we are making sure that your content is both easily editable while still being highly available, because this is our expertise and this is our service, there's a big emphasis on usability. We are not a monitoring company. We are not going to invest a lot of effort into monitoring. It's not that we are not going to do it, it's just that we are not going to write our own solution in it from scratch because our monitoring problems are standard and standard tooling should handle it.

Viktor Farcic: So, you should focus on your specialty and then try to get the rest in through a standard way. But what confuses me is that it's a bit contradictory because, on the one hand, we can agree we should have standards, so we don't waste our time, but on the other hand, if things are changing on a daily basis, you're never increasing speed, and thus standards cannot also be long-lasting.

Júlia Biró: Usually every problem domain has a smallish set of standard solutions that you can choose from, maybe three to five, that are very well documented and very well supported. But like you said, the bottleneck always moves. All new solutions are about improving some bottleneck, but they're not solving the same problem over and over again. They are solving the next problem.

Viktor Farcic: So, whenever we solve a problem, there is another one to solve, and so actually the ever-increasing speed of new processes and tools are a reflection of us raising the bar.

Júlia Biró: For example, there are currently five big tools in container scheduling and orchestration. I don't think there's going to be 50 industry standards in that thing, and the new technology is not going to be about container orchestration anymore. It's going to be about something else, something on top of it.

Viktor Farcic: Like a cake?

Júlia Biró: Always like a cake. For example, once virtual machines become an easily accessible resource, you can grow your infrastructure to the point where you need to have personal negotiations with AWS about how much of the residual nodes you are using. People will probably have 6 billion Kubernetes clusters, but then after that, it will just become an easily scalable resource again, and then the complexity will go somewhere else.

Viktor Farcic: I agree.

Júlia Biró: I mean, people are still writing UNIX tools, but that's because we are using UNIX tools that are 30 years old, on a daily basis. Why? Because they are in every bit of software that we write, and we are not adopting new standards on that one because they are the same standard solutions. For servers, you use NGINX, HAProxy, or Apache server, and they all do the same stuff and then you know, it's OK, it works, you don't need to have a sixteenth one.

Viktor Farcic: That's brilliant. I am wondering, though, what makes you click?

The engineering constant

Júlia Biró: I've had the privilege of working with some very experienced engineers, like yourself for example. I'm also very new at this, but we've already said that technologies change a lot and I am very interested in seeing what is the "engineering constant".

What are the things that will probably come with experience? They're not really knowledge of specific technologies, but skills, thinking patterns, and best practices that can be used overall and don't get outdated. Whether some of those are something that can be picked up to the benefit of my work without having to spend five years learning two or three single technologies in depth. The question from all this is, "What are the things that I can learn without having to spend 10 years in tech, and which will not get outdated?"

Viktor Farcic: You can learn Kubernetes in a year.

Júlia Biró: But Kubernetes will get outdated in around three to five years' time.

Are there constants in the tech industry?

Viktor Farcic: I'm kidding. But is there such a thing that will never become outdated? If you move outside of tech, is anything cultural that is continuously changing our perception of everything? Are there such things as constants in the tech industry?

Júlia Biró: There are basic ideas, such as the depiction of female beauty, which seems to be a very constant thing in the past around 3,000 to 5,000 years in art and across the entire world. Methods for manipulating masses (for making a bigger part of your population stand on your side) are also mostly unchanging ever since the history of written politics.

Viktor Farcic: OK, fair enough, you can have that.

Júlia Biró: I do feel that as I talk to engineers around me who might have experiences from different fields, there are some approaches that they apply uniformly, regardless of the field or of the actual problem. Approaches that don't change. Whether you're doing programming in 1983, 2003, or in 2013, sometimes the questions are the same, but the answers are different, and then the solutions are different. I'm interested in that part, the part that separates engineering from programming.

Viktor Farcic: But isn't that partly a sign of immaturity in our industry?

Júlia Biró: It's partly a sign of maturity, and I see that all around me. It's also something I learn mostly from people who have more experience in the field than me. But I also think that it is something that can be made conscious and that it's something that you can steal a bit, so you try to use it even when you don't have that experience.

Viktor Farcic: It was not long ago that I spoke with an acquaintance of mine, who is an architect, and I was telling him how only yesterday we were using Java, and today we're using Go, and god only knows what's tomorrow. He explained to me, "Yeah, because what I do as an architect has existed for a couple of thousand years and we've had time to figure it out, and you haven't."

Júlia Biró: I mean, the laws of aesthetics are not changing, but the way in which buildings are built has changed very much in the last two centuries because of the change of materials.

Viktor Farcic: But you just said, architecture has existed for two centuries, and we've only been around for 50 years.

Júlia Biró: No, and here's the thing. An ex-colleague of mine who works in a remote-only company with all senior engineers told a story: "We're going to dinner. We meet once a year in person, and we go to this off-site/team-building event, and we try to architect problems. It's ridiculous the amount of advancement you can get by asking, 'what is the problem we are trying to solve?'"

> *"That's like a super simple trick that senior engineers do. They're not letting themselves be dragged into the small details or down rabbit holes, but from time to time they take a step back and try to ask, 'Are we getting closer, and could there be a shorter way?'"*
>
> —Júlia Biró

That's like a super simple trick that senior engineers do. They're not letting themselves be dragged into the small details or down rabbit holes, but from time to time they take a step back and try to ask, "Are we getting closer, and could there be a shorter way?" This all comes with maturity, but if you're sneaky like me, then you try to use it early. I'm interested in these things. Basically, is there a fast track to becoming a senior engineer? This would be my interest. Because I don't have that much time.

Viktor Farcic: That's a great point of view. Thank you for sparing some time to talk to me today.

12

Damon Edwards

Cofounder and Chief Product Officer of Rundeck, Inc.

Introducing Damon Edwards

When Damon Edwards founded Rundeck, Inc., he helped create a platform that transformed thousands of global IT operations by enabling them to run more efficiently and scale much faster, all while maintaining security. These are hallmarks of the DevOps journey. You can follow Damon on Twitter at @damonedwards.

The journey to DevOps

Viktor Farcic: I'd like to start with a quick introduction. Can you tell us a little about yourself and how you got into DevOps?

Damon Edwards: Between 2005 and 2007, I was a part of a boutique consulting organization that focused on what are now called deployment pipelines. Back then, web-scale services were still a fairly new idea, but we were experts in configuring and deploying applications at scale.

When the industry started to become more cloud-oriented, whether it was virtualized in VMware or the nascent AWS EC2, everything became part of the software stack. We found that this actually suited us as we mostly came from an operations-heavy background. Between 2007 and 2009, it became obvious that scale was no longer the issue; the technical aspect of deployment was becoming a solved problem.

The challenge, as we were being told by our customers, was they wanted to be able to get things done more quickly, moving at a pace where they can learn and outpace their competitors.

This led us to become accidental Lean consultants, with clients saying, "This automation works great, but we've noticed that we're not as fast as those other people who have the same automation. Why aren't we getting any better while they are?"

That's what got us into the whole Lean movement. We were looking back, past Agile, at things like the Toyota Production System, Deming, Goldratt, and more, decoding why one organization gets stuff done, goes faster, and produces things of higher quality when other organizations can't. We were self-taught and learned a lot through the trial-and-error method as there wasn't much of a body of knowledge around applying these techniques across the full development and operations life cycle.

Viktor Farcic: From the timeline that you're talking about, it seems that was right at the same time the DevOps movement took off. You must have been at ground zero when this whole concept first kicked off.

Damon Edwards: I was, along with people like Patrick Debois, John Willis, Andrew Shafer, and John Allspaw, right as Patrick lit the DevOps spark by organizing the first DevOps Days. In fact, I was the one that sent the email to get Gene Kim, known then primarily as the author of *Visible Ops*, to come to the first DevOps Days, a conference he had never heard of before.

> "We were especially interested in DevOps in the enterprise because that is where DevOps problems—the ones that are really sticky and problematic—really live."
>
> —Damon Edwards

What my colleague Alex Honor and I brought to the conversation was an enterprise-centric, operations-first perspective. A lot of people were interested in extending Agile all the way through deployment, but instead, we were more interested in operations reaching back toward development. We were especially interested in DevOps in the enterprise because that is where DevOps problems—the ones that are really sticky and problematic—really live.

If you're a small organization or even a high-scale, single-purpose-built web organization, your DevOps problems all have simple answers. Yes, it takes effort and thoughtfulness, but the path forward is clear. All you need to do is get everyone into the same room, tell them to stop doing it the old way, and instead do it the new way, and your problems will generally go away with straightforward effort.

Now, try that in a large, complex enterprise where you have multiple business lines usually gathered—some by acquisition and some by organic growth—over decades. You have one of everything of every kind of technology, in addition to having a huge spread of people, skills, mindsets, and processes, and it's this large, distributed organization with thousands of people across dozens of political structures all over the globe where it's difficult to implement system changes. That's a whole different animal that's very hard to deal with; those are the big nasty DevOps problems.

Viktor Farcic: You're now based at Rundeck. Can you talk a bit about your work there?

Rundeck, Inc. and DevOps

Damon Edwards: Rundeck was born as an open source project in 2010. It filled a gap in the automation toolchain and had what we thought was a modest and helpful community, so we kept it going. Around 2014, we discovered there was something special going on. The first indicator was that we had all of these large, household-name companies calling us for help with Rundeck, and not our consulting services. They would say, "We know that you're consultants, and maybe we'll get to that later, but we're using Rundeck, and we need help here and there."

Eventually, we figured out that Rundeck was being used by companies to fix the operations end of their DevOps problems. After enough people told us that Rundeck changed their lives, Alex Honor, Greg Schuler, and myself, the three founders of Rundeck Inc, decided to shut down the consulting company and focus on Rundeck. The deciding factor was that we could help a lot more people at scale with a product company than we ever could as consultants.

Viktor Farcic: I have a very rudimentary understanding about Rundeck. Correct me if I'm wrong, but from my understanding, it's kind of like a task executor.

Damon Edwards: Technically, that's correct but it's not the exciting use case. Self-service operations are the big value of Rundeck. Operations teams will use Rundeck within their team to create standard operating procedures out of all of the various scripts, tools, commands, and APIs they already have. That delivers a lot of efficiency gains within a team, but things really get interesting when they use the access control feature to give people outside of operations access to those procedures, because that's when they can really rethink how their organization works.

Viktor Farcic: So, teams use it, but self-service is the main goal?

Damon Edwards: Yes, but teams see a lot of benefits from standardizing how they work. The standardization encourages ongoing improvement and experimentation; this is a known Lean technique. Instead of me having a bunch of scripts, you having a bunch of scripts, and someone else having a bunch of scripts, let's put them all into Rundeck. Let's collaborate and say, "Hey, let's just come up with a good way to do these things." So, plug in whatever you have now—scripts, tools, commands, APIs—and Rundeck provides the workflow, notifications, error-handling, user input management, the UI, the API, the logging, and much more.

Rundeck's access control features are really what got people excited because now they're saying, "Well, hey, let's enable teams to do operations activities that traditionally don't do operations activities." A simple example is the classic DevOps idea of letting developers do restarts in production environments. It's a pretty shocking concept in most enterprises. How are you going to do that? You can't give them logins to production environments and say, "Here are your SSH keys, sudo access, and some scripts... good luck!" because that doesn't cut it in the enterprise. It's a complicated enough problem and involves so many groups that most people give up.

But now, with Rundeck, developers can just say, "Well, let's use Rundeck. Plug in the restart script, run the health checks to make sure it worked, and run the commands to quit the monitoring and manipulate the load balancers. Then, put some extra guardrails around it like constraining user input options, notifications, and error handling." Then they would use Rundeck's access control to safely give the development team the ability to do restarts in production. Likewise, you could just give them the permissions to watch the trusted SRE do restarts in production. Either way, they have better control and visibility, which enables them to distribute the ability to perform operations tasks throughout the broader organization.

This self-service capability unlocks all these DevOps organizational changes that you see being driven in forward-thinking enterprises. They want to decouple and push control closer to these delivery teams so they can move faster, and operations just stay out of their way.

Viktor Farcic: It's like centralized management with a strong focus on the empowerment of the rest of the organization.

Damon Edwards: That's an interesting way to put it. We recognize that the expertise and capability of operations are not going anywhere, but the idea that there is a central operations organization that does all of the "operations work" can't keep up with today's demands. You need a mechanism where control is distributed, but there are operations experts who maintain oversight.

That's something that shows up in the Rundeck design philosophy as well. We don't want to be another thing that moves the bits around because you've already got plenty of things out there that do that well, whether it's Chef, Puppet, Ansible, or container orchestrators. We let people use what they want to use and then create the logical procedures out of it that need to span all of those different tools. I think we have all lived under this delusion that one automation tool is going to rule them all, but what we did was embrace the idea that heterogeneity is the preferred reality. Let people do what they need to do to get their job done and focus on helping them to coordinate that work and make it safe.

> *"Let people do what they need to do to get their job done and focus on helping them to coordinate that work and make it safe."*
>
> *—Damon Edwards*

Viktor Farcic: What are your thoughts on the commercialization of DevOps and the wider idea of DevOps tools?

The commercialization of DevOps

Damon Edwards: It is definitely an interesting topic, because people love to throw their hope into tools. First, it was Puppet. Then, it was Chef. More recently, it was Ansible, but now it's cloud-native and serverless. Each new automation tool is going to take over the world, but then the special project team working on it moves on and it becomes legacy. Now we have one of everything. Meanwhile, someone is saying that if they can bring in another new tool, then that will solve all their problems. It's a cycle that has always been there.

Nowadays, there are a lot of companies with DevOps initiatives, and their people are following the pattern that they've always followed and are looking for a DevOps tool to help them. I don't blame the vendors for offering their tools up as DevOps tools, because most of them are perfectly fine tools that solve specific problems. But don't be surprised when your DevOps problems don't go away, and you have yet another tool to support.

> *"If anything, there's a Lean lesson in this; you're going to need to let teams make the choices for the tools that they feel like they need to use."*
>
> —*Damon Edwards*

If anything, there's a Lean lesson in this; you're going to need to let teams make the choices for the tools that they feel like they need to use. They need to worry about how they integrate, worry about the toolchain architecture, or worry about how you let others plug their tools into other people's tools. This has been a major design point for Rundeck since we first recognized the heterogeneous nature of the enterprise as something to be embraced.

Premature optimization or tool standardization is actually bad for the organization. If you're forcing a team to do something they don't want to do, and they have a good reason for not wanting to do it, then you're just putting an unnecessary burden or friction on top of that team. Heterogeneity is not only a fact of life; we think it's actually a feature. Let the teams do what they need to do in order to be successful, and just worry about how they integrate it with the rest of the organization, making sure the right security and compliance controls are in place.

Viktor Farcic: I completely agree. From my own experience, I'm still having trouble finding a big enterprise that is actually bent that way. I've always had the impression that that's what it's like with DevOps. Everybody talks about DevOps, and every single company in the world has a DevOps initiative—yet nobody's doing it.

Damon Edwards: Changing how you work is very difficult in itself. For those who are owning the change, it can feel risky and scary. That's not just from an organization point of view; I'm talking from the personal perspective as well.

Here's an example. You tell people, "Okay, we are going to distribute operational capabilities to delivery teams, so we should make these delivery teams cross-functional. That means we take the headcount out of operations and convert it into more of an SRE skillset. We'll leave some SREs taking care of both the platforms and the specialties that we can't distribute for practical reasons in central teams." That's the idea of cross-functional teams, and it sounds logical, but what are you doing on a human and political level? You're taking away headcount from one group and giving it to another.

A secret that few will admit in large enterprises is that it's really difficult to know what anybody else is doing. Executives in large organizations need indirect measures to identify performance at different levels of management. Say you're at the director level of a theoretical company—you're four to five levels down from the C level, and you're three to four levels up from the people with their hands on the keyboards, and the senior executives want to know if you are any good: "Is Viktor any good? Is he going places or has his career topped out?"

Viktor Farcic: It's great that we're getting into the day-to-day discussion of DevOps, but one thing I would love to know is how it would work in this theoretical company.

Damon Edwards: By traditional corporate measures, they might say, "Oh, Viktor seems pretty good. He keeps getting more headcount and more budget. Viktor must be doing something right; we should keep an eye on that Victor, he's going places."

You're a rational human being. You care about your career and your family depends on your career. What's the last thing you're going to want to do? Give up a budget or people! You've been conditioned throughout your career to know these are signals that you're either a weak or bad manager. Suddenly, you are a lot warier of an idea to move people out from under you and into other teams. Organizational change is difficult because people have personal and political motivations that often don't align with those of the organization, which is what I find to be the number-one problem.

Viktor Farcic: Then, what's the second problem?

Damon Edwards: The second problem is that much of the rewards in corporate culture are designed around delivery. For instance, you landed a huge sale, or you cemented a key partnership—here's your bonus. You delivered a major IT project, took us to the cloud, or you delivered the new Foo service we promised Wall Street, so here's your raise. News of delivery makes it all the way to the boardroom, and so delivery on business-oriented projects is another way to get yourself on that up-and-comer list.

So, now imagine that you're a development leader incentivized to deliver. You want that glory and the spoils, right? The last thing you want to do is anything that's not delivering! Taking on a bunch of SREs and a shared responsibility for production services means that you're being judged on and committing resources to something other than delivery.

The right thing for the company to do is to stick with the stuff you've built, keep it running, and evolve it to meet the customer's future needs. But, personally, you're compelled to say, "Forget it, it's done, let someone else worry about that and get me on to a whole new project," because then you'll be Viktor who delivered customer value X last year and then delivered customer value Y this year, which is a fast track to promotion.

> *"The reality of all of this is that it's very hard to change how people work, which means it's very hard to change large enterprises."*
>
> —*Damon Edwards*

The reality of all of this is that it's very hard to change how people work, which means it's very hard to change large enterprises. You'll have a much easier time if you can just bring in that DevOps thing by just painting some existing boxes on the organization chart with some DevOps freshness.

This is how DevOps has been pigeonholed as a new name for release and systems engineering in so many enterprises. They're not actually doing what makes the DevOps high performers very successful, which is changing how they fundamentally operate. There are a lot of vendors out there who will gladly reinforce this behavior. Why complicate the sale? Just let them do a "DevOps" paint job and declare victory. At the end of the day, this really isn't a technology organizational culture problem; this is a business culture problem.

Netflix works the way it does because of the technology organization; that's how they run their entire business. Amazon works the way it does because that's how Amazon runs their entire business. The same is true of Google. Unless your business wants to change how it operates and what it incentivizes, don't expect the technology organization to act much differently. We can still make a lot of improvements within the walls of the technology organization; just don't expect the business head to be wagged by the technology tail. They still have to figure it out on their own.

Viktor Farcic: At least from what I've seen, the business side that makes the decision is still used to making that same decision for software development as they are for making any other decision.

Damon Edwards: A valid point, because they just see the world from what they do and they're working to their incentives. Because of that, they'll be running things according to their current beliefs. Too many times, you'll see a technology organization telling the business how they should be run and that they need to do things in what is described as the right way, and when the business doesn't do it, there are generally some grumblings about "idiots." Well, the thing is that the business sees it their way too. They know what they need, and they think their way is the rational way to do it, and if the technology side disagrees, then they are being whiney or just don't get it.

Of course, conflict ensues. Everyone thinks they're the rational ones and that what they're doing is best for the company, which is something that we really have to keep in mind. Very few people anywhere in the world show up to their job saying, "How can I screw things up and what stupid thing can I do today?"

Viktor Farcic: But in big companies, are people really trying to do the best for their company? I say this because, the way I see it, big companies are actually a collection of smaller companies, whether you call them silos, departments, companies— whatever you want. Do you have the impression that actually doing right for your department is not necessarily right for your company?

Damon Edwards: Most people think they're doing the right thing, but I think you bring up a good point. Perspective and context really matter from a business viewpoint. You can look at a big company as more of a portfolio of companies, because the parts can often live somewhat in business isolation, and that isolation encourages siloed behavior. In that situation, you wind up with people who only see a small piece of the larger puzzle, and with that limited view, they do their best for that piece of the puzzle, but not their best for the overall business. To the people in the other pieces of the puzzle, they might think those others aren't acting in the best interest of the company, but those people only have their own limited view. This same silo problem repeats itself all the way down to the classic development and operations divide we see today.

Viktor Farcic: That's very true, because if you go even deeper, everybody has their own objectives. What is the objective of operations? Never to go down. How do you never go down? Well, by never deploying a new release. I mean, developers want to release every second because they don't care if we go down.

Damon Edwards: Exactly. It's easy to think about the thing you are being paid to do and not strive to see the end-to-end system; or equally, it's easy to be accidentally disincentivized to not act in the best interests of the end-to-end system.

The most striking way to illustrate this is to ask how the customer sees your organization. They see a point of transaction and perhaps a horizontal line of everything that has to happen to make that transaction happen. They don't care about your functional silos or who does what. Does it satisfy them? Is it giving them the functionality that they wanted at the right price? Are the right features at the right price at the right time for them? That's what they care about; it's a very horizontal view.

But how do we think about work internally? We think about it by job function and whatever is printed on our business cards, which is usually a vertical, functionally aligned view. It's generally human nature to group like with like. Let's put developers with developers, operators with operators, testers with testers, and security with security. Then from there, let's manage those people for their own efficiency inside those groups. What happens is that as soon as you do that, people lose sight of what the customer cares about, which is the end-to-end capability. That's what happens when people optimize, not realizing that they are doing a localized optimization and actually deoptimizing the whole end-to-end system. The problems just fall from there.

Perceptions of quality and its impact on work

Viktor Farcic: Do you think, then, that those people get incentivized based on the customer's perception of quality?

Damon Edwards: Ideally. But do they know what that is? Do they know how their work actually fits in the whole system, and how that impacts this quality? Let's use an example of a siloed firewall team.

This firewall team might just offer the best firewall rule changes in the Western Hemisphere. Their job is to make sure they make only the best and safest rule changes. They do this by offering limited change windows. If you give them your firewall rule change by Tuesday at 2:00 p.m., then by Thursday at 4:00 p.m., your change will be complete.

Now, imagine I'm a developer and I need a change. I may well be thinking that while I'm not a firewall expert, I'm going to try to figure out what to write on this support ticket. I submit the ticket on Monday, but then it gets kicked back to me on Wednesday because of some problem with my request. I do a few go-arounds with a network admin to figure out how to request what I want, but then it turns out that I've missed the window and have to wait until next Thursday.

The support team won't do it sooner as it isn't a production service yet, so now I have to wait until the change takes place. The problem there is that you've now got everybody waiting on this firewall rule change because they're working in this disconnected, isolated manner. The optimization for the firewall change rules was made from the firewall team's siloed perspective, not the perspective of the end-to-end system.

Viktor Farcic: Definitely. It's like that quote: if you want to really understand a society, you need to understand its prison system. To me, this translates to the ticketing systems you just mentioned. If you want to see how Agile or Lean a company is, just go to their ticketing system.

Damon Edwards: Ha! I've never likened the ticket systems to a prison, but I can see where you are going with that. The destructive tendencies of silos and ticket queues really play an important part in the Rundeck view of the world.

We noticed back in our consulting days that ticket queues accelerate silo effects, where people lose shared context, start to focus inward, and optimize for their siloed view. In the end, the company suffers, even though everybody looks really busy and their individual areas are highly efficient.

Viktor Farcic: All of those request queues just add all kinds of economic cost to the company because you're injecting delays; you're adding breaks in context.

Damon Edwards: Exactly. We know from other fields that work queues cause delays, quality problems, increased overhead, demoralization, decreased learning, and greater risks. For some reason, IT operations ignore this and act as if ticket-driven request queues are expensive or cause destructive behaviors.

Viktor Farcic: Yet the ticket system has become the way that we run our lives, especially in operations.

Damon Edwards: Exactly. I mean, the ticket system was originally called the trouble ticket, because it was supposed to be for when something went wrong. It was there to handle the exceptions. But along the way, it has become the way that we govern work and grant permission for operations to do their work.

What we've ended up doing is taking organizations who want to be high-velocity learning organizations and dropping ticket-driven request queues all across that value stream. We're taking the queues that are at the epicenter of our existing bottlenecks, delays, bad hand-offs, and knowledge loss and we're spreading them everywhere. It feels like a real industry blind spot.

A big theme of ours has always been that you've got to design your organization and the underlying work in a way that limits the number of handoffs. You must get rid of the need to hand off work to other teams as much as possible, and doing that often means driving more toward cross-functional teams. However, the cross-functional team idea has its limits, and there are situations where you just can't get rid of those handoffs.

This is especially true in operations. We're not going to be able to have enough of those people from that great firewall rule-changing team to put one on every team, we're not going to have enough security people, and we're not going to have enough systems engineers, database administrators (DBAs), or storage experts. If that's the case, then we're going to have to take what they do and turn them into pull-based, self-service interfaces. This means that other teams, when they need those operational activities, will have a self-service interface, whether it be a GUI, API, or command line, to do what they need to do, get fast feedback from the system, and move on.

Viktor Farcic: You mean, for example, getting a virtual machine when you need one?

Damon Edwards: Yes, that would be a low-level example. I shouldn't need to open a ticket for somebody to go do it for me, because I have an API or a web button and I can get what I want, and it builds from there. How do you let environment teams do schema updates without a DBA ticket? How do you let developers do their own restarts or health checks in production? How do you let business analysts run their own catalog update procedures?

The key idea is that self-service operations can't only be the ability to push the button to run something. The people who would want to push the button are going to need the ability to define their own buttons, just like in Amazon EC2 where you can define your own Amazon Machine Images. EC2 would've been useless if they told you the five types of instances that you can spin up and that was it. Let people define their own procedures, and they can still have security and operations do code reviews on those buttons.

In the EC2 example, they make it useful because they give you the framework and guardrails that allow you to take charge and be useful. The self-service model is not just the ability to push the button, but is also the ability of those teams to define the button; it's a strong design pattern.

The best definition of DevOps

Viktor Farcic: This question is going to sound silly, but I like it because everybody gives me a different answer. We've already mentioned it countless times throughout our discussion, but what is DevOps?

Damon Edwards: The best definition that I've heard is from Adam Jacob. He says that DevOps is a cultural and professional movement, focused on how we build and operate high-velocity organizations, born from the experience of its practitioners.

> *"DevOps is a cultural and professional movement, focused on how we build and operate high-velocity organizations, born from the experience of its practitioners."*
>
> —*Adam Jacob (quoted by Damon Edwards)*

I think that's as good as any description because I think it captures the essence of the DevOps movement. DevOps really is an umbrella over a bunch of evolving problems and solutions, all based on the idea of creating higher-velocity and higher-quality organizations. Trying to make it a more detailed description than that loses the point because DevOps is a movement, not a static thing.

I think people who try to make it more specific than that are inventing something that was never really there. That's fine, they can try to do that, and perhaps they'll bring something new to the movement, and everyone will benefit. But they shouldn't complain if the movement ignores them. I think it was Charity Majors who I first heard describe DevOps as an open source movement; the community goes where the community goes.

Viktor Farcic: That's a great definition.

Damon Edwards: It works for a lot of people and keeps them focused on what matters: improving how technology organizations work and the lives of the people inside those organizations. Definition battles in DevOps are useless.

Viktor Farcic: What do you think about the commercialization of DevOps? When I go to conferences, there's no software anymore that doesn't have a DevOps sticker attached to it.

Damon Edwards: I have mixed feelings about it, because at first, I was more of a purist and declared that it just doesn't make sense to label everything as DevOps. It's like saying a person is Agile or that a robot was going to make a factory Lean. But over time, I've softened my stance—partially because I've realized that the market eventually decides that those tools are just slapping the DevOps label on the box, only to get found out. I've also realized that it at least signifies at the macro level that the industry needs to change how it works because if even the tools vendors are talking about it, then a lot more executives will listen.

Viktor Farcic: Aren't most of these vendors making the claim that DevOps is all about deployment?

Damon Edwards: A lot of vendors are pushing that narrative because that is what they sell. It's not all of them, but there are many that do. That's probably the one negative of the tools-vendors jumping into DevOps; it plays into the urge for enterprises to just apply a fresh coat of DevOps paint to their old processes. If DevOps is just deployment, then we can just make it an engineering project and not worry about dealing with those messy things called people.

> "If DevOps is just deployment, then we can just make it an engineering project and not worry about dealing with those messy things called people."
>
> —Damon Edwards

This also plays into how large companies like to solve problems. The higher you get in the food chain, especially in large companies, the more transactional management becomes. They'll say, "Tell me the problem. Tell me what check I need to sign and tell me what I get out of it. I'll weigh that against the other checks and sign the ones I think are the right ones." Tools fit into that model well, and the vendors know that. To be fair, I'm a software vendor, and I know that. However, we think that the tools-vendors who last are the ones who actually solve problems and are clear about what problems they can and can't solve. "Buy my tool, and I'll solve your DevOps problems" isn't possible unless you frame DevOps into very narrow and largely unhelpful terms. We didn't all get dressed up to just move some software bits around faster.

Viktor Farcic: To me, that sounds like the reverse of Scrum. People jumped into the Scrum way thinking that changing people's human processes will solve the problem, and now we have the reverse of that: buy this tool, and it's going to solve your human problem.

Damon Edwards: That's a really interesting way to look at it. I think the parallels go even deeper. How many companies "went Scrum" without really changing how they worked? They bought the tools, did some minor training, and then just Scrum-washed their existing Waterfall processes and mindset. Those who did that eventually joined the "Scrum didn't work; it must not be working" backlash. We are going to undoubtedly see the same thing with DevOps, with SRE, and any other movements that come along. It's just how it is.

Viktor Farcic: That's kind of normal, but perhaps your expectations are too high. Let's say you accomplish 15 percent of something. That's still 15 percent of something.

Damon Edwards: That's a fair point. We can lose sight of the net positive. At least people are recognizing that they have problems and they're trying something. My concern is when they use those efforts to declare a premature victory. Actually, nothing has changed, that or they use it as fake proof that it didn't work.

Viktor Farcic: There are always people like that, which reminds me that a long time ago when one of the QA managers came to me, and I was pushing for automation, they said, "I've found the test case that is not automatable. This is all kind of worthless." But to me I'm like, "You've found one, so what?"

Damon Edwards: Humans are tricky, and changing how humans work is downright hard.

The industry today

Viktor Farcic: I heard a theory that a big part of our problem in the industry is that we are carried today by people not appreciating operations. Kind of like, with Agile, suddenly we now have rockstars. The industry is saying, "It's a rockstar developer, that's a rockstar tester, that's a rockstar product owner," but nobody ever mentions operators in any context of a positive prize.

Damon Edwards: There might be something to that. I'm not sure if it's that certain people get rockstar status, but I'm more concerned with the mistreatment of so many IT workers than I am with the cushy lives of a few.

> *"I'm more concerned with the mistreatment of so many IT workers than I am with the cushy lives of a few."*
>
> *—Damon Edwards*

You can go to the far-flung corporate technology centers all over the world, really, and there are a lot of people in this business only because it pays better than selling insurance. I mean, that's it. They just want to get through their day, provide for their families, and get to their kids' sporting events on the weekends, and here they are in organizations that are highly dysfunctional doing what is often demoralizing, repetitive work. They're burning out left and right because of all the pressure and the conflict that's hoisted upon them.

That's a lot of human potential that could be put to better use. If we can tap into better ways of working, then that will be good for the individual and great for the company's bottom line. This is why I am so bullish on topics like Lean, DevOps, and SRE; the focus is on how people work and how to make it better.

Viktor Farcic: I think this is a great place to leave our conversation.

Damon Edwards: We've certainly covered a lot of ground. I've really enjoyed this.

Viktor Farcic: Me too. Cheers, thanks.

13

Kohsuke Kawaguchi

Creator of the Jenkins
software project

Introducing Kohsuke Kawaguchi

A respected developer and popular speaker, Kohsuke Kawaguchi is perhaps best known for creating Jenkins, a CI platform that has become a widely adopted and successful community-driven open source project. Kohsuke's principles behind the Jenkins community—extensibility, inclusiveness, and low barriers to participation—are many of the driving factors in DevOps. You can follow him on Twitter at @kohsukekawa.

Viktor Farcic: Before we delve into our conversation about DevOps, could you tell us a little about yourself?

Kohsuke Kawaguchi: I'm probably best known as the creator of the Jenkins project, which started at the CI server, and is now more broadly used in the general computational industry and automation. Currently, I'm the CTO of Cloud-Bees, a company that's involved in a number of things, among which is productizing Jenkins, and helping companies through their digital transformation.

What is DevOps?

Viktor Farcic: So then, a simple question for you: what is DevOps?

Kohsuke Kawaguchi: If I'm totally honest, I feel like DevOps is a bit of an overused word today. In fact, even I sometimes wonder what people really mean by it. What DevOps is truly depends on several factors. I personally associate DevOps with this growing trend of, over the last few decades, more automation and shorter and shorter feedback cycles.

> *"I feel like DevOps is a bit of an overused word."*
>
> —*Kohsuke Kawaguchi*

In the last five years, this automation feedback cycle has become all-encompassing in everything from writing code to managing Quality Assurance (QA) in order to push it out to production and run it. I think people generally default to practices like that and then call it DevOps. When I talk to these people working in the larger enterprises, I think they immediately see DevOps as erasing the organizational boundaries that are in place, which I think is obviously an important problem for them. I know some people like to emphasize that point and make it more of an organizational thing.

The DevOps toolkit and its organizational impact

Viktor Farcic: Moving on to the DevOps toolkit, what tools do you see as empowering workers? Do you think that some tools fit better than others into whatever definition of DevOps people have?

Kohsuke Kawaguchi: In the context of broader automation that goes across a number of different things and this ever-expanding need for automation with human control, the tool is obviously the primary means of enabling automation. I know a lot of Jenkins users see the world that way.

Software developers like myself enjoy inventing tools. That's what we do. So, given that world view, it's only natural that we come up with our own tools to bridge those gaps and expand automation even more, because without automation, you can't create shorter feedback cycles, which is a critical part of DevOps. For me, this is the interesting part. It feels closer to what we can solve, as opposed to the organizational structure problem in enterprises, which is not only dictated by those technical concerns, but lots of other factors. For example, there's a good compliance reason why development and operations are separate; it's because it's seen, historically, as a well-maintained compliance necessity. Fundamentally, it's not a technology fight.

Viktor Farcic: You're the creator of Jenkins, one of the most popular open source tools out there, and you're also the CTO of a company that, as you said yourself, works with enterprise companies. Do you think that there is a significant difference between how the tools and processes operate on smaller greenfield open source-type companies versus those found in enterprises?

> *"There's a good compliance reason why development and operations are separate; it's because it's seen, historically, as a well-maintained compliance necessity. Fundamentally, it's not a technology fight."*
>
> *—Kohsuke Kawaguchi*

Kohsuke Kawaguchi: The kinds of problems and challenges that the enterprise people need to deal with are just in a different layer from the smaller guys. For the smaller folks, time is money. As I said before, these smaller operations often don't have too many people on staff to begin with, so they have a lot more flexibility in choosing how they work.

Compliance is usually not as real; it doesn't mean you can ignore it, but you can fly under the radar. In other enterprises, when provisioning new employees, the segregation you have to think about is like optimizing for a global, not just a local, team. It's no wonder one group feels the other group is a bit of an idiot. They each have different challenges.

Viktor Farcic: As an example, when I go to different booths at DockerCon, it's "DevOps, DevOps, DevOps." All of the software vendors have some form of DevOps associated with them now. What do you think is driving that?

Kohsuke Kawaguchi: I want to say two things.

First, if I look at the decade-long march toward more automation that I talked about, then we're talking about more than just DevOps. It now includes infrastructure, services, VMs, or software-defined networks. In this broad trend, you can include a practice such as continuous integration, which, at this point, is about 10 years old. Today, DevOps is used as the go-to label for this march. I think this march will continue, but at some point, it'll take on a different name.

Second, we, the engineers, might roll our eyes at the fact that everyone is saying DevOps and twisting its meaning to whatever fits their agenda, but we also underestimate the importance of communicating this stuff in a way that a broader audience understands, which is very difficult to do.

In order to achieve changes that we know are necessary, as engineers, you have to rally your organization, which means communicating with people who are not engineers. Terms such as "DevOps" are rather useful ways of capturing the ideas, and when a lot of people say the same thing in different ways, it puts some weight behind the credibility of the idea. In a way, therefore, all of these vendors saying "DevOps" are doing us a favor.

Viktor Farcic: I've heard a lot lately about those organizational changes where they're moving everything to the left. What do you think about that? I mean, tools to me are obvious, in that you pick a tool that does the job; you learn how to use it and implement it. In your view, what are the other changes that need to be applied?

Kohsuke Kawaguchi: Yeah, there are obviously things at the technology level as you say, and then there's other challenges. One example I can give you is that the infrastructure around the Jenkins product itself has only a somewhat limited capacity, so when we wanted to shift more QA to the left, we could only do so much. In other words, it takes money, and that's a hard thing to come by in an open source project.

Then, there's a challenge fundamental to QA. QA is actually a never-ending challenge to automate most things, and it's not easy. I used to work on a compiler, and so I used to think naively that testing was super easy—that it's actually completely deterministic. I have an input, I run it through the program, and I get output. I then compare that with what the output should be and then I'm done. But most of the interesting apps that people are writing are very difficult to actually measure out in this way.

> *"QA is actually a never-ending challenge to automate most things."*
>
> —*Kohsuke Kawaguchi*

Once, I went to a car manufacturer where they had this tower full of headlights. They were testing a little microcontroller that controlled the headlights. Imagine the challenge of mounting them up on a tower, verifying that a light actually turned on, resetting the hardware, and so on. All of that is work. Just on the technology front, there are still tremendous challenges like that. Every time we want to do more QA, there's a never-ending list of problems like this that need to be tackled.

Viktor Farcic: Not to mention those organizational challenges if you're in those companies.

Kohsuke Kawaguchi: Exactly! You have those people in different groups, and you are used to operating in certain ways, and your left-shifting happens at a different pace and at different parts of the project. If you think about somebody who is working on an operations team and is interfacing 100 different operations teams, and only one wants to do things differently, the reaction is, "Look, I can't accommodate things just for you."

Those things can always be challenging. I'll give you another example of faster delivery creating a friction downstream. The marketing team: the things they do, such as running marketing campaigns or events, are more compatible with big releases. You don't want to issue a press release just for one feature, right? Same thing with the customer-facing guys. They don't want to bombard customers with communication. You want to batch things up. As engineering work becomes more continuous, those people also need to change the way they work. That's nothing new; it's not as if I made this amazing discovery that nobody else knew before. It's easier said than done.

The hype around containers

Viktor Farcic: Speaking of technology, all the hype over the last couple of years has been about containers. How do you see that fitting into this whole picture?

Kohsuke Kawaguchi: When I worked at Sun Microsystems, we had our own operating system there called Solaris. I remember an internal conference where they talked about this thing called Solaris Zones. They would say, "Oh, we can split the user space into different portions, and we can allocate different CPU sizes, RAM, and so on to them. They will be like a different set of computers with virtually zero overhead." So now, looking back, I can see that what they were doing was actually putting in place the building blocks of what became containers.

The Solaris guys must have designed this feature, fully aware of the impact it can create. But it had zero traction. There were a number of other similar examples. The thing that I took away from Solaris is that we, as open source engineers, often tend to think that if you just put the code out there and explain what it does, then other like-minded developers are able to look at it and get the same perspective as yours and then be able to use it. It turns out that's completely not true, and that's something I didn't appreciate before.

The Solaris guys put all of the nuts, bolts, and engines together to do this new hard thing of isolations and they expected the rest of us to grok the point of it, and we didn't. It took this certain packaging and positioning for the mainstream to really see the value of it, so that was, for me, an interesting history lesson.

Viktor Farcic: But what are your views on containers? That's obviously a key part of everything that we do in this field.

Kohsuke Kawaguchi: Obviously, I think containers are great. I just can't believe we still have to actually say they're a good thing, but this landscape is moving very rapidly. I remember going to one of the DockerCon conferences and feeling like these guys are going to be the next VMware, as they will own the corporations and the large enterprises that are going to deploy containers in the hundreds of thousands. Yet, within just a few years, what we have discovered is the interest in layers moved up. Containers are considered a good thing, but now it's only as exciting as Unicode. Everyone uses it and nobody cares.

> *"Obviously, I think containers are great. I just can't believe we still have to actually say they're a good thing, but this landscape is moving very rapidly."*
>
> —*Kohsuke Kawaguchi*

I was shocked at the pace of the amazing work in this space. Right now, I think that Kubernetes is all the rage. But, on the horizon, if you look at what Amazon is trying to do, they are essentially hiding Kubernetes almost like an implementation detail.

As soon as something dominates one layer, that dominance immediately moves the conversation upstack. Now, people will be talking about all of the higher-level values, integrating those, and how to hide them behind. Unicode and TCP—it's all the same. I think this is already happening with Kubernetes. That's what I mean by "boring."

Viktor Farcic: The point of good technology is that if it becomes boring, but everybody still uses it, then it's accomplishing its mission.

Kohsuke Kawaguchi: I think that's the ultimate hall of fame for engineers—achieving "good technology" that's become so boring nobody talks about it. I live in San Jose, so I occasionally cross the Golden Gate Bridge, which is a magnificent piece of engineering. I have no idea who built it, but I'm sure that a lot of hard engineering work went into it. Most people don't pause to think about the work involved, even though they benefit from it.

Sometimes, I feel that the world should recognize these people's work more, but then I also think these people probably don't need the validation from the whole world. I bet they know they've done a great work.

Conferences, open source, and the US versus China

Viktor Farcic: Right now, you're the CTO of CloudBees, where you're in charge of technology. I'm curious; how do you follow up with all of that? I'm asking this simply because I don't know how to do it myself. Every time I visit a conference, I have the impression that I need another year just to learn what each of those programs does.

Kohsuke Kawaguchi: I wish I knew the answer. I, too, struggle with keeping up with what's going on. I find it useful to go to conferences because people there are trying to explain things to you, as opposed to expecting you to grok things on your own. At the same time, in the grand scheme of things, people like you and I are probably good at making sense of the rough bits out there, so from that perspective, going to conferences is a bit of a waste of time because we'd probably learn a lot more on our own in the same amount of time it takes to travel. Also, when you are a producer of a technology, conferences are great ways to hear from people who are using the product. It's always worthwhile to listen to them.

Another reason I go to conferences is that I personally can't watch a recorded video. I just can't keep my attention for anything longer than a minute. I start watching a YouTube video and then within 15 seconds I start multitasking, and then, next thing you know, I completely lose track of what the video is saying. If I could fix that about myself, I'd be a lot more efficient in ingesting information.

I also think there's some truth in the idea of "tested by time." If I continue to hear about something for a long period of time, then it's probably worth paying attention. It's the same with "word of mouth." If people you trust are excited about something, it's probably worth paying attention, too. I think, realistically, those are the only ways that normal people can use to filter signal from noise.

Viktor Farcic: I don't know how they manage, and maybe they don't. What's your feeling about open source? When you started your career, it wasn't a thing, but now it is. Is there still a future in projects that are closed source from the start?

Kohsuke Kawaguchi: Before we go into that, I just need to correct you. Open source has been around for a good amount of time, long before I started Jenkins. I think it still demonstrates my previous point about finding more viable ways to socialize DevOps. I really do believe that, fundamentally, open source is a better way of developing software. I've seen first-hand a number of proprietary software defeated by open source. We've talked about Sun and Solaris, so there's my case.

When I think about what made open source so successful, I think a key is that open source allowed new ideas from anywhere to be tested out more rapidly and thus quickly converging into a better working solution. Innovations happen everywhere, and that was a key differentiator.

But I feel, nowadays, there's another emerging differentiator in the different axis, which is the scale of the problem that they are dealing with.

Viktor Farcic: Can you clarify that a bit?

Kohsuke Kawaguchi: I've spent a good chunk of my professional career in Japan. In the worldwide software development market, Japan has about 10 to 15 percent share, so it's no small chunk, but it's not a majority either. Because of the various challenges related to language and time zone, Japanese software companies are by and large only solving the problems for their domestic market. It's a closed market.

Japan has around 100 million people. If you're running a service and you're serving the entirety of Japan, your scaling challenge is capped at 100 million. I attended developer conferences in China and what I realized is that even though their domestic market is just as closed, it is far bigger. So, their biggest service companies are facing and solving the kinds of scaling problems that Japanese companies haven't even thought of.

I was quite impressed that China was talking about how they need machine learning to help our operations. In Japan, that's a science fiction problem, whereas in China, that's a real problem today. The only other market in the world that rivals that is the United States. So, I'm convinced that our technology landscape in the next decade will be a duopoly between the US and China.

Because of the scale, when a new problem first gets discovered in those markets, they get solved, and they become available to the rest of the world, so the rest of the world doesn't get to really innovate.

> *"I was quite impressed that China was talking about how they need machine learning to help our operations. In Japan, that's a science fiction problem, whereas in China, that's a real problem today."*
>
> —*Kohsuke Kawaguchi*

What I'm trying to say is that the exposure to challenges at the frontier is becoming as big a differentiator as open source, if not more. I said innovations used to happen everywhere, but I feel innovations are happening closer to challenges of large markets. People say end user companies are now the source of innovations, not vendors, and I think this is for the same reason. So that's something of a prospect that I try to keep in mind.

DevOps in the next ten years

Viktor Farcic: Where do you see DevOps going in the next ten years?

Kohsuke Kawaguchi: I wish I had a better sense of the future to say interesting things about it. Like I've been saying, I would say the obvious direction is more automation.

There will be more demand for software and technology all over the world. For example, every time I have to go through the airport and show my driver's license to authenticate myself to the system, I think, this should be a solvable problem. So, yeah, there will be more software, and there will be more automation.

I guess I just can't get away from automation! Beyond that, I think data and machine learning should play a central role in the way we develop software as well. Those technologies have been disrupting so many things, it's silly to think our own profession is immune from that. But I don't know how quickly those things will happen. If I had that magic 8-ball, I'd be working on it and not talking to you now.

> *"There will be more software, and there will be more automation."*
>
> —*Kohsuke Kawaguchi*

Viktor Farcic: You've mentioned automation a couple of times. When I visit companies, there's always a huge number of people doing repetitive manual tasks over and over again. I was even involved in conversations where people are questioning automation, which completely doesn't make sense to me. What's not to like about automation? Why aren't we automated already?

Kohsuke Kawaguchi: Yeah, that's funny. The truth is sometimes I feel the same way. I feel like, as the outsider, we're landing into some places, and we do sometimes underestimate the rationality of the status quo. There's always more to it than what meets the eyes—consideration for things I don't understand, nuances that I don't get, the context, those sorts of things. I don't think it hurts for us to be a little humbler to those things. I'm not surprised if my parents think that our work is completely automatable. You go to the office, you sit in front of a computer, and then you come back. You seem to be repeating that every single day. What's not automatable about that?

Viktor Farcic: Exactly.

Kohsuke Kawaguchi: We need to be careful because we might be falling into that trap ourselves when we look at other people. That is not to say nobody is doing repetitive manual tasks that should be replaced. I'm sure there are some people who resist changes and what not. But my first reaction is always to assume that they see something I don't. So, I don't know. Personally, I don't come across people who genuinely perform this repetitive work. Most of the time, I think people see their work as not overly repetitive.

The other interesting perspective is, if you think of Japan, they've got traditional cultural things such as the tea ceremony, kendo, or judo. These are art forms, where they emphasize repetition, following the certain *kata* and repeating the same tasks to perfection. You start by mimicking a master, then you slowly develop your own style. What might look like circling in the same place to untrained eyes is actually a spiral movement upwards. What's implicit is the respect to the wisdom that your predecessors have built. There's also something deeply satisfying about the feeling of "this time I did it better than the last time." I think it's a key to motivate oneself for a long run. I think those are beautiful, though maybe it's just a part of the Asian psyche.

Viktor Farcic: As we start to wrap up, I would love to know, is there anything that really excites you in the industry right now?

Kohsuke Kawaguchi: As technology people, we're always excited to play with new toys. So, I guess playing with these new tools and new services is one thing that really excites me. Yesterday, I was playing with Google's new text-to-speech engine, which was pretty good. It's a kind of a black magic, and that's cool, then I think about all of the things that we could do with that, such as an audiobook, voice navigation while driving, or whatever. You just never know what comes out of it. New technology is always fun like that.

I do enjoy playing with these toys, but at the same time, some mundane problems also excite me. I go and see larger companies struggling with the problem of deploying their large hairy software quickly. Everyone has this problem of tests not being very reliable, or that they have too many tests and, most of the time, they are not doing anything useful. They are starting to question whether running all these tests is actually useful. I'm interested in seeing whether we can intelligently pick the subset of tests to run in the right order. I have a feeling that we can reduce the average turnaround time by an order of magnitude.

Another example of a mundane problem is the way that we track bugs, do the code change and then we get that verified. It's something that happens everywhere, and it's held together by people manually communicating and collaborating. I feel like some of them are ready for automation.

The connection between cross-stitching, Lego, and DevOps

I guess one person's mundane problem is somebody else's exciting challenge. Aside from that, cross-stitching.

Viktor Farcic: Cross-stitching? What exactly do you mean by that?

Kohsuke Kawaguchi: Cross-stitching is needlework. I started doing this because my wife picked it up and I thought it would be good to have a common hobby with her. It's generally an old woman's hobby. Let me explain cross-stitching in a way that geeks understand. Imagine a screen, and there are the pixels. Each pixel can be a different color. That's how we build graphics. Cross-stitching is the exact same thing; it's just on the piece of cloth, instead of a screen, and instead of pixels, you're using colored threads. It's just the analog version of a video screen. So, I stitch some video game characters and so on for fun.

Now, obviously, the actual stitching is incredibly manual and repetitive. I feel like I should be able to automate this. If there's a programmable machine, as in a sewing machine, I want to see whether I can control it to do the right things. A machine that takes a JPEG or a PNG as an input, then it would cross-stitch things for me. I think that'd be awesome. That would allow me to say, I master everything about cross-stitching, and then I can move on to another hobby. I wish I could do something like that. I have never been able to find anybody in the cross-stitching community who has any passion for this kind of automation. Most fans of cross-stitching are there for enjoying conversations with others while they are stitching things, and so for them, the idea of automation is horrifying. They would say, what's the point of doing it? That's why I'm itching to find a venue in which to talk about it.

If I get to do that, Lego will probably be the next.

Viktor Farcic: Lego and DevOps? That's a conversation that I wasn't expecting to have with you.

Kohsuke Kawaguchi: I'm a big Lego fan, and among the Lego community, you can have a never-ending conversation about how to sort and store your Lego blocks. You build something, and then you disassemble the model you've built. Most of you put Lego pieces in a big packet when you were small, and then you grow out of Lego and move on to something else. But for the rest of us who never grew out of Lego, and who continue to buy more and more Lego sets, the pieces get too many to just fit in the one packet. It'll take forever to find pieces you want.

I have several drawers full of Lego blocks, and as I was sorting them, naturally I started to think, "Wow, there's so many pieces, I need to automate this." People are actually doing that sort of thing. So, they build the machine, not just the software. It has a webcam that takes a picture of a brick on a conveyer belt, it matches the shape against a catalog, and then some sort of nozzle blows the air to push the piece into the right bin. That kind of automation is really fun, but then again, I just find myself trying to automate everything and anything possible. It's just how I am wired. I don't know if every other software developer feels the same. This story has no conclusion, but that's what excites me.

Viktor Farcic: I have the impression there's a fear that if you do those things, then you're automating yourself out of a guaranteed job position.

Kohsuke Kawaguchi: Wouldn't that be perfect? Because now I can die since I've completely automated myself! Of course, we know there's really no such thing as fully automating yourself away on anything, not even cross-stitching. I mean, what software development teaches us is that if you solve one problem by automation, you then get to face the next problem, and this ladder never ends. That's kind of fun for me.

Take cross-stitching, for example, if I someday manage to produce an ultimate cross-stitching machine like I described, the next thing I'll start thinking about is probably how do I automate the management of my inventory of threads. At that point, I can stitch any design, so I'm pretty sure I will be using threads like crazy, at an unimaginable scale. Today, it takes a trip to a local store to get threads of the right color, which can take several days. That's okay when a stitching project is taking months, but not if it only takes 15 minutes. So, how do you optimize that?

> *"What software development teaches us is that if you solve one problem by automation, you then get to face the next problem, and this ladder never ends. That's kind of fun for me."*
>
> —*Kohsuke Kawaguchi*

Or think about all the secondary problems that the Minecraft people get hang up on. I had a mod that can create a programmable robot inside a Minecraft world, so I could program it to do mining or building. Once you automate the mining part, then great, but we have this almost infinite inventory of raw iron ore, and then you start to think, "Oh, now I need to automate the smelting part. Otherwise, I'm smelting this forever," and so you kind of keep going like that.

Viktor Farcic: That's the freakiest story I've heard.

Kohsuke Kawaguchi: I hope it'll be at least somewhat entertaining to people who are reading this.

Viktor Farcic: Oh, I think it will be. I mean, for many people, I think relating it to both Lego and Minecraft will be a really good way of relating DevOps to the real world.

Kohsuke Kawaguchi: Thanks, Victor. This was fun. I'm looking forward to seeing your book.

Viktor Farcic: Thank you for taking the time to talk to me.

14

Sean Hull

Cloud Architect

Introducing Sean Hull

A seasoned industry advisor, author, speaker, and entrepreneur with over 20 years' of experience, Sean Hull specializes in DevOps cloud automation, scalability, Docker, and Kubernetes. His experience scales from small start-ups to Fortune 500 companies. You can follow him on Twitter at @hullsean.

Sean Hull and the world of databases

Viktor Farcic: To kick things off, tell us a little bit about yourself and how you got involved in DevOps.

Sean Hull: I'm based in New York, and I've been working in technology and alongside start-ups for over a decade. I got my start back when I did database work, scalability, and performance tuning for high-scale websites, such as the *Hollywood Reporter* and *Billboard*, sites that got a hundred million unique visitors per month. Back when Amazon started getting bigger, a lot of start-up companies were either migrating to the cloud or natively deploying their applications in the cloud, and so I saw an opportunity there to specialize in automation.

My background really is in Unix and Linux, and so it was a good match for me to shift gears and pivot in that direction, but I still do a lot of database-related work with MySQL, Postgres, and Redshift. These days I also do a lot of Python programming and all the automation stuff like CloudFormation and Terraform, which allows you to script all the objects in your cloud or in your AWS account, and that in turn allows you to version all the changes that you're making.

Viktor Farcic: I always get asked the same question in every talk I do: what do we do with databases?

Sean Hull: I read articles sometimes about people trying to put MySQL databases inside of a Docker container and the horrible performance that results, so that's absolutely a good question. A lot of the types of things that automation attempts to remedy with repeatability and so forth don't necessarily apply equally to databases. For instance, if you have a large MySQL database made up of users and activity, those tables have evolved over time. I mean, you have inserts, you have deletes, and the database tunes and optimizes a lot of that I/O to the disk based on usage.

Now, if you were to go ahead and rebuild that database, the layout on the disk would be different. So, the presumption is that a rebuilt database is exactly the same as the other, which isn't necessarily the case. In microservices, when you do a backup, you have to either version or timestamp all of those backups, and then the question arises of how do you restore across your entire application at a particular point in time. It might potentially become much more difficult when you have 10 microservices databases if you wanted to restore them all.

Dev versus Ops – how to define DevOps

Viktor Farcic: Moving on to a more general subject, how would you define DevOps? I've gotten a different answer from every single person I've asked.

Sean Hull: I have a lot of opinions about it actually. I wrote an article on my blog a few years ago called *The Four-Letter Word Dividing Dev and Ops*, with the implication being that the four-letter word might be a swear word, akin to the development team swearing at the operations team, and the operations team swearing at the development team. But the four-letter word I was referring to was "risk."

To summarize my article, in my view, the development and the operations teams of old were separate silos in business, and they had very different mandates. Developers are tasked with writing code to build a product and to answer the needs of the customers, while directly building change into and facilitating a more sophisticated product. So, their thinking from day to day is about change and answering the requirements of the products team.

On the other hand, the operations team's mandate is stability. It's "I don't want these systems going down at 2:00 a.m." So, over the long term, the operations teams are thinking about being as conservative as possible and having fewer moving parts, less code, and less new technologies. The simpler your stack is, the more reliable it is and the more robust and less likely it is to fail. I think the traditional reason why developers and operations teams were separated into silos was because of those two very different mandates.

They're two different ways of prioritizing your work and your priorities when you think about the business and the technology. However, the downside was that those teams didn't really communicate very well, and they were often at each other's throats, pushing each other in opposite directions.

But to answer your question, "What is DevOps?," I think of it as a cultural movement that has made efforts to allow those teams to communicate better, and that's a really good thing.

Viktor Farcic: What about infrastructure?

Sean Hull: What I see happening is that as the infrastructure code has caught on, a lot of companies don't have operations at all, or DBAs, or even operations teams. All they have are developers. That's fine insofar as you can build the infrastructure, but we've lost some of that mindset of stability, reliability, and the conservative thinking that would have come out of the operations teams. And now everything is on a developer's shoulders to not only write the code but often to deploy the infrastructure as well.

In larger companies, there is a separate DevOps team, so hopefully, they still carry some of those operations, but I'm thinking in terms of keeping things simple. "What is DevOps?" is an interesting question. I think it means different things to different people.

> *"It [DevOps] means different things to different people."*
>
> —*Sean Hull*

Viktor Farcic: I agree. Everybody has a different answer, so nobody knows what it is. What you just said leads me to an interesting, or rather horrifying—I don't know which—case that I once heard. I was speaking with a guy who said, "Oh I love that. That's really interesting for us because if we implement the serverless approach, we can get rid of all the operations because we would have no servers." What do you think of that?

Sean Hull: Actually, that's a great question, but it's a bit more complicated than that. I wrote an article called *The 30 Questions To Ask a Serverless Fanboy* where I talked in-depth about the question of whether we have to worry about anything if we're serverless. While being serverless definitely does simplify operations, there's still a lot to be mindful of. For instance, in a serverless framework, you may have one service to do authentication, and another, let's say DynamoDB or Firebase, as your data store. And then you have your Lambda functions that are running. As you add more components into the mix, you have more surface areas that become vulnerable to malicious code.

For example, in the traditional three-tier, the database is hidden behind a VPC. But in serverless, that database is on the internet, so how do you test and deploy your API gateway changes? In a traditional application, you have the web server, and you deploy your application code and so forth—while in serverless, you have to deploy the API gateway configuration.

For Lambda, there's a serverless framework that takes a serverless YAML file that you can configure the API gateway for and then when you deploy it, it will do all that for you using CloudFormation. But testing is another area that's more complex in serverless applications. You can test locally to some degree, but it's quite a bit different than testing an application that runs with the database on which you can run those web servers and databases locally.

Viktor Farcic: But with serverless, you're typically tying into a database somewhere else, so where do you run that development database?

Sean Hull: You may not be able to have all those components running locally, because it turns out the serverless framework has built stubs to provide Amazon-types of resources running locally on your computer. In terms of the management of a serverless framework, I definitely think that serverless simplifies certain things but makes other things more complex.

Exploring serverless functions, SQL, and the cloud

Viktor Farcic: How do you load-test serverless functions?

Sean Hull: You're paying every time that function is called, so do you really want to load-test it on a hundred thousand customers? I don't know. Then, there are timeout questions. You have resource limitations across your AWS account, so maybe you're going to hit a wall because you can only run a certain number of Lambda functions for the month, or you have 10 Lambda functions, and one function runs off the rails, which then takes all the other ones offline because you've hit some resource limit.

I think that there are still things to manage, for sure. I think that DevOps, infrastructure as code, and serverless have changed the nature of systems administration, site reliability engineers, and operational engineers. It changes their day-to-day jobs, but I still think there's a lot of work to do.

> *"DevOps, infrastructure as code, and serverless have changed the nature of systems administration, site reliability engineers, and operational engineers."*
>
> —*Sean Hull*

Viktor Farcic: How can we integrate database processes with all the automation that we're doing?

Sean Hull: Database management is quite a bit more complex than automating, say, a web server deployment, a caching server, Memcached, Redis, or even a search server or any of the other types of components. There's definitely more complexity. Another thing too with continuous integration is that your code is often deployed with code that affects the database.

For example, maybe you have a user's table, and a cell phone number, and you want to add a work phone number. So, you write the code around that, and then you write the DDL, the SQL statements that add the column, and you deploy those together, with the Python or Node.js code along with SQL. Those are called migrations. So, you're migrating the version of the database forward in time so that now that table can support that additional column.

The thing is, migration scripts typically include a roll forward and a roll backward script. But with a database, you can see how with code that's no problem. You roll back to an older version. That's not a big deal. However, if you roll back the database now, you may have data in that additional column.

If you've just added a work phone number, and maybe 10,000 of your users added their work phone numbers, if you roll back, you would drop that column and lose the data.

In some cases, roll forward and rollback scripts are managed by a DBA or somebody who's tasked with managing the database. But if you're an enterprise who's built your own application, then you don't have the luxury of that. Maybe you write your code blindly, and it drops the column, and you lose data? That's just another example of how the automation that we do in other parts of the enterprise doesn't necessarily always work the same way around with the database tier.

Viktor Farcic: As I said, it's not my expertise, but I always have the impression that I would prefer not to have a rollback feature at all rather than having people relying on such a thing with databases. It seems more dangerous than actually having any real value. The moment that the first transaction enters your system, how do you roll back? You can't.

Sean Hull: That's definitely a complicated question, and one that lots of folks have thought about. But at the same time, it used to be that database schema changes were done sort of ad hoc, in that you'd hand the script to the DBA and say, "Hey, add these columns," and it was not tightly bound to the version control system, because it's hard to do that. Databases don't have versioned schemas—at least MySQL and Postgres don't—and as far as I know, Redshift doesn't either. So, at this point, they're not really supporting that.

Viktor Farcic: Do you have a preferred tool, or just plain SQL, when you're doing migrations?

Sean Hull: Some languages support that. For example, Ruby has migrations built in, so when you're making code changes you can also deploy SQL. The response is that those chunks of SQL DDL (data definition language) commands are then set alongside the other branches of code, so that when you check out a particular version of the application, you're also checking out a version of the database.

Viktor Farcic: How about zero-downtime deployments of applications, where people are using a blue-green deployment or rolling updates, which effectively means that you will have multiple versions of your application running at the same time. How do you handle that on a database level?

Sean Hull: That's another good question. A lot of companies are using Amazon Relational Database Service (RDS) now. It's a managed MySQL, Postgres, or Oracle, and because it's managed, you don't have access to the command line, or to the server itself.

A few years back, I was working for a company called ROBO, and I had to do a database upgrade of RDS. With a MySQL installation, you log into the command line, and you have direct access to the MySQL instance. With this, you can restart it in a matter of seconds, and with replication you can have two masters. One is read-only, and you're replicating data back and forth so that you can do both zero-downtime deployments and zero-downtime upgrades while having the database set in read-only mode for a very short period of time.

My experience in trying to upgrade RDS was that it took at least five minutes to restart after the upgrade and we didn't really have much visibility in terms of what was going on behind the scenes because Amazon controlled the server. We only had access to the MySQL database; we didn't have access to the instance, so we couldn't really see what the status of that restart and that upgrade was, and whether it was held up by something such as corrupted data.

Viktor Farcic: So, how did you deal with that?

Sean Hull: We ran through a number of fire drills, and created the database on another AWS account, then upgraded it and timed it to see how long it took. It's a very cumbersome way to go about upgrading a database, and not only was it not zero downtime, it was in fact guaranteed downtime. There was no real way to avoid that. For some start-ups it's worth it because you have this managed solution: the database is always running, you have a dashboard, and you can see what's going on.

However, if you don't have a database expert around to manage your database, it's a lot simpler. But if you do have a DBA, it's much better to roll your own MySQL or Postgres and manage it because you can reduce your downtime quite a bit.

Viktor Farcic: How about the other case? Let's say we're not upgrading the database, but instead, are rolling out a new release of an application that speaks to the database and potentially changes the schema. In that case, we would have two releases of an application that potentially requires a different schema. Let's say that release 1 and release 2 introduced a new column. Do you have any suggestions about how to handle that?

Sean Hull: Yes, so the migration scripts that I was talking about before, alongside your code changes; so, when you check out that newer version of the application, you would also check out a newer version of the SQL and the DDL statements that add that column. So, if you're starting from scratch, you would start from a database dump and then apply all the migration scripts that point to that.

Viktor Farcic: Would those changes need to be backward-compatible with the previous version of the application, or would you just go straight ahead with a new schema?

Sean Hull: Usually you're rolling forward. If you were to go backward, you may or may not need to apply the dropped column because, for example, in the case where I described before, we added the user's cell phone and work phone numbers. If you go back to a previous version of the application, it just won't access the work phone.

It won't be a problem if that extra column is there, except in one particular case if you do `select *` in your application, and the `select *` is very frowned upon for exactly that reason. If you're selecting star and you change the database columns, you're going to get a different number of columns back, and your code could break. You never want to use a select star; you want to specify all the columns that you're accessing.

Viktor Farcic: Definitely. So, in your experience, when companies you've worked with are migrating to the cloud, what would you identify as the biggest problem that's waiting around the corner for them?

> *"I think the biggest obstacle is cultural; everything is done completely differently in the cloud now."*
>
> —*Sean Hull*

Sean Hull: I think the biggest obstacle is cultural; everything is done completely differently in the cloud now. In the traditional computing world, you have physical servers where you set up the server, you give it a name, plug it into your network, and you configure all those things the same way you would in the real world. It's almost like physical things have names.

Before we had managed hosting, people had a cage or a closet in their business, and you could physically see the machine to plug a cable into. But in the cloud, everything's virtualized, and that ends up being a completely new paradigm that doesn't only challenge the business people, it also challenges the technology people to think in a new way.

Viktor Farcic: You say challenges, like security?

Sean Hull: Yes, let's take security. In AWS, you have VPCs, and it's like virtual networking, so you can set up private and public subnets, and you can control access to servers inside of those subnets through two methods: one being security groups, and the other being access control lists. That's very different from the way you would control access to servers in the old world where you need to have a firewall, which the networking team manages and configures, and/or you would have a firewall on each server like, for example, iptables.

In the Amazon world, it's definitely as sophisticated, but the configuration of those firewalls is in the form of security groups and ACLs on your VPC, so its virtualized networking is very powerful, but it's also very complex and troubleshooting is difficult. When you try to access the server, and you get no response, and you're trying to figure out what could be the cause of that through debugging and troubleshooting, those problems are big challenges.

But back to your question, the biggest challenge to migrating to the cloud is that for enterprises, there's a big learning curve, not only in understanding how an EC2 server spins up and how it uses disk, but how it accesses Amazon's Elastic Block Store (EBS), how it stores files in S3, and how you write Lambda functions that respond to events taking action in that environment. It's a completely new paradigm and a new set of technologies, so it's a big learning curve for both the engineers and the business folks.

Viktor Farcic: I've seen quite a few of these tools that tell you if you buy our tool, we're going to transfer whatever you have to the cloud. For example, Docker announced in the last DockerCon that they're going to put in containers without a single change and everything will work. What do you think about that?

Sean Hull: Salespeople often simplify things quite a bit in order to sell a product; in my experience, the devil is in the detail. It's not to say that an automation tool like that might not be valuable and useful. It might be a good first step to getting your application in the cloud, and it might be an easier way than to rebuild everything one by one. But I doubt that it's going to work magically just with one script.

EC2 instances, for example, have different performance characteristics, not only in terms of the disk I/O, memory, and CPU, but in smaller instances, they actually throttle network access so you might spin up an instance and it just might not behave well. It might take time. In fact, all sorts of things could happen. You might have written MySQL scripts that assume you have root access to the server and then you rebuild that in an RDS and you get errors because you don't have access to those resources on the RDS. There's a lot of things to consider.

Viktor Farcic: How about applications? Say I'm a company and I have OpenFrame applications that were developed in the last 10 years. Does that require some kind of changing paradigm or architecture? What are your thoughts on that?

Sean Hull: It may. For example, a lot of applications might use shared storage. Amazon now has something called Elastic File System (EFS), which is meant to mirror the functionality that you see in traditional datacenters. But really, the right way to do it is to store your assets and your content on S3, but S3 didn't exist in those old applications in that environment, so you have to rewrite portions of your application to use S3. I worked with a media publishing company last year that used an NFS server to store some of their content.

> *"A number of years have passed since a lot of companies were locked in with Oracle, and so much time has passed that there's a new generation of folks that haven't been bitten by that."*
>
> —*Sean Hull*

The right way to do that would be to use the plugin—in this case, it was WordPress—to access those files in S3. But they wanted to move it to Amazon with a fewer number of changes. For the short term, we set up EFS, which is Amazon's version of NFS. The only reason Amazon built EFS in the cloud is because, exactly as in the use case you're talking about where you have applications, you're moving them, and you don't want to. The native way to do it in Amazon would be to store it in S3 because S3 has life cycle control and infrequent access. It also has Glacier and all the rest so that would be the native way to do it in the cloud.

Vendor lock-in, AWS, and keeping up with the DevOps world

Viktor Farcic: With the companies you work with, do they express concern about vendor lock-in, for example, when they go to Amazon?

Sean Hull: Yes, actually I think a number of years have passed since a lot of companies were locked in with Oracle, and so much time has passed that there's a new generation of folks that haven't been bitten by that. I sense that there's less fear right now around Amazon lock-in than maybe there should be. There are tools like Terraform that can plug into Google Cloud; it can talk to the IBM Cloud, Azure, and AWS, among others, so you can deploy resources in any of those clouds if you've built your infrastructure code in Terraform. Terraform is like a layer on top of CloudFormation that implements that stuff in a generic way.

Viktor Farcic: What's your take on container schedulers: Kubernetes, Mesos, Swarm, and so on?

Sean Hull: I haven't done much with Kubernetes and Docker Swarm. Docker is awesome, and containerization has been around for a long time, since the late 1970s. In fact, I think there was an original BSD project that really popularized containers, but obviously, Docker is the modern version that everybody knows so well, and it does a lot of powerful things.

You can spin up development environments and QA test very easily, and so you can encapsulate all the code to rebuild everything you need to get your application working, and that makes everything more repeatable, and so forth. I don't think containers are going away anytime soon because they serve a really big need.

Viktor Farcic: I have the impression that the speed with which new things are coming is only increasing. How do you keep up with it, and how do companies you work with keep up with all that?

Sean Hull: I don't think they do keep up. I've gone to a lot of companies where they've never used serverless. None of their engineers know serverless at all. Lambda, web tasks, and Google Cloud functions have been out for a while, but I think there are very few companies that are able to really take advantage of them. I wrote another article blog post called *Is Amazon Web Services Too Complex for Small Dev Teams?* where I sort of implied that it is.

I do find a lot of companies want the advantage of on-demand computing, but they really don't have the in-house expertise yet to really take advantage of all the things that Amazon can do and offer. That's exactly why people aren't up to speed on the technology, as it's just changing so quickly. I'm not sure what the answer is. For me personally, there's definitely a lot of stuff that I don't know. I know I'm stronger in Python than I am with Node.js. Some companies have Node.js, and you can write Lambda functions in Java, Node.js, Python, and Go. So, I think Amazon's investment in new technology allows the platform to evolve faster than a lot of companies are able to really take advantage of it.

> *"Amazon's investment in new technology allows the platform to evolve faster than a lot of companies are able to really take advantage of it."*
>
> —*Sean Hull*

Viktor Farcic: That was my impression when I heard the announcements from their conference. I was like, it would take me a year just to go, and if I would dedicate a year, I would still have trouble keeping up with everything they announced in just a single day.

Sean Hull: I had a customer recently ask me if I have experience with Lambda. I said, "Yes," and he said, "We want to use something called Lambda@Edge," and I said, "I have no idea what Lambda@Edge is as I've never even heard of it." It turned out Lamba@Edge is a product released four or five months ago that is actually kind of cool. Normally, in your applications, your content is either fed off of the web server or in S3, and then you have CDNs that can then fetch that content and keep it closer to where the traffic is coming from.

Say I'm hosting an application in New York, but I have a customer in Japan, and they're hitting that piece of content. They would hit a CDN endpoint that's closer to Japan, and therefore the application would be quicker. All the graphical images and CSS and the other things that it can cache, it would keep them cached at the endpoint. Lambda@Edge allows you to write Lambda code that executes at the edge, so you can examine a cookie that the user authenticated with and then see at the CDN if they have permission to access something. You can write Lambda code that executes at the edge, hence further speeding up your application. If most of your application is in Lambda, you'd be completely distributed at point, and you'd see really huge performance improvement there.

Viktor Farcic: I haven't even heard about Lambda@Edge until today.

Sean Hull: Lambda@Edge exposes four new events: there's both a before and after endpoint, and a before and after origin, so you can respond just like any other Lambda code would respond to events in the AWS world, and Lambda@Edge exposes those four new events to allow you to write code that runs at the CDN endpoint.

The future of DevOps and closing remarks

Viktor Farcic: I'm going to ask you a question now that I hate being asked, so you're allowed not to answer. Where do you see the future, let's say a year from now?

Sean Hull: I see more fragmentation happening across the technology landscape, and I think that

that is ultimately making things more fragile because, for example, with microservices, companies don't think twice about having Ruby, Python, Node.js, and Java. They have 10 different stacks, so when you hire new people, either you have to ask them to learn all those stacks or you have to hire people with each of those individual areas of expertise. The same is true with all these different clouds with their own sets of features: there's a fragmentation happening.

Let's look at the iPhone as an example. Think about how complex application testing is for Android versus the iPhone. I mean, you have hundreds of different smartphones that run Android, all with different screen sizes, different hardware, different amounts of memory, and the underlying stuff. Some may even have some extra chips that others don't have, so how do you test your application across all those different platforms?

> *"You have hundreds of different smartphones that run Android, all with different screen sizes, different hardware, different amounts of memory, and the underlying stuff. [...] How do you test your application across all those different platforms?"*
>
> *—Sean Hull*

When you have fragmentation like that, it means the applications end up not working as well. I think the same thing is happening across the technology spectrum today that happened 10 to 15 years ago, where for your database backend there was Oracle, SQL Server, MySQL, and Postgres. Maybe somebody who's a DB2 enterprise customer uses DB2, but now there are hundreds of open source databases, graph databases, and DynamoDB versus Cassandra, and so on and so on. There's no real deep expertise in any of those databases.

What ends up happening is you have cases like what happened with customers who were using MongoDB. They found out the hard way about all of the weird behaviors and performance problems it had, because there just weren't people around with deep knowledge of what was happening behind the scenes, whereas in Oracle's space, for example, there are career DBAs that are performance experts that specialize in Oracle internals, so you can hire somebody to solve particular problems in that space.

There aren't, as far as I know, a lot of people with MongoDB internals expertise. You'd have to call MongoDB themselves; maybe they have a few engineers that they can send out, so what's the future? I see a lot of fragmentation and complexity, and that makes the internet and internet applications more fragile, more brittle, and more prone to failure.

Viktor Farcic: Do you think that trend will continue, or will it kind of reverse itself?

Sean Hull: I don't know if it would or how it could reverse itself; it seems like it's a more general trend of all human knowledge. Look at science and the different specializations; that have gotten more complex across the spectrum, and I think that complexity can lead to very unexpected surprises.

For example, I recently read a research paper that talked about depression among teens. I know this is a long side note, but the researchers believe teenage depression is related to the overuse of smartphone devices, because they're messing up how people socialize. I think that more complex fragmentation across the technology spectrum can lead to very unexpected surprises. I don't know how we wrestle that and how we rein that in, because it just seems to be growing more and more every day.

Viktor Farcic: I share the same impression. I think that nothing ever goes away, like how we still have mainframes to think about as well. But to finish up, is there anything else you would like to talk about?

Sean Hull: Not long ago I wrote an article titled *How is Automation Impacting the DBA Role?*. I was talking to a colleague of mine who works in the Oracle space, and they were lamenting how things are changing so quickly, and a lot of companies don't hire a traditional DBA role anymore. That's partly because there are managed services like Amazon RDS that simplify that process, so you don't need a dedicated resource person just for that role.

To summarize, in the article I wrote that there's a lot of opportunity for people with deep database knowledge, but they need to step up, pivot, and present their skills and their knowledge and frame it in a new way.

I do think that deep database knowledge is very valuable for companies, especially as they adopt microservices and try to put databases into containers, and you have other weird performance issues around multi-tenant, Amazon-related stuff. I think someone who has deep database knowledge and performance should still be able to apply that and be of value in today's technology landscape. I just think it's a matter of packaging it and selling yourself in a new way.

Viktor Farcic: I have the same impression. I think it actually goes way beyond specific examples like databases. I feel the same thing is happening in other areas, and I'm seeing more and more Java developers who actually know how to write getters and setters and stuff like that. I have the impression that's happening all around, and to me, this is a very big warning that we might get into trouble.

Sean Hull: I think what is happening is that hiring managers are starting to realize that they're not going to find somebody with the exact specific skill that they're looking for, and they have to look for a more general skillset and someone with more general computing understanding and knowledge. Once they've found them, they need to ask, "Hey, do you want to step up and learn this new stuff, or do you feel confident to solve this problem?"

Viktor Farcic: That's a great place to end the interview. Thank you.

15

Bret Fisher

Docker Captain
and Cloud Sysadmin

Introducing Bret Fisher

Bret Fisher is a freelance DevOps and Docker consultant, Udemy instructor, trainer, speaker, and open source volunteer. He also teaches courses on Docker and container technology. You can follow him on Twitter at @BretFisher.

What is DevOps?

Viktor Farcic: I want to start by asking if you could give us the elevator pitch as to who you are, and how you're involved with the DevOps community.

Bret Fisher: Firstly, I would say that I'm a DevOps consultant who mainly focuses on Docker. That being said, I'm actually a Docker Captain, who both works and teaches the program. I guess you could say I live and breathe Docker 24/7.

Viktor Farcic: Last night, I was talking to three self-proclaimed DevOps engineers who were all from different companies. You'd think they would all describe their jobs in the same way, but they didn't. In fact, each of them described their jobs using different terms. So, my question for you is, and it's something I've asked everyone in this book, what the heck is DevOps?

Bret Fisher: The definition of DevOps today is not what people who do DevOps actually do, so it's funny that you've asked me this question. People have asked me to inject more

DevOps into my Docker course because they're self-proclaimed beginners in DevOps. But they're actually not beginners of DevOps, they're beginners in IT.

> *"The definition of DevOps today is not what people who do DevOps actually do."*
>
> —Bret Fisher

If John or Jane, who are just starting out in IT, comes to me saying that they want to do DevOps, I find it difficult to do. Why? Because, to me, DevOps is something you can only do after you've been in operations or in development for a while, because you have to know both in some form before you really get the overarching idea of DevOps. You can't really be a part of DevOps if you're new to either area.

Viktor Farcic: So, really nobody knows what DevOps actually is?

Bret Fisher: To me, DevOps is literally if you're a developer, you're working with operations, and you're sharing the same concerns around the concept of getting the software off of the developer's laptop, into production, and everything in between. Then, after the software is in production, the job of DevOps is making sure that the project remains up and that you can update it reliably, and that there's this continuous feedback loop between everyone involved in the process. The loop is how the software is getting from the developer all the way through to the servers and then getting updated in an ever-increasingly faster loop.

But let's, for a minute, imagine that I'm in a DevOps team with you. If, in the future, we're still shipping software at the same pace that we're shipping it now, I would say that we're not doing very well as a team. We should be optimizing and making the system more efficient, assuming of course that we wanted to go faster. If the company's not trying to go faster, then that's fine. I find it funny that DevOps is now becoming this entryway thing for people want to get into technology. Everybody's saying that technology is awesome and that DevOps is something we all should be doing, but I just don't see how that works. If I don't know how to be a developer, and I don't know how to be operations, then how could I possibly do both of them and DevOps?

Viktor Farcic: That's the issue I keep coming across. I'm continuously meeting people who are just starting their IT journey. At that stage of their career, they know nothing about anything. They're starting from scratch.

It would be as if my first introduction to IT is me saying: "I'm going to become a DevOps engineer." It's as if I'm choosing whether I'm going to become a tester. I'm going to become a developer, and I really don't understand how that happened. You said earlier that you do Docker courses, but to me, when you've completed them, you're certified DevOps, and you have an ability to say: "I'm a certified DevOps beginner."

Bret Fisher: If someone said that he or she was new in the industry and wanted to get into DevOps, then I could hire them with the idea of training them towards that specific goal. If I had to make them a DevOps engineer, their first job would obviously be to learn the developing language that the team is running and effectively become a very junior developer.

I would stick the newbie on the build team, so they would have to be someone involved with using Jenkins and either building or testing the app and automating that part. For me, that's the only role where they don't have to develop the code but, instead, have to understand the code just a little bit. They don't really have to know the operations, but they're going to have to talk to the operators, and as a result, they're going to learn a little bit of the operators' pain.

> *"If I had to make them a DevOps engineer, their first job would obviously be to learn the developing language that the team is running and effectively become a very junior developer."*
>
> —*Bret Fisher*

Fast-forward a year: I would now say that you've done all that for a while, let's actually have you be responsible for some servers, and from there, you get a little bit of operations sysadmin experience. Fast-forward another year, and now you can say: "OK, maybe you can start focusing on DevOps-related issues." People that are new to operations find it a tough thing because they don't understand software and servers, which raises the question of what exactly are they operating?

I'm sure there are some job descriptions out there that say they're looking for a junior DevOps engineer. I just have to ask, who would do that job well? Is it somebody who's a developer and likes to tinker with servers, or is it a server admin who knows a little bit about how to script and code? I really don't know, but what I do know is that I don't have a good answer to your question. What's funny is that there are all of these courses that say you can do DevOps now, but all they do is teach you a tool like Jenkins, which doesn't make you DevOps.

Right here, right now

Viktor Farcic: I find that interesting because, when I've gone to conferences—say, over the last two years—all I'm seeing is every single vendor and every single product being labeled as DevOps. Yes, it has already existed for years, but today, every single product is called a DevOps product. Just look at Jenkins. I know that you go to a lot of conferences, so I was wondering what your thoughts are on this?

Bret Fisher: DevOps is like the new cloud. Remember when we were all joking in 2013 about what is the cloud? All we knew was that it's just servers on the internet. That's all it is. But we had this new term, and everybody had to use it. All of these companies came out with all of these products, and they all had the word "cloud" in it somewhere.

So, now, what is the cloud? The cloud doesn't mean anything. It's just the internet. I feel like that's what the word DevOps is going toward, though I must put my hands up as I'm guilty of this because my course has DevOps in the title.

Viktor Farcic: Even my previous books have DevOps in their title—the *DevOps Toolkit* series.

Bret Fisher: My title is *DevOps Dude*, simply because

it works. I get more requests to interview for jobs on LinkedIn simply because DevOps is in my title.

Viktor Farcic: I can tell you if I named my books *Operations Toolkit*, instead of *DevOps Toolkit*, it would just sell seven copies, and six of those seven copies would be bought by my relatives. But let's shift focus onto containers. I don't ever recall seeing something becoming so popular so quickly, so I'm left wondering why is that?

Bret Fisher: Whenever I do a Docker 101 talk, I talk about how we've been around in IT for a long time, and that, in the past, we never got paid for it, but actually we were still doing it. We were doing it just for fun, but now we get paid to do it for fun. I was in technology back when we took out the mainframe and put in PCs, which were actually just DOS operating systems. We also had to actually put mice on the PCs because they were going to get Windows, which is something we then had to install on the machines—machines that didn't have the internet. Then, eventually, we finally got the TCP/IP suite of communication protocols and were able to simply plug up all of the computers to the internet.

Then, after the internet, we had virtualization, and during those times, I was the guy in the big company with half a million employees that was walking around saying, "Virtualization is the future." Meanwhile, everyone else was saying, "You're stupid, you're crazy, the servers will run slow, we're never going to be able to build security." It's the same arguments we hear today for containers, and last year, for the cloud. Now, with the cloud, it's basically all about putting our data on the internet.

You're taking your data out of the data center, putting it on the internet, and letting someone else take care of it. Even though that was 11 years ago when Amazon's AWS service launched, it's still happening today. Even though we were all like, "Oh, everybody's going to be there." The truth is, not everyone is there yet.

Viktor Farcic: Out of interest, what would you say is today's version of the cloud?

Bret Fisher: I would say containers. It was only three years ago when I changed my entire career to focus on containers. Why? Because I've been a part of enough of these transitions to know that this is the next one. If you look at these waves, every single one of them—from mainframe to PC, PC to the internet, PC to virtualization, virtualization to cloud, and now containers—seems to happen faster than the one before it. At least, that's my theory.

Virtualization took a decade, but it was taken on pretty quickly. But moving to the cloud for a lot of companies happened much quicker than virtualization. Today, we're seeing containers having a much faster adoption rate, at least when compared to virtualization. I think that's the nature of where we're at in the industry, and so whatever the next thing is going to be, it's going to happen faster than containers.

Viktor Farcic: And when I think about it, it's probably going to last a shorter amount of time as well.

Bret Fisher: It might just as well last that long. But here's the thing: it might be more volatile, where we'll eventually get containers that will be so good that we won't even need most virtualization. Maybe in the future, virtualization will become unnecessary.

Viktor Farcic: But then, if it's happening so fast, how can humanity keep up with that?

Bret Fisher: It doesn't.

Viktor Farcic: Each time I read about the next release of something—say, Docker—I feel like I'm in a position where I haven't even finished with the last one, and yet there's already a new one to learn, and I end up having no idea what's going on.

Skipping a generation – a good or bad idea?

Bret Fisher: Exactly, so you'll have companies that skip a generation. For example, company X might now be doing virtualization. They didn't really do cloud, so they skipped it, but now they're going to do containers instead of just virtualization in the cloud.

Viktor Farcic: But can you do that? Is jumping a generation a good idea?

Bret Fisher: Not without your pain increasing. The pain increases because you're part of a team, and organizational learning means that we've both got to know that you're never a silo of knowledge. The entire team has to learn together and so, even if you were to hire a container expert, in a good-sized organization, it's going to take them years to get the entire team up to speed on all of that tech.

If the companies aren't doing cloud yet and you're going to take them to the cloud, but now they're also going to do containers too, that's going to suck. They're probably going to make more mistakes, but it's still going to get there, eventually. You're just going to incur more pain and more suffering. Laura Frank, the Director of Engineering at CloudBees, actually has a new term for this. She calls it the laggard tax.

> *"We still have people using mainframes, and we still have people that are not fully virtualized. There are still companies out there running 10-year-old servers that were never virtualized."*
>
> —Bret Fisher

If you've ever seen that bell chart diagram where you have your people up at the front when the technology first starts, then there's also the people at the very beginning of it and, after that, the majority of us, and finally, there are the laggards. Laura describes laggard tax as being if you're so slow to adopt the technology—let's say, as in our case, the cloud—it's actually going to cost you more in the long term because you might have to completely skip a generation of technology. But the thing is, none of these are absolutes. We still have people using mainframes, and we still have people that are not fully virtualized. There are still companies out there running 10-year-old servers that were never virtualized.

Viktor Farcic: I know people, and I'm not joking, who are still graduating in the COBOL language.

Bret Fisher: Even looking forward a decade, there will still be people that are not yet doing containers, and instead only doing virtualization or something along those lines.

There was a good session at GOTO Chicago a couple of weeks ago where the keynoter talked about how 30 years ago in technology, life was great because you could be someone who, if you were fully invested in the community, knew a little bit about most things. You could know a good amount about most languages and most technologies. But what stood out was how he said that now no one knows anything about anything. We all have just a fraction of the knowledge available about current technology. Even in a team, you probably don't even know a tenth of the languages out there. How can we possibly make educated decisions fully aware of everything that's available to us? The answer is just we don't.

> *"No one knows anything about anything."*
>
> —*Bret Fisher*

As an industry, we're stumbling through the dark, only engaging with whatever works for us right here and now. There's no right or wrong until you've been hacked and then you're wrong. The number one way to fail in this industry is to just wait until your product has been hacked, and then suddenly everybody will blame you for everything at that point. But until you've been hacked, as long as it works, it doesn't really matter.

I believe it was back at GOTO where I got on a rant about how you walk in the average company—and by "average", I don't mean the Google- or Netflix-type companies—and you start critiquing all of the different parts of their technology stack. There's going to be at least a half a dozen things at that company that would be front-page-worthy. Company A still stores their passwords in a spreadsheet, while company B doesn't even monitor their most critical DNS servers. Or company C has had the same root password for their servers for the past five years, while in that time period, 30 people have been fired from the company, and yet they've never changed the password. You're going to find these issues in every company. If it's all that mixed up, if it's all horrible, or if it's simply just luck that we're not all doomed to crash and fail, then I think, at the end of the day, all that really matters is getting stuff to work and doing the best you can at that moment. It's never going to be perfect, and it's never going to be great.

Using containers

Going back to your earlier question though, I think that the definition of DevOps itself inherently means compromise. The operations and developers at any company have to compromise to get the stuff to work together and to go faster. Maybe that's compromising on security or on testing. Maybe our testing lifecycle isn't four weeks' worth of user testing anymore; maybe it's just four days before we go to production? But in a lot of cases, we can't just speed things up without making some sort of eventual compromise that every party involved in would be okay with.

Viktor Farcic: Let's talk more about you, Bret. From my understanding, most of the time, you're helping companies or people adapt to using containers. Do you think we should be shipping everything in containers? As someone who's so invested in the concept, do you ever sit back and say that, actually, no, this stays as it is—we're not going to use containers?

Bret Fisher: Obviously, we can say that, technically, everything can run in a container. The real question that needs to be asked is about how much pain and suffering you want to go through in order to make your "thing" run in a container.

In my own experience, if I'm starting a project with a client, I'll look at whatever tool or technology they're going to run, and together, we'll try to imagine what the end goal is. If that's in a container, how will that make their product or service better? If their goal is a database and we only update that database's engine once every six months, they don't need to patch it every month. They're not moving it around in the environment, it's already on a server with redundant power supplies, redundant memory, redundant switching, and redundant NICs, which is a lot of data centers.

> *"I will always prefer the thing that they're going to update every day/week versus the thing that's just going to sit there reliably and never change for months at a time."*
>
> —*Bret Fisher*

A lot of private data centers are still very hardware redundancy focused, unlike the cloud where it's the complete opposite. For me, I will always prefer the thing that they're going to update every day/week versus the thing that's just going to sit there reliably and never change for months at a time. Usually, that means your web APIs or your new worker jobs for your PHP workers on the backend of your system are constantly changing; those are always the things that I try to get them to do first. Then, by the time we get to the things that require really big and complicated databases, the companies are usually out of money, and so we won't ever do those things, and they'll stay where they are.

A lot of companies, especially if it's a new product or app, will containerize the database to begin with. But I'm always telling them, "Don't make this database the first thing you put in a container!" Anything with persistent data is always going to be harder no matter what you do, whether it's in or out of a container, so I would try to avoid that at first. But if it's brand new, and if I can give them a Docker file that they can put in a container—even if it's not in orchestration, it's just on a server in a container and that's the only thing on that server, and it never moves—then that's fine. I'll be happy. Because, at least, at that point, it's in a container and they're not writing shell scripts to do apt-get installs of MySQL.

Viktor Farcic: Let's say somebody doesn't know anything about containers. Would you recommend still teaching them to start from the beginning, in a similar way to what we experienced with containers four years ago? Let's get them started with containers, then move onto schedulers, or should they just jump straight into schedulers? Where should the newbie go today?

Bret Fisher: I would always want to teach them the local-host. I feel that maybe because it's universal, even if you're not a developer, and you're just a sysadmin, showing how your Mac/Windows machine can run an Ubuntu container or a CentOS container and then having all of those tools right there in front of you so that you don't have to figure out how to put curl on your Windows desktop. I feel like that is valuable for everybody regardless of your background.

Maybe I'm a traditionalist, and I don't want to teach you an orchestrator because I feel that sometimes, by teaching orchestration first, it would be like telling you the solution before you even know the problem. To me, it's like if you're a Windows admin in a data center. Traditionally, you would use something like System Center for Microsoft or some big enterprisey server management tool, but if you're new to server admin, showing you that tool at the start would be confusing. To the newbie, it would seem very complex, because the newbie doesn't even know how to run one server much less a thousand servers. If I'm teaching you that tool and you don't even know how to manage one or two servers, I feel like the tool that's going to help you to manage a thousand servers isn't going to seem very useful.

> *"Maybe I'm a traditionalist, and I don't want to teach you an orchestrator because I feel that sometimes, by teaching orchestration first, it would be like telling you the solution before you even know the problem."*
>
> —*Bret Fisher*

Viktor Farcic: It's kind of a doubt that I have. I've been in a number of situations where I explain containers and then it turns out that I'm explaining it to somebody who is very new to IT in general. "What's the benefit of me explaining this to you?" I feel like asking them, "How can you see the benefit if you haven't experienced the pain first?"

Bret Fisher: That's tough, but it's possible. If you go back to 2013, you'll remember that Solomon Hyke, who founded Docker, talked about why we all teach Docker. He talked about the matrix from hell with all of the little question marks in the boxes, and he also explained the matrix of hell and why we have all of these systems and patches for various things.

Let's say you want to install a Ruby app on my local machine and my development team has a mixture of both Windows, Mac, and Linux machines. But then, I also have servers that are Linux, and some of those servers are in the cloud running a different distribution of Linux, and I have a different package manager. Now I have all of these different environments. My goal is to install the same thing on all of them and to ensure it works exactly the same way when you hear someone describe that. Hopefully, this will make sure that you realize you have two options. You can think: "OK, that sounds very painful," or equally, "I could just do this one thing and keep doing it over and over." So maybe, if you're brand new, you should go through that whole "why Docker?" thing.

Viktor Farcic: Yeah, shouldn't that be included in courses? That's kind of like saying: "I'm going to make you do everything without Docker to realize how beneficial Docker is, or even containers in general."

Bret Fisher: Exactly, it's like saying that, first, we're going to do this on Ubuntu. We're going to install your Node.js app on Ubuntu, and then we're going to use Node v10, which means you can't use the latest `apt-get`. Sorry, but you're going to have to go get something else. You have to build it yourself, and then we're going to make you do it on CentOS. After that, we're going to make you do it on Red Hat, Enterprise, and Linux. Oh, and by the way, we're also going to make you do it all on Windows. But we're not done yet. After all four of those, we're now going to do it on Docker on those same four systems. That's going to waste a lot of their time. And the simple fact is, they may not want to do that at all. But maybe you would just be good enough to show an installation document that says: This is what you would have to do. You just show them these 12 pages of documentation for how to do this, and maybe that's enough.

The future of the OS

Viktor Farcic: I have the impression that many OSes, apart from being Docker containers, made us question quite a few things, such as do we even need Ubuntu and Red Hat?

Bret Fisher: That's the distribution issue. The Linux distributions don't want to hear the fact that they're becoming less relevant, but the truth is that they are becoming less relevant. I have no doubt that several of them will succeed in making themselves more relevant in the container space, and that they'll come up with tools that will make it worth me using Ubuntu to run containers instead of choosing something else. To an extent, it's already true today because I would choose one over the other simply because it comes with a more modern kernel that's going to work better with Docker. If you've got a five-year-old kernel that's still on the 3 series, I know I'm not going to prefer you just because I now have to go and update the kernel before I even want to put Docker on it. So that's step one.

> *"The Linux distributions don't want to hear the fact that they're becoming less relevant, but the truth is that they are becoming less relevant."*
>
> —*Bret Fisher*

Viktor Farcic: Back to your question about learning the basics first, and learning the problem before you can learn the solution. I've been saying this about things such as TCP/IP, for example. You've been around long enough to know that when we got started, we were reading a book literally called *TCP/IP*.

Bret Fisher: I've actually been trying to suppress that memory, and you've just brought it back. Thanks!

Viktor Farcic: I remember that the book was actually called *TCP/IP Unleashed*, and it was either the 4th or 5th edition because they just kept re-releasing the books because that's how we all learned before the age of Google. This meant that, for years and years, I kept thinking I was lucky to build networks for the first time. We were switching mainly from IPX to TCP/IP, Thicknet and Thinnet, and all of these different protocols and standards to Ethernet. Because of that, I had to learn about TCP packet size, headers, different protocols, and all of that stuff.

Bret Fisher: But today, the issue is that you can ask anyone younger than 30 years old to break down what the OSI layers are and they're probably not going to know any of it, yet they can still get employed and do the work.

Viktor Farcic: Which is a good thing.

Bret Fisher: It's both a good thing and a bad thing at the same time. I was convinced for the longest time that, eventually, we're going to have this world where very few people even understand how networks work. It's all going to start to just crumble underneath the weight of the lack of knowledge. In your team, when things start to go wrong, you're thinking we don't know how any of this other stuff that we use works because it's always just worked.

It's like public infrastructure. How many of us know how to fix an electrical grid? None of us do. Yet, when it breaks, we're all wishing we really could help. But we haven't yet had a problem, so I don't know. Maybe it's just not a big issue. When I interview people though, I still ask them questions like, "Which layer of the OSI stack does a switch operate on?" or "Which one does a router operate?"

Viktor Farcic: Do you ever get the answer?

Bret Fisher: Sometimes, but it really depends on who you ask. If they're going to be a developer, they're not going to care about that. But if I'm hiring a sysadmin or something, then they should. They all have to really think about it, because to me, it's the foundation of how everything talks to everything else. If you don't even know the basics of that, how could you possibly troubleshoot a computer even in Docker?

We're creating all of these virtual networks in Docker, but then the minute you have an IP address conflict, suddenly you must start caring about subnets and subnet masking.

Viktor Farcic: It opens an issue.

Bret Fisher: Yes, which is for somebody else to solve.

Viktor Farcic: I have a feeling that this is actually where we are moving in the industry. I see the same thing with programming. Nobody knows how to program anymore, and instead, we all just know how to use the libraries to do stuff.

Bret Fisher: That's a good point. If you're doing nothing but libraries, and you had to write it all by yourself, how would you do it? It sounds like we both learned originally by copying code out of books, which is how I learned BASIC.

Viktor Farcic: I don't know whether it was happening in your part of the world, but when I was a kid, I would get those computer magazines that featured around four to five pages of code that you would read and write.

Bret Fisher: I don't remember the name of the magazines, but I do remember my dad bringing home this huge 3-inch book, and within it, there would be five or six programs. What I do remember is spending an entire weekend never going outside, just sitting at the computer typing from the book, line for line, just to make an app or game.

Viktor Farcic: Let me guess, it's not a strongly typed language. You needed to finish it before you could discover if something was wrong?

Bret Fisher: Yes! Because if it didn't work, you had to go through line by line, all 600 of them. This was done on the Tandy color computer, TRS-80. The biggest problem was that the saving device was a tape recorder. Because of this, you had to plug in an analog line, which would make a sound like a modem to record to the tape. The only way to know if your save worked was to turn the computer off and then back on, play back the tape and then hope your program ran. If it didn't run, you had to type all 600 lines of it all over again.

I just remember the weekend that I left the computer on overnight because I wasn't finished. I recorded it to tape on Sunday, I played it back, and it didn't work. I had the sound up too loud or something, and there was distortion. So, I had to retype the whole program just to play it again, which was a horrible way to learn.

Viktor Farcic: I found myself telling the stories in terms of saying: "You kids have no idea what you're doing." But then I find myself thinking I sound like my mother saying this new generation has no idea what to do.

Bret Fisher: Yeah, your story is boring, but you're exactly right, and that's why this story is boring. Because everybody's first website is very exciting, no matter how old you are. That first time you make a program or anything you've coded work, it's always super exciting to you, and it's always incredibly boring to everyone else.

Looking into the future

Viktor Farcic: If you had a crystal ball, where would you predict we're going to be in the next year, next decade, or even further out? Obviously, now the leading-edge tech is containers, but what's coming after?

Bret Fisher: I think it's going to take us a long time before orchestration is normal.

Viktor Farcic: I mean, with that, we're just starting.

Bret Fisher: It's a lot harder now than it's going to be, and it has to get a lot easier before most people are going to use it. I'm really a fan of the whole one container per VM concept, such as Clear Containers with Linux. VMware is doing a little bit of it, Microsoft's doing it, and Docker's doing it with the LinuxKit. I don't necessarily know if we're going to end up with a world where it's a lot of just one container per VM or if it's going to be this world of mini containers in a VM. But I think locked-down apps, whatever the future of containers is, will be the norm.

> *"I don't know what the next thing is, and I don't have the pulse on what's going to replace containers. But I think it's going to take us a long time to come up with a new concept at the OS level."*
>
> —*Bret Fisher*

It'll be weird in 10 years for you to be a software company that sells software that doesn't ship in some form of container image. I mean, it's kind of weird now, depending on where you are in the industry. It'd be very normal to download images. It wouldn't surprise me if we somehow got to the point where we had a bunch of package managers that were downloading. Right now, you have to use `docker pull` to get a Docker image, but I can see it as the future `apt-get`. The future of `yum` is it's downloading of images, tarballs of container images, and it's running containerd or something in the background, but that's just normal for those apps.

But I think it's going to take us a lot longer. I don't know what the next thing is, and I don't have the pulse on what's going to replace containers. But I think it's going to take us a long time to come up with a new concept at the OS level. Everyone talks about unikernels, but I'm not entirely convinced.

Viktor Farcic: I haven't heard anybody really talk about using unikernels.

Bret Fisher: No, I think the distribution wars are over. The future is roll-your-own distribution. All of the distribution packages will become much more modular, and so it won't really matter what distribution you're running. I love the LinuxKit idea. That's something I'm behind.

Viktor Farcic: Likewise.

Bret Fisher: I hope that the idea of building your own distribution catches on and that it becomes more mainstream and popular. I'd love to be able to say that I'm on DigitalOcean, or I'm on AWS—wherever I am—and just have my preferred distribution. I would have a YAML file that makes it, and I just give it to this instead of me choosing Ubuntu, Amazon, or CentOS. I'd just upload my YAML, and then they'll make my OS for me and put it on a virtual machine. I don't know that it's going to be the future, but I'd love for that to be possible.

Viktor Farcic: Is serverless computing going to kill containers?

Bret Fisher: I personally think serverless and containers go hand-in-hand. You really can't do serverless well without containers.

Viktor Farcic: Thank you! You're the first one to say that. I try to explain to people how serverless and containers support each other, and they all look at me like, *no*.

Bret Fisher: Serverless is to me containers as a service.

Viktor Farcic: But does that mean everything below the level of orchestrators and containers is going to be commodities? Do you even have to care about what's happening below it, for instance, the operating systems that you commented on?

Bret Fisher: I really don't think so. We've had this talk before. If we're looking out, five years is a long time. I mean, five years ago, there were no container orchestrators. Five years would be two to three times the current lifecycle of these tools. So, certainly.

Let me back that up. For me, any new tool that I'm going to recommend to someone has to be able to replace at least one other tool. It can't be a net add because nobody has any time for anything new. They can't add another tool to their stack if it doesn't replace at least one—if not ideally two—tools, it's very unlikely they're going to adopt it. But right now, I don't feel like orchestrators will really replace any single tool completely.

Viktor Farcic: That's very true.

Bret Fisher: I still need Ansible, Chef, or Puppet to deploy my servers. But now, you look at something like InfraKit, which has not yet taken off, but is like a Terraform plus Swarm. It's basically the idea that the same tool could be my orchestrator and yet also deploy my infrastructure and manage the infrastructure all at the same time. That sounds like a better play and a better pitch to someone.

Now, you've got this tool that you already manage your infrastructure with, but it's a real big pain to do updates to that infrastructure. So, what if I gave you a tool that does that, plus updates and daily automated management of everything? Maybe that's where we end up in five years. I know today it can manage your infrastructure, but that's not the always-on default option.

Perhaps, eventually, whatever tool we're using will be the same tool to create your infrastructure, update your infrastructure, and deploy your apps. All of those things happen by default without any extra packages or any extra tools on top of it. It just comes as a single distribution of tools. I feel like that's the only way we're going to get people to adopt it. Because you've got to get rid of something. And maybe that means you truly have tools that aren't being used anymore. Like, we can get rid of Puppet, Chef, or Ansible, and we only really need this tool.

Viktor Farcic: Because that's kind of a problem. I have the impression that I'm yet to find a big enterprise company that ever removed anything. Maybe I was unlucky, but I've never seen that.

Closing thoughts

Bret Fisher: The last thing I'll say is that it's both hard, and rare. A tool has to be extremely awesome in order to be a net add, on top of everything you're already currently doing Docker did that. Docker was beneficial enough by itself that you could still use your Ansibles and your Puppets. You were also able to still have your VMware, all of your `apt-get` and other package install tools such as your npms, and your composer. What you had was this extra tool in the stack and people used it. It's not going to happen very often, so whatever's next probably won't be able to do that. But again, I don't know, and it might just be because I'm skeptical.

Viktor Farcic: Great! I know we're out of time now, so I just wanted to say thank you for taking the time to talk to me today. I really enjoyed talking to you, and I hope to talk to you soon.

Bret Fisher: No problem! It's been great talking to you too, Viktor.

16

Nirmal Mehta

Technology Consultant

Introducing Nirmal Mehta

Nirmal Mehta is Chief Technologist in the Strategic Innovations Group at Booz Allen Hamilton specializing in research, implementation, and integration of emerging technologies to Booz Allen's federal government client base. He leads the firm's efforts in digital research and development, immersive machine intelligence, and emerging technology strategy. In addition, he is a containerization subject matter expert and thought leader for DevOps practices. He was the lead architect on the high-profile GSA Integrated Award Environment AWS cloud platform, implementing a first-of-its-kind production open source, data-centric, microservices-based distributed application in the public sector. He is passionate about machine learning, immersive tech, open source, DevOps, and integrating emerging technologies to answer client needs. He focuses on bringing leading edge technologies to enterprise systems for commercial and public sector clients. He is a member of Docker Captains group. You can follow him on Twitter at `@normalfaults`, on LinkedIn at `https://www.linkedin.com/in/nirmalkmehta/`, and on the web: `https://nirmal.io`.

Viktor Farcic: I want to start by simply asking you to say a little bit about yourself, Nirmal, and your relationship with DevOps.

Nirmal Mehta: Throughout my career I've had the opportunity to see many organizations follow IT transformation paths, and through those experiences, I've seen what works and what doesn't in our industry. I strive to distribute knowledge around emerging technologies, methodologies, and solutions—especially through DevOps!

Viktor Farcic: So Nirmal, what does "DevOps" mean to you?

The meaning of DevOps

Nirmal Mehta: DevOps is the application of process improvement techniques from the last century to our modern IT culture. If I had to offer a fuller definition, I'd say that DevOps is an IT operating model that focuses on using tools and cultural change to streamline and automate the delivery of IT services. It's modeled after optimized manufacturing models from the last century by the likes of W. Edwards Deming.

More simply, DevOps is transforming the culture of an organization into a mindset of achieving a shared goal, versus the tribes that are traditionally set up in an organization.

> *"DevOps is transforming the culture of an organization into a mindset of achieving a shared goal, versus the tribes that are traditionally set up."*
>
> —*Nirmal Mehta*

Viktor Farcic: Thanks, Nirmal, it's interesting to see how everyone has such different ways to define DevOps. So, what do you think is the difference between DevOps and Agile?

Nirmal Mehta: I think the twelve principles of Agile are guidelines. More importantly, I don't think Agile was meant to be commercialized and taken over as it has been to the extent we see today. I think the organizations that are adopting Agile have been overthinking it a little.

DevOps, on the other hand, is Agile applied across the whole organization, rather than just its developer process. Perhaps my distinction is merely semantic, but broadly speaking you could say that DevOps encompasses Agile methodologies. DevOps is like a superset.

Viktor Farcic: Yes, I think DevOps is like inviting more expertise to an organization, or even more automation. This can open new positions in an organization, of course—and sometimes I see an absurd number of DevOps engineers in an organization. I honestly don't even know what one of these is—how would you define a DevOps engineer?

What is a DevOps engineer?

Nirmal Mehta: This is where it gets controversial because there's no such thing as a DevOps engineer. There shouldn't even be a DevOps team because to me, it's more of a cultural and philosophical methodology. It's a process and a way of thinking about things and communicating within an IT organization.

> *"There's no such thing as a DevOps engineer. There shouldn't even be a DevOps team because to me, it's more of a cultural and philosophical methodology."*
>
> — *Nirmal Mehta*

But going back to a definition, I think that a DevOps engineer is a job that signals that an organization, instead of hiring both a developer and an operator, just wants one less person to do twice as much work.

Viktor Farcic: I love that description. Even though no one but you will admit it, that's often how it is in reality. You can tell just by looking at advertised job descriptions for DevOps engineer roles.

Nirmal Mehta: I think organizations just want somebody who is willing to both build and operate the software. These DevOps engineer roles are all over the place, but there just isn't a single accepted definition for what a DevOps engineer is.

The reason is that DevOps engineers are really engaged in two distinct things: tools and culture. I believe that DevOps is mostly about culture, but there are also some tools involved in the DevOps process that will naturally tilt your organization toward more DevOps practices. A DevOps engineer could then be defined as a person who is implementing those tools and some of those philosophies.

Of course, simply installing some tools won't mean that an organization is automatically DevOps—you can misuse a tool regardless of how much magic is in it. So, it's important to also say that a DevOps engineer is more like a consulting role than someone who simply operates those toolsets and keeps those tools running.

Usually, organizations just want someone to come in and implement those tools. And then eventually they're asked to just be a developer who also operates stuff.

Viktor Farcic: Yes, I often see cases when existing teams simply get renamed. They continue performing the same set of tasks using the same processes and tools but under a more popular name.

Nirmal Mehta: I was once on a project where they required a separate DevOps team, which to me didn't make any sense at all. The DevOps team was on a separate contract, so they didn't even work for the organization. So, this project had developers, a security team, operators, and a DevOps team.

Now, you tell me, what was that DevOps team supposed to do? Their only job was on the last step before deployment to production. That DevOps team didn't do anything except handle the sign off before the code went into production. That was not a DevOps team. They were just a random team, a random authority, that didn't have a purpose.

Viktor Farcic: That makes me think about sysadmins being renamed DevOps.

Nirmal Mehta: Yes, that DevOps team was essentially a neutered quality assurance team that was renamed DevOps because it sounded sexy.

There is still a lot of whitewashing in terms of DevOps today. As I've said in one of my talks, if you've spent more than a month trying to figure out your organization's DevOps, or you've already spent 15 meetings trying to figure out what your DevOps is, then you're overthinking it.

> *"If you've spent more than a month trying to figure out your organization's DevOps...then you're overthinking it."*
>
> *—Nirmal Mehta*

Not everything has to be complex! It's up to you how much complexity you want to put into the mix at any given time. Take a good look at your organization, pick some pain points, and just go from there. Reading some books and implementing one or two parts of those processes is probably a better start than debating what DevOps is for a month, which is something we love to do in IT. We love to just argue about stuff but get nothing done.

We like to be in our tribes, we like to shed responsibility, and we have this need for argument and for some oppositional force, and I think DevOps and Agile help to redefine who that opponent is. Instead of friction between internal groups, DevOps directs our confrontational energy toward the problem that we're trying to solve for our customer. DevOps brings us into conflict with the actual problem, rather than with each other.

Viktor Farcic: But then we end up with consultants selling us month-long training that is supposed to convert us into Agile experts?

Nirmal Mehta: True, and that's something I can get very philosophical about: why do we have to have so much training for Agile? I think all that training is contrary to the goal of Agile in the first place! We find ourselves enveloped in the minutiae of all that complexity and we forget the core principles of Agile.

I think that's why the Agile people came up with the manifesto, to force us to print it out and put it on a wall. They knew that if we weren't reminded about the whole point of Agile, then we'd forget what we're really trying to achieve.

Viktor Farcic: That sounds like a misunderstanding and over-complication of Agile, which is in its essence, very simple.

Overthinking DevOps

Nirmal Mehta: As an industry we love to overthink everything, and I think that DevOps has the same kind of issues.

DevOps is very simple. DevOps is the application of techniques for process improvements that some start-ups, well-functioning organizations, and smart people implemented. These were shown to other people who said, "Yes, that sounds great; that's helping us be more efficient, reduce cost, or make better quality and, you know what, we might as well adopt it!"

> *"As an industry we love to overthink everything, and I think that DevOps has the same kind of issues."*
>
> —*Nirmal Mehta*

Let's not overcomplicate DevOps. When it's time to lose weight, simply put more calories out than you put in. That is the simple fact. Don't be distracted by complex diets because you want an easy way out. It's the same with DevOps, the philosophy is simple: get out of your own way.

The DevOps philosophy – get out of your own way

The DevOps philosophy is to get out of your own way. But this is too hard, of course, so we try to find a shortcut. This shortcut might be a tool, a consultant, some YouTube videos, or a book. At the end of the day though, we cannot get away from having to follow the philosophy. We can implement Jenkins all day, but we won't achieve anything unless we also follow the philosophy.

> *"The DevOps philosophy is to get out of your own way. But this is too hard, of course, so we try to find a shortcut."*
>
> —*Nirmal Mehta*

This is the fundamental shift that's taking place today in organizations—it's a realization that actual, productive change must be a little bit more painful. This is a deep cultural shift, and we must deal with people, their attitudes, and all that— including people who just don't want to change.

There's a lot of misinformation about what DevOps is in our industry today, and that is because no one wants to hear that it's all about simple but important truths like "more calories out," and a lot of people don't want to face change. Do you think organizations such as Facebook and Google are having those kinds of debates?

Viktor Farcic: I expect that Google and Facebook are having some important debates, right now, that the rest of us will have in fifteen years, about machine learning and neural networks. But Google has also been discussing SRE, for example?

Nirmal Mehta: Yes, organizations such as Google have been taking some of the most recent debates and codifying them into service level agreements and Site Reliability Engineering (SRE) philosophies. There's no escaping the pain.

DevOps and SRE

Viktor Farcic: Let's explore how the Google SRE thing relates to DevOps then. How do you define an SRE?

Nirmal Mehta: A site reliability engineer is an IT operations engineer who supports development teams and production systems based on Google DevOps methodologies.

One of the big things to come out of the SRE philosophies is that there's a risk associated with the budget of how many hours the SRE team gives their project team for fixing whatever happens.

You can deploy as risky a piece of software as you want, but if you burn through that budget, that's on you. If you're providing a service that isn't as critical, you have a higher budget, and so you can take more risk. Or you could say, "You know what, I need to save that up for certain times of the year, or certain events, and balance that out."

This approach in Google's DevOps methodology removes the ability to skirt around the pain because it puts the pain at the front and center.

Resolving key pain points is something that a lot of organizations have difficulty with, and it's a very common problem with Agile. For example, if you're transitioning from Waterfall to Agile, then the project managers, leaders, and owners will all want Agile—but Agile with deadlines!

Viktor Farcic: You're saying that managers want others to adopt Agile, but they don't always want to adapt their own way of working?

Nirmal Mehta: Yes, exactly, those people want Agile with deadlines because deadlines allow someone to put the blame somewhere else.

Deadlines are an escape route, whereas Agile just forces you to think about implementing at a more regular pace, or with prioritization, and to make decisions more frequently.

Not one person in leadership likes to make decisions at the frequency that Agile requires because decisions mean responsibility. And a lot of organizations and the folks working within them are masters at the craft of dodging responsibility. Agile forces that discussion at the beginning instead of having discussions about priority after the deadline or closer to the deadline.

> *"Not one person in leadership likes to make decisions at the frequency that Agile requires because decisions mean responsibility."*
>
> —*Nirmal Mehta*

DevOps is the same because it forces you to understand how to put your projects into production and to pay for it at the beginning of the cycle. In DevOps, you're trying to catch things at the beginning of the cycle, not the end.

A lot of problems we face today are because somebody was able to avoid making a decision until the very last minute—that is, when they were forced to make a decision. They probably knew what their decision was going to be, they just didn't have the confidence in that decision until they were forced into an answer.

Agile and DevOps force you to make decisions more frequently, and from the beginning. I think people have a hard time with the confidence that is required or the *okayness* with failure that one needs to feel, in order to be able to do that. Ironically, DevOps and Agile will tolerate you making bad decisions more frequently than the older methodologies!

Make [bad] decisions more often

Viktor Farcic: Are you saying that organizations and people in IT departments should make bad decisions more often?

Nirmal Mehta: If you're deploying four times a year, then you only have four opportunities to make a decision, and therefore each of those decisions has a big impact. If you are in Agile, you're making a lot of smaller decisions. If you make a bad decision, you can just correct it at the next deadline, and you've lost very little. That's the irony.

> *"If you are in Agile, you're making a lot of smaller decisions. If you make a bad decision, you can just correct it at the next deadline, and you've lost very little."*
>
> —Nirmal Mehta

Of course, it's still painful if you've made a bad decision, but for some reason we humans find it more painful to have to make a decision every two weeks.

I think these kinds of things happen in other industries as well, sometimes when there's even more on the line. In the aeronautics, manufacturing, or construction industries, for example, where when you make a big decision that goes wrong, there's a multi-million dollar consequence. Those kinds of organizations have evolved their own techniques to force incremental decisions to be made.

Viktor Farcic: Over the last couple of years I've seen a huge growth of interest in DevOps at conferences. This interest is often centered around a particular set of themes—immutable infrastructure, containers, and schedulers. Is there a relationship between them that explains so much interest?

DevOps patterns

Nirmal Mehta: Yes, there is a relation between them. And there's a lot of interest around them because they reflect some important patterns that people are starting to adopt right now.

Maybe only ten percent of people out there really know what they're doing in IT today, and they can't be in every organization at once. It's debatable whether anyone *really* knows what they're doing, of course, because I bet if you asked those ten percent, they would say, "I don't know what I'm doing!"

What the ten percent *do* know is that when they do *this*, they're less stressed out. When they do *this*, their website is more reliable. When they do *that*, they get one more extra customer every time. So that's how they see it: "If I do this, I get an extra million dollars of investment funding; if I do this, my evaluation goes up; and if I do this, I have not closed the door because I'm still competitive." Those are the only heuristics that we have as an industry.

Now, let's take a person in their IT career, maybe they work on average at between three to six different places, across their peak career time.

Viktor Farcic: Yes, it's difficult to strike a balance between being locked in a single company all your life and never experiencing what's happening outside or just switching companies every few months.

Nirmal Mehta: Yes, so what do we do across our career? Every year we're like, "Hey, that kind of worked, I spent six months doing it, and it worked." What we're trying to do, in DevOps, is gather as many heuristics from each person and somehow distill them down so that one day we say: this is *the* winning heuristic.

For example, Aaron Huslage, who was formerly at Docker and is now at Red Hat Ansible, comes over to me and he says, "Why are you guys patching? Just destroy the server and move the containers to a new patched server. Don't patch retroactively; always move forward." Okay, that's a good idea! That saves me time because now I have one less piece of software that I need to worry about.

I think that all we're doing in DevOps is hunting, hunting, and hunting for these ideas. With each of these ideas, there's an associated cultural change that needs to happen. The cultural change that happens when you adopt these practices is called DevOps.

Viktor Farcic: Are you saying that DevOps only exists in relationship to new ideas and that new ideas need DevOps to manage organizations toward cultural transformation?

Nirmal Mehta: I think DevOps can be there with or without those ideas. I mean you can patch with DevOps. And you can have the traditional operations of DevOps. Just as long as you understand the communication mechanisms involved, and that you're going to have to continuously inspect and understand your processes—and be ready to improve them.

After all, there's no timeline for the adoption of DevOps, and there's no manifesto that says you must achieve greater deployments of your software.

> *"There's no timeline for the adoption of DevOps, and there's no manifesto that says you must achieve greater deployments of your software."*
>
> *—Nirmal Mehta*

In my client space, deploying software *faster* is not always the real need. And some organizations don't even care about *cost*. Across my customer base, it's quite a common situation that if they don't spend the money that they were given this year, they will get less money next year, so they *want* to spend more money.

That doesn't mean DevOps has no application for organizations in those situations: they can still have other things they need from DevOps, such as being more *secure* and thus more *reliable*.

Reliability is a big topic. At its core, the reliability of services is what drives a lot of the interest you see today in DevOps. Reliability with fewer people is what I think DevOps is. There's a risk that all these things will reduce the need for people like us.

Viktor Farcic: Who do you mean when you say, "people like us"?

Nirmal Mehta: I mean developers and operations. As these services become more SaaS-based, I think greenfield development of new software is going to be much closer to junior-level, pre-canned business object stuff, like Azure or Amazon Web Services, at some point in the future.

Viktor Farcic: So, you wouldn't bet on the future for developers and operations?

Nirmal Mehta: My gut says that in the future we'll see less bespoke software being developed in the majority of IT organizations. Instead, new software development is going to be in the hardware.

The only caveat on that is machine learning, which is already blowing up into a whole new world of software development. Programming by combining different deep learning and neural networks together could become a new field of software development, and that might be a transition for a lot of people. Instead of making APIs for web apps all day long, we're going to be just optimizing machine learning, and we'll become much more programmatic. Eventually, eighty percent of services will be filled from four overlord service providers, and that's it.

> *"Eventually, eighty percent of services will be filled from four overlord service providers, and that's it."*
>
> —*Nirmal Mehta*

Viktor Farcic: To be honest, I would be very scared if I was young and had my career years ahead of me because I think that most people just won't be able to follow the ever-increasing pace.

Those people who are specialized in a single field are at greater risk of becoming obsolete. I mean, what will happen to those who spent years working on infrastructure when companies decide to move to the cloud? Sure, they can apply for a job in AWS, Azure, or Google Cloud, but I'm afraid that the bar might be too high for many.

Nirmal Mehta: We've already seen that in the industry; look at how many organizations are moving to Office 365, and how many places have their own Exchange Servers. That number gets smaller and smaller. That was a core role of IT for a long time, managing Active Directory, Exchange, and MS SQL, but those days are in the past.

Viktor Farcic: I guess that it puts companies in a sweet position where they can dedicate most of their resources into something that really brings value to them. When you think about it, does it bring value to a company to manage Exchange?

Nirmal Mehta: No, it doesn't. But what I think is interesting, and this is a kind of a cynical point of view, is that there is so much low-hanging fruit in a lot of these companies!

This is especially true for companies that have either established themselves in a monopoly or have created a big enough wall through competition or where there's a consolidation of who works or even competes in that field anymore. For such companies, there might not have even been a reward for increasing value. For such companies, there's been no need for perfection. It's not even that they don't need non-buggy code; they just need to get something out there, even if it's just bad.

The true enemy of DevOps

We're talking here about the true enemy of DevOps and Agile. This true enemy is not the benders, it is not the mislabeling of what DevOps is, and it is not all those difficult IT shops. The true enemy of DevOps is when the fundamental balance of everything that we're trying to achieve no longer matters. The true enemy of DevOps is when higher quality stuff doesn't matter—when an organization is just trying to get shit out there.

> *"The true enemy of DevOps is when higher quality stuff doesn't matter—when an organization is just trying to get shit out there."*
>
> *—Nirmal Mehta*

A lot of the people I meet at conferences are IT people, and most of them are obviously trying to derive more value, to make their mark, to reduce costs, or to keep their job. But at a certain level in most organizations, if you find a non-IT person, they will probably consider that whatever is there right now is perfectly fine and that they can squeeze that apple for longer.

Viktor Farcic: I think that we have a serious discrepancy in velocity. While we're used to the fact that things often change, and with ever-increasing velocity, the world is still trying to figure out what that means. Non-IT personnel are still not used to the fact that whatever was valid yesterday might be completely different today.

Nirmal Mehta: Yes, they need to just change the color of the website every six months, and they're good to go. And to change the name of the product.

That's why competition is a good thing because the real enemy of DevOps shows its face in IT organizations where "good enough" is of a lower quality than any of us want to work in.

In this sense, DevOps is just a way to do a good enough job with two or three fewer people, before an organization transitions to an entirely Software as a Service (SaaS) arrangement. This is the real adversity, and apathy, that DevOps is trying to fight.

Agile is also trying to fight the apathy. Waterfall was all about making decisions at the last minute possible, right before going to production. Agile is forcing those decisions earlier so that you can't be apathetic to whatever. Instead, you have to make that decision today about what you're going to work on and what you want people to work on. Agile is about creating an incentive to make decisions.

DevOps is very similar in that we're creating an incentive for people and organizations to make decisions about what kind of code they want to deploy or what kind of service they want to deploy.

Viktor Farcic: I think you're right about the role of DevOps, but I also think that decision-making is what many people are trying to avoid. This may be the reason why we have such a huge discrepancy between what we say DevOps is about and how DevOps is really implemented in practice. A critical decision area for many organizations today is security. So, how does DevOps fit into IT security departments?

DevOps in security departments

Nirmal Mehta: I think that IT security is very important, but I also know that we can very easily underestimate how many people don't give a damn about security right now. And that's because, to many people, the problem of security is just the same as the problem of pollution. IT security and climate change are in almost the exact same position from that perspective: there's a negative externality to what happens.

Let me explain. If Equifax, the consumer credit reporting agency, gets hacked, which it did, and all our credit information is breached, but there is no cost associated to Equifax for doing that, then it's the same thing as if I build a power plant and I don't pay the price of the pollution I give out. This is a negative externality that is not associated with the cost, and it's a situation that doesn't fix itself without the government. That's essentially what government is for, to eliminate that tragedy of the commons. I see security as absolutely stuck in a tragedy of the common situation where there is no consequence.

> *"I think that IT security is very important, but I also know that we can very easily underestimate how many people don't give a damn about security right now."*
>
> —*Nirmal Mehta*

If I put 100 dollars into improving my security, and my competitor puts zero dollars to improve their security, and we both get hacked, then we both have no consequences. The only thing I lost is 100 dollars, and my competitor didn't lose 100 dollars. That's the only difference.

Viktor Farcic: My experience from working with enterprise-based companies is that security always has the last word, but at the same time most don't really understand. Too often, security is about marking some fields in an Excel sheet and not really helping IT teams develop secure applications. Too often, it seems as if the only goal of a security department is to be able to say, "It's not our fault."

Nirmal Mehta: That's the unfortunate situation we're in, and this is something I would say we faced even before the Spectre and Meltdown vulnerabilities. These kinds of massive security bugs aren't going anywhere, but we do not have the headspace to rationalize how bad the security is. We therefore just bury our heads in the sand as a civilization and as a modern society, when it comes to privacy and IT security. I think that we will absolutely continue to do this unless there are real consequences to the industry, and even then, I don't think change will happen because it would essentially mean killing IT.

Just imagine if developers had to get insurance on the code that they wrote, just like a doctor must get malpractice insurance. If there was a computer or developer engineering malpractice insurance, like this, it would kill the industry overnight. Some developers would buy it if they had the money, but we're already aching for talent and resources now as an industry, and this would eventually eliminate ninety percent of developers in the field.

On top of that, all those people who we promised could become developers because we destroyed their job with automation must then get insurance against how bad their initial code could be as they switch careers. The whole idea is just not practical unless everything becomes more expensive, and security is not going to be any different.

Viktor Farcic: I'm surprised that I haven't heard this idea about code insurance before. The more I think about it, the more it makes sense. Why would software be any different than anything else that has insurance? We all use it, we all depend on it, and malfunction can result in serious damage or even death. It fits the description of many other things that we take for granted as being insured.

But, as you say, guaranteeing code quality would ruin a big segment of the industry overnight. We have somehow become used to the fact that software doesn't always work, and that hacking is part of life. There's not a big incentive to make what we create truly secure—at least not everywhere.

Nirmal Mehta: That doesn't mean that a company can't differentiate themselves on their security. It's nice to see companies such as Apple and others where they don't treat us like products.

> *"I don't think change will happen because it would essentially mean killing IT."*
>
> *—Nirmal Mehta*

Now, when you come to the business-to-business side of security, or the e-commerce side of security, I think the answer is that things will just move to more SaaS-based services.

When you do have conversations with organizations about moving to the cloud, you start to see how it really is going to make everything more secure. Why? Because the organization is then forced to face reality: they must actually do the security things that they said they were doing, but they're not! Of course, Amazon Cloud is also way more secure than a lot of the places that do it in-house because Amazon has a massive financial incentive that's missing from many government services.

DevOps has this real opportunity to increase the security incentive that is missing in a lot of organizations. However, good IT security still requires strong leadership.

Viktor Farcic: What's missing in IT that needs this strong leadership? Is it more money being invested, more education, or better practices? What do we miss in security today? I ask this because in the companies I visit, I continually find partners who will say, "Look, you need to fulfill those 35,000 requirements, and then you're secure." Nobody I know ever manages to fulfill their bulk.

Nirmal Mehta: There's a couple of different problems here. The first one is that there's no glory in fixing a bug or a security issue, whereas there's always glory in deploying a feature.

The second thing is that fixing bugs, finding security holes, and doing things the *right* way often takes more patience, more thinking, more engineering, more time, and more cost.

These are things that most organizations don't even have to begin with. Most organizations don't even have enough money or resources to do what their original goal is with respect to their software. That stuff is way further down on the list.

> *"There's no glory in fixing a bug or a security issue, whereas there's always glory in deploying a feature."*
>
> —*Nirmal Mehta*

The third thing is experience and understanding. How many people even really understand speculative execution and processors? If you went to those coding boot camps to become a web developer, and you sat there and imported 15,000 npm JavaScript libraries, did they explain to you how a CPU works? No, they didn't.

Viktor Farcic: And you don't even know what those libraries do.

Nirmal Mehta: Right, and so people who *do* understand are expensive and they're few and far between. Their experience and knowledge are not codified in any software suite currently. The security software industry is very far behind in terms of its ability to adapt to more frequent deployments and to bring that whole entire picture together about common bugs and penetration testing.

And, of course, this all costs an organization more than their competitor who decides not to do any of that. There's still a consequence to maybe losing a customer, but there isn't really a global consequence.

Viktor Farcic: That is until it happens.

Nirmal Mehta: Yes. My gut feeling is that a lot of places are less secure than we think and that the insurance model just pays that problem away, instead of them just dealing with it. It's still cheaper to just pay for the problem than it is to pay the 250,000 dollars a year for a security person.

There are a lot of issues with paying for the problem, and just one of them is that a security person in an organization that's not a top-tier place such as Google, Facebook, or Apple is probably not an expert at all. They've quite likely just done some training and got certifications. Yes, they're probably smart on SQL injections and phishing scams, but they're probably only one member of a small team tasked with that, and they care more about having dinner after work.

They do have this secret weapon, of course, that no one else in the IT organization has, and that is the ability to say "No" unconditionally.

Viktor Farcic: Thou shalt not pass!

Nirmal Mehta: It's like a cognitive bias, and it's like a false power... but it's not actually a false power—it's true power! And it's much harder to fight a negative.

Security is not a justice system; you're not innocent until proven guilty. There are good reasons why you're guilty until proven innocent with security, and that's why we have those checklists.

> *"Security is not a justice system; you're not innocent until proven guilty. There are good reasons why you're guilty until proven innocent with security, and that's why we have those checklists."*
>
> —*Nirmal Mehta*

But this means that both your false positives and false negatives are also going to be through the roof because it's too hard not to say no.

Viktor Farcic: If I'm guilty until proven innocent then I can't prove myself innocent.

Nirmal Mehta: Exactly, there's no such thing as 100% infallible and bug-free software. We have non-deterministic complex systems, and that's a challenge because everyone wants 0/1, yes/no, but there's no yes/no in a non-deterministic complex system. There is only a percentage of acceptance and probabilities.

The problem is, security wants to treat everything like yes/no with a certain amount of risk, but everyone needs to treat security more like a probability. At the same time, no one wants to work on the hard thing.

The hard thing here is writing good software without having to import all these things, and to actually look at all the code, to look at your open source tools that you're using, to validate what you're doing, to implement mutual TLS, to renew your certificates, and to make sure your domain names use two-factor.

These things are so fundamental to security that it's the same thing as "more calories out than in," but we're all just looking for a shortcut. And the shortcut for the security person is just to say "No, here's a checklist of symptoms."

The checklist is just symptoms that have been seen in the past. It's not a cure, and it's not a diagnosis of a system. It's just a symptom checklist. Are you sneezing? No, okay. Are you coughing? No, okay. Do you have a fever? No, okay. Then you're no security risk.

Fighting security threats

Viktor Farcic: How do we fight security threats, if we can at all? A single person can do serious damage by exploiting our system vulnerabilities. How many people, if you can even put a number on it, do we need to prevent that person from attacking us?

Nirmal Mehta: That's all we've come up so far with, isn't it: how do we pay for the problem? How many people? That's because everything is reactionary.

There's more to this problem though. The core of security in IT leverages that same power that allows our modern technology companies to do amazing things with 100 or 1,000 fewer people than ever before. But here's the rub: that ability for technology to so dramatically increase the leverage of a single person also works for the person attacking you.

It's the same problem we have with terrorism. It costs 500 bucks for someone to become a suicide bomber, but it costs 1.5 trillion dollars to prevent that suicide bombing from happening. The attackers who are attacking your infrastructure have the same 1,000x or more advantages that you use to make your company exist.

> *"The attackers who are attacking your infrastructure have the same 1,000x or more advantages that you use to make your company exist."*
>
> —Nirmal Mehta

It's impossible to really secure against this unless you send your stuff to space. So, what does all this mean? It means that you must decide where on the spectrum of 0% to 100% probability of security failure you are comfortable.

You're still not going to put the equivalent percentage of actual money toward your security risk, because that is a lot costlier than you think it is. There needs to be a balance—some sort of cost/benefit evaluation that puts us in a situation where we gain as much benefit with as little investment.

Viktor Farcic: What's waiting for us in the next ten years from now?

Future technologies

Nirmal Mehta: Part of my job is to look at future technologies, and nowadays I'm doing that for the cloud. At a certain point, it really hit me hard about the cloud.

Let me tell you. It was when I saw a slide at *AWS re:Invent*; it was just a bar chart, and on the x-axis was *2011, 2012, 2013*, and *2014*—the years; and on the y-axis, it wasn't new services, but instead it was the year-over-year percentage increase in features that AWS will provide. The first year on that chart, it was 50%. They added another 50%, so the next one was 100%. Then it was 500%. The following one was 1,000%, and after that, it was 4,000%.

If you're an internal IT organization and you're building services, and you see that graph, and I'm selling the cloud and the ability to use cloud services to compose and build your own applications, how do you resist?

It's pretty clear to me that Amazon, Azure, and Google are making their way vertically. They want to vertically integrate as much as possible because every time they move up that tier, they get higher value, so commodities and value bump up.

> *"It's pretty clear to me that Amazon, Azure, and Google are making their way vertically. They want to vertically integrate as much as possible..."*
>
> —*Nirmal Mehta*

Now you do that at 4,000% or 5,000% a year, you eventually run out of stuff to develop. Are you telling me there's not going to be a service where you just drag and drop three things onto a screen, and you get a full business application? Of course. That's the inevitability of that graph.

If that's sustained, and even if it wasn't sustained, even if they went back to 50%, then they just need to add little bits and pieces here and there and do a better job of connecting their existing services together, and there would be no reason to develop your own software. You'd just have your business use case, pick the language and the container format, pick the

CICD pipeline, and you'd be done.

I took some Azure training a year ago, and we had to build a web API that had authentication. It would take a JSON-formatted string, convert it into Chinese, do sentiment analysis, search Twitter, and then provide a machine learning prediction on what the next word would be in that phrase.

If I had got that challenge five years ago, I would have had to build an architecture with maybe some machine learning. I wouldn't know how even to spin up some EC2 instances. This were pre-containers, but there was no Docker yet, so I would have had to cobble the thing together and spend 99% of my time authenticating web connections and running EC2 instances, just getting that stuff up and running.

By contrast, we managed to do all this in our training in fifteen minutes. We dragged a box onto this window; we then dragged another box containing Cortana translation services and drew an arrow, so sentiment analysis was done by Cortana. We put the API key in there, and we were good to go. We clicked deploy, and it was a fully load-balanced API, automatically created, with authentication and certificates already all there. We hit it with some JSON and boom. Now we could package that and put it in the marketplace, where we could sell that to you for 1% per API call.

Viktor Farcic: I would need to make a couple of zillion API calls, but at the end of the day that would still be a fraction of what it would cost me to probably never actually succeed in making it myself.

Nirmal Mehta: Exactly, and so it was during that training that I said, "We will probably be consultants and build this stuff for maybe fifteen more years, but there is a point in the future where there will be no more greenfield; it's just going to be business intelligence applications with us composing them on Amazon, Azure, or Google Cloud."

> *"We will probably be consultants and build this stuff for maybe fifteen more years, but there is a point in the future where there will be no more greenfield."*
>
> —*Nirmal Mehta*

There will be some other service that maybe combines those services together, but at some point, this is going to be completely vertically integrated. In fact, you can already see it in Amazon's video editing tools. They released a bunch of 3D web VR tools, so they're already starting to go against these industries where it would have been impossible to think that this would be done in the cloud, but here you are, and so at a certain point there's no reason not to just to build your own service anymore.

I mean, Lambda allows you to pay by the call, so if you're a start-up you don't even need to run a server anymore, and your costs can become perfectly linear with your customer acquisition.

Viktor Farcic: The cost as a start-up, right at the beginning, is basically zero because you're very unlikely to reach the limits of what is free in those first few months.

Nirmal Mehta: I predict that this will be the future. There will no longer be a conversation between the business owner and the internal IT team. The business owner will just go right to Azure. Then the business user—not the developer, not an operations guy, and not a security guy, but the business user—is going to have their Azure account.

The business user is going to be some savvy intern and the business owner is going to say something like, "Okay, I need something to tell me the logistics shipping route of our competitor." To which, the business owner will say, "Okay, boom, here's a geospatial service." The business owner will then add a little bit of a machine learning block, put an API in, click deploy, test it, and that's it. They'll then simply pass a bill to the business owner.

That's something that scares me, but our DevOps careers will nearly be over when this stuff really takes off. If I was starting my career now, I would just do DevOps with data science and machine learning because if you can collect data and you can learn from it, that's where the real value is today and in the coming years.

> *"If I was starting my career now, I would just do DevOps with data science and machine learning."*
>
> —*Nirmal Mehta*

Viktor Farcic: As you say, it's okay, right? It's like climate change; it won't happen before I retire. Do you have any final remarks?

Nirmal Mehta: My final remark is that I sometimes overestimate the impetus for change to newer systems, against the inertia of keeping older systems running. I mean, people are okay with really bad stuff in IT for a lot longer than you might think.

That's my parting thought. We can get excited about containers, CICD, and DevOps itself, but one way or another, at some point in the future, there will be no need for all this.

17

Gregory Bledsoe

Agile, Lean, and DevOps Consultant

Introducing Gregory Bledsoe

Having recently joined MThree Consulting, much of Greg's focus is in helping businesses achieve delivery of agility transform. Previously, he's worked as an Agile, Lean, and DevOps consultant at SolutionsIQ. Greg has also written extensively about DevSecOps, kernels, and virtualization. You can find him on Twitter at @geek_king.

Viktor Farcic: Hi, Greg! Before we delve into the world of DevOps, tell us a little about yourself.

Gregory Bledsoe: My career up to this point is entirely down to the fact that I was a very successful engineer, and because of this, people promoted me to management positions. That being said, however, I don't think it's the best approach because good engineers don't always make good managers. Nobody ever gives us engineers any training on how to manage, nor do they take the time to explain what we're actually supposed to be doing as managers. Because of this, I had to reinvent myself into this manager role, where I've actually applied the engineering principles of fail fast, experiment, and measure the outcome to see what happens. This all took place in a time before DevOps was even a word; but, looking back, I see that I was already incorporating the principles of DevOps as a core part of my way of doing anything in the industry. Through that process, I learned that you couldn't do the engineering and the management role at the same time.

> *"What the word DevOps means is probably the most fundamentally misunderstood question out there."*
>
> —*Gregory Bledsoe*

Over time, I continued to work at various companies, and gradually, I got invited to speak at more and more conferences. Fast-forward to today. My latest ventures have been with Accenture/Solutions IQ, the management consulting and professional services firm, and MThree Consulting, where I'm concentrating on training and providing emerging talent to the Fortune 100. But bringing it back to the idea of DevOps, I find myself perfecting the DevOps+ methodology in my new job. It's worth adding, and I'm sure we'll come back to this, that I included the "+" because the methodology includes DevOps, in addition to both Agile and Lean.

DevOps and Deming's ninth principle

Viktor Farcic: That nicely brings me to the first question I have for you, which is: what does the word DevOps actually mean? I've spoken to a number of people, many of whom are featured in this book, and when I come to this question, I don't think I've ever received the same answer. What's your take on it?

Gregory Bledsoe: The whole idea of defining what the word DevOps means is probably the most fundamentally misunderstood question out there. That's not to say that the question itself is wrong because, while there are many valid answers, there are infinitely more invalid answers, and that's fundamentally the problem we have. Even when people are giving valid answers, they're only partial answers, and those giving the answers don't fully understand the overall scope of the question. As an industry, we're constantly learning new lessons and incorporating new things, and DevOps is a way to collect the best practices of everyone. Because of that, I've stopped trying to define it simply because the definition changes every day.

Did you know that, at its core, the word DevOps comes from the 14-Point Philosophy of William Deming, an American engineer and statistician? In that list, the 9th principle is, *Breaking down barriers between departments*. That's literally where the names Dev and Ops come from. Thus, you can't define DevOps without including Deming's concept in said definition. When we started with DevOps, we didn't know if we were specifically implementing DevOps or Deming's 14 points, but at some point, we figured it out. Let's say you're applying a Lean methodology; in 2018, it grew so far beyond what it was originally. We realized that what we're really doing is progressively implementing Deming's 14 points into software development. And once we've done that, we've then got to move on and drive out the fear, while continuously improving and getting everybody on board. Then, we've got to make everybody agents of transformation. If you don't understand that all of those things are implicitly included in defining what DevOps is, and they're not included in your DevOps definition, then your DevOps definition is probably wrong, or at the very least, incomplete.

Viktor Farcic: I actually think that's a great view. What you've managed to do is show a lot of thinking behind the meaning of the word, which is often omitted. But in the Gregory Bledsoe dictionary, what's the definition next to the word DevOps?

Gregory Bledsoe: As we discussed, before I give you my answer, I need to come up with a definition of DevOps that won't change. Because it's the overarching umbrella that all of DevOps falls into, my definition of DevOps is "reorganizing IT around business value." Within this definition, we've included Lean by reference, and likewise, we've also got all the canonical DevOps elements that we've already incorporated, but we haven't excluded any other future best practices. I think that's the one that should propagate now, and that gives us great freedom not to exclude new innovations. Because, when that happens, and something, such as DevOps, becomes so defined, it ends up squeezing out the new innovations.

> *"My definition of DevOps is 'reorganizing IT around business value'"*
>
> —*Gregory Bledsoe*

I'm not a big fan of prescriptive frameworks that purport to solve every possible problem, because the problem set that we as an industry face changes too rapidly for that to be true. Whereas really, everything has to be open to interpretation and to change as the context itself changes. What we all want out of a definition of DevOps is something that tells us fundamentally what it is but doesn't exclude all the new innovations that we haven't even thought of yet that are coming our way. We've already got this pipeline of possibilities out there, with the likes of serverless and unikernels beginning to make their way into more and more places. But the way that we interface with the technology is going to change so unpredictably over the next two years that all of that might get thrown out the window for something else.

A great example is the direct neural interfaces that are starting to come along. We've already got artificial reality in the form of virtual reality, as well as artificial intelligence. If we feed artificial intelligence feedback directly into, say, an artificial reality or a virtual reality environment, then we're using a direct neural interface. The issue we have is that we have absolutely no idea what the world's going to look like in two years, and we have no idea how to adapt our processes to that upcoming change. The fact is, what we all need to do is abandon the idea that we can build a five-year roadmap for DevOps because, as we've just talked about, we can't even predict two years into the future. Instead, what we can do is begin implementing the best practices now, trying to mature it as best we can, but to ultimately be ready to reinterpret, unlearn, and relearn as quickly as possible.

Viktor Farcic: That was a great answer. It's really good to get behind the thinking of the question. The only problem I see, which is similar to when you mentioned how we don't know what's going to happen in two years, is that I get the impression that a large number of companies, especially the bigger ones, don't even know what's happening today.

Passing the baton between generations

Gregory Bledsoe: Do you want to know a secret? The truth is that many of the big companies out there don't actually have an idea what their actual environment is today. There are elements of those environments that have become a black box, and the people who originally built those elements of that big company's environment have left. The issue is that, now, no one at the company actually knows how that element works. The scripts and the deployments are all scriptures that were handed down from past generations that in the current generation, nobody really wants to dig into and try to change.

The holy writs are beyond question. You don't even really know how it works after a certain amount of time. So, I think you're exactly right. Even the bigger companies don't know what's happening in their own environment today.

Viktor Farcic: That being said, I don't personally think that's a bad thing. The worst case is that some companies are convinced that they know what's going on today.

Gregory Bledsoe: This is one of my big points. I always paint it in a way that says the executive management in these companies is sitting at the end of a game of Chinese whispers. In the game, you have a long line of people where one person whispers something to another person, then the next person whispers it to the next person, and so on. The idea is that they're all trying to whisper exactly what they heard, but by the time it comes out the other end—in this case, to the executive management—you end up with something radically different, and everybody laughs when he or she compares what came out of the two ends.

All of their information is filtered through so many layers, and the incentives for filtering are not to be transparent and not to give accurate information. So, the best case is that they can't have the best and most accurate picture of what's happening. Meanwhile, the worst case is that everything has been filtered through the lens of: *what does my boss want to hear?* It's inevitable that, at the top of the chain, you have no idea what's really happening on the ground, and the more you think you do, the more you find yourself being wrong. Unless you actually measure it—which is one of the components of DevOps—and you're doing culture and satisfaction surveys, you'll find yourself having to really put some deep thought into the metrics that matter.

Furthermore, unless you know that you're validly gathering them and unless you know what they mean, and what action you're going to take if measurements go up or down, then you really can't have any idea what's happening. We can pretend we do, but it's totally impossible. To me, the whole advance of IT in the last 15 years is starting with extreme programming. And then, with Agile and both the formal Agile Manifesto and the Agile principles, it means we're progressively learning to stop pretending we know what we don't know.

Viktor Farcic: I like that idea of effectively learning to admit when we don't know something.

Gregory Bledsoe: Right! We're crushing the hubris of these few people—this aristocracy—that are better enabled by education, breeding, birthright, or whatever the factor is, that somehow gives them a better ability to make all of the decisions and filter all of this information.

We have to make every decision at the highest point possible because the ones at the top are the only ones that actually know what's going on. What we need to do is stop pretending that that's true because, in actuality, that's the complete opposite of what's true. The real truth is that we need to make every decision at the lowest point possible because that's where the accurate information can be found.

Our organizations have to develop an autonomic nervous system, where most of the decisions are being made below the level of attention to strategy. If they find that the executives have to get involved in day-to-day operations, then there's something desperately wrong. Your executives should be doing a meta-analysis, setting a strategy and asking the right questions. Then, the alignments to our predictive autonomics are all wrong, and that's one of the things where DevOps, Agile, and Lean are fundamentally correct.

We're trying to collapse those silos and remove the cover-your-butt culture of finger-pointing, credit-taking, and blame-shifting to create these empowered cultures where people actually feel like they own a piece of the outcome, and not just this tiny little slice of the process. If people are able to solve their own problem—and they have to destroy the entire rest of the process—fundamentally, they will, because then you get the response of: "It's not my job; somebody else is supposed to worry about that." This is what these cross-functional collaborative teams fundamentally solve, by making everyone an owner of the outcome.

Nokia – the fall of a giant

Viktor Farcic: A while ago, I spoke with a friend who worked at Nokia. I asked him, is it really possible that Nokia didn't see the smartphone coming? Because you'll remember that, back in the day, Nokia was at the top of its game. Their Nokia 1100 series of phones have, to this day, sold over half a billion units and remains—combining the 2003 and 2005 model—one the two most popular handsets in the word. In fact, seven out of ten of the best-selling handsets of all time are Nokia devices. Yet, in Q4 of 2017, the company only grabbed one percent of the market share, shipping only 4.4 million units.

I asked my friend if it was really possible that Nokia didn't see the coming smartphone wave and the impact smartphones would have on the industry. He answered by saying that everyone at Nokia knew what was coming and, more importantly, what needed to be done, but nobody dared tell that to management. That's the crux of the problem we have. It's what I refer to as a cultural artifact because everybody knows what the people above them want to hear. They know what they'll be rewarded for, but equally, they also know what they'll be punished for, and telling upper-management the truth and having the hard conversations is something they know they'll probably be punished for. But then, to me, the question is: in such an organization, who can actually initiate that change?

Initiating change/taking responsibility

Gregory Bledsoe: Everyone and anyone can initiate that change because, at the end of the day, it's all our responsibility. If you're dancing with your dance partner, and you want to change the dance, you can't force your dance partner to change their steps but you can change yours, and when you change yours, your partner has to adapt.

I remember the very first conference I keynoted was themed on overcoming obstacles to DevOps. One of the things I pointed out is that anyone can initiate change, and there's a ripple of that. If you understand this ripple effect, you can take advantage of it. You can identify your allies; you can influence the influencers and manage your managers and spread this good change. This is something you can do from anywhere in the organization. You're able to inspire people; you can articulate the argument in economic and mathematical terms and through measurement. You can always start doing that. You can nudge the bar, and that's the only way to do it from anywhere in the organization.

> *"Everyone and anyone can initiate that change because, at the end of the day, it's all our responsibility."*
>
> —*Gregory Bledsoe*

Now, obviously, you can do this more effectively if you already have the positional power within the organization. But even from the bottom of the organization—and this is one of the things that I feel made me such a good engineer—I was able to get people on board with what I wanted to do. I could get people who had no personal incentive to help me to accomplish something. Now, why was this? It was because we could then both go and sell that to our managers as a part of the value that we produced. But I had to sell them on the value; I had to make the economic argument.

If you're at the bottom of the organization, making this economic argument and starting to change your dance steps by beginning to pull in more collaborators and starting to nudge the bar by setting yourself up is designed not to win *today's* argument, but to win *tomorrow's* argument by playing the long game. Change is incremental, so people don't actually know that things are changing until they hit a critical mass of people who want this change. Then, the change becomes inevitable, no matter what the executives want.

People who don't have positional power underestimate the power they do have. At the same time, executives underestimate their power as well because they're used to going into a meeting and saying: "Tell me the problem and tell me all your potential solutions," then simply asking people to do a given solution. It's a fundamentally backward way of managing, but it's the customary way we do it.

It's the artifact of Taylorism, the idea that, after the Industrial Revolution, Frederick Taylor was the only management game in town, and we all absorbed that. But it's time to move on. I know I've said it before, but in a large corporation, you've got to identify your allies, you have to influence the influencers, and you have to manage your manager. If you manage to do all of that, then you can start the transformation, and you can lead it at any point in the organization.

Viktor Farcic: But then, there is the problem of time. When I speak with people, and then I start giving them stories, I often get the answer: "Yes, but I don't know what to do. I don't know where to start, and for 20 years I've been continuously working on a project that was supposed to be done yesterday."

Gregory Bledsoe: So, that's another point where you have to make the economic argument. This is the Agile principle of sustainable pace. A lot of people who are implementing Agile into their projects want to do a flexible scope but fixed date, which is actually the opposite of what you want to do. What you want are a fixed scope and flexible date. When you do a flexible scope and fixed date, you just keep pouring things on people, and those people become overburdened. Now, no one has the time to even think about how to make things better, much less actually work to make things better. This is another one of the Lean principles, where, again, you can make this as an economic argument. You have to sell it to your manager, and you have to help your manager sell it to *their* manager.

> "You have to sell it to your manager, and you have to help your manager sell it to their manager."
>
> —Gregory Bledsoe

What we have to do nowadays is carve out time for improvement. Again, this is purely economics. You can make the graph showing that your technical debt grows because you're only ever building things and never fixing them. Eventually, that'll make the system grind to a halt, where you can't touch anything without breaking everything. Over time, the system becomes more fragile. These are economic arguments that you can make because they're mathematical and certain; there's not even any doubt about this.

Viktor Farcic: So, to change the environment in which they work, people need to make the economic argument to their boss?

Gregory Bledsoe: Exactly. If you want to start changing the environment in which you're working, then you must carve out time for improvement. You have to educate yourself on the mathematics and the economics behind the changes that need to be made. This is something that you may have to do in your own time because, again, you're underwater with delivery demands.

Once you start doing that and once you begin making and eventually start winning the economic argument, which will happen if you make the argument consistently enough because it's a mathematical certainty, then that's when you can really start to roll out the change. Here's another fundamental thing about people: we copy what works. Even when we don't know why it works, we'll still try to copy it, and if over time, enough people get it right, we'll be able to articulate why it works. Only then does it start to really be adopted, and the uptake really picks up.

You only have to look at how Edward Deming's theory was rejected in the US because they thought they already knew what to do. Edward went to Japan, and suddenly Japan started kicking the US manufacturers' butts in the market. Only then did the Americans take notice and start trying to copy what Japan was doing, but it took them a really long time to adopt that. It wasn't until 30 years later that they worked it out because they didn't bother to try to understand why it worked fundamentally, they just tried to copy process examples. But the difference was far deeper than that.

What makes the difference between somebody who comes into work and cares about the outcome of their work versus somebody who comes in, punches the clock, does what they're told, and then leaves, not caring? Drucker and Deming pointed out that, if you can take a clock puncher and put him in another environment where he becomes invested in the outcome, his performance is totally different. The same person in two different cultures will produce vastly different results.

That's the secret the Japanese learned from Deming really early on, that when you take these ideas, and you root them in your cultural soil, it allows you to empower people to improve the process. You reward them for pointing out problems, instead of punishing them because we don't care about the perception of failure. We care about the reality of success.

Viktor Farcic: But in your view, what prevents us from understanding, instead of just blindly copying, things? Is it vanity or a lack of capacity?

Gregory Bledsoe: It's a mixture of pride, hubris, vanity, laziness, and greed. Nobody wants to say to themselves that the way they've run their career for the past 15 to 30 years has been wrong and that they've managed to succeed in a pathological system by adapting to it. But, in today's world, that's not going to work, so we fundamentally have to change the way we do this. It's an extremely difficult thing to come to grips with. People always want to make the economic determination that they want to do the easiest thing. But we're wired that way. We want to do the easiest thing to get the results we want, and if we don't take the time to really try to figure out what is the easiest thing to get the results we want, then we do the thing that looks the easiest to us.

> *"Collaboration only ever happens when the incentives are aligned. Misaligned incentives are an artifact of corporate culture and the incentive structure produced by the silos."*
>
> —*Gregory Bledsoe*

For example, as a company, we'll just install Jenkins. We'll start with tools that are trying to copy these process examples. But if that doesn't work, we'll get a pilot team, give them everything they need for success, and put all of this focus on them. We've put a lot of attention behind it. We clear out all of the obstacles and then, it's a smashing success and you build this pipeline of continuous delivery. But then, you try to replicate those results outside the pilot, and you can't because the pilot had all of the intention and all of the focus on clearing the obstacles, and all of the rest of the teams don't. When the pilot team no longer has that, all of the integrations they build in the pipeline break, and then it's like: whose job is it to fix them? Well, it's nobody's job because integration is a function of collaboration.

Collaboration only ever happens when the incentives are aligned. Misaligned incentives are an artifact of corporate culture and the incentive structure produced by the silos. In a nutshell, in order to reorganize your culture, you have to attack the incentive structure. But again, it's fundamentally different and not at all compatible with how we've always done things, and that's hard to come to grips with.

Fixing the digital transformation

Viktor Farcic: Part of what you're saying reminds me of the digital transformation. Every company has been doing the digital transformation potentially for years, and they've all made a new department but with the same people. They've brought in Jenkins, Kubernetes, and whatnot, but I'm yet to find any improvement to come from those digital transformations. Maybe I'm paranoid, and I'm exaggerating, but I just don't see any improvement.

Gregory Bledsoe: Firstly, you're not paranoid or exaggerating. In a Fortune 500 company, what you've described is normal. These companies have been trying to make these changes for years, but they're in exactly the same position that American manufacturing was in, where it's just not working, and they have no idea why, because they fundamentally don't understand it. Remember Deming? It was he who specifically was asked: "Well, if Japan can, why can't we (America)?" He responded by saying that Americans simply expect miracles. They want to copy the process examples and expect to get the same results, but the issue here is that these companies don't know what to copy.

> *"Corporate America is not giving people incentives to collaborate."*
>
> —*Gregory Bledsoe*

This is the story of the new digital transformation that's going on right now in most of corporate America. There's been no deep thinking or sharing of a vision across the organization to build consensus or incentives to collaborate. People are putting a lot of work into building this sophisticated automation framework, but they're not building a sophisticated collaboration framework that incorporates the sharing part of DevOps. Corporate America is not giving people incentives to collaborate.

But at the same time, the people that you want to give incentives to in order to collaborate don't necessarily understand the secret sauce either. You can make them sit in a feature refinement meeting, but you can't make them start thinking about what they actually need to do together until the work arrives on somebody's desk as a work item. That's what they're used to doing. We wait for it to be thrown over the wall to us, and then we start thinking about what we actually need to do with it. But the whole purpose of feature refinement, story refinement, and Agile is that we want to start unearthing as early as possible what we don't know that we need to know.

Viktor Farcic: So, how do we go about fixing this? Because, to me, it sounds like this would solve a lot of the issues we've been talking about.

Greg Bledsoe: We need to start using a shift-left mentality. I've sat in story feature refinement meetings where nobody asks any questions, and nobody has anything to say. The first meeting has just burned. It's useless because people are used to just waiting for work. For instance, the developer will open up the IDE, start a big `if` loop, and then start thinking about how he actually needs to do the work to accomplish this. But by this point, it's way too late.

You're still going to run into the same problems that you would in a Waterfall culture, where you don't understand that you didn't have everything you needed. But now, at the last second, everybody's going to be scrambling to try to make things work and make fundamental changes to the other components. The whole point is to develop as early as possible.

Changing that mindset from the top down is not an easy move, but it's the first thing you must do in order to understand how it has to change. We haven't even cleared this hurdle most of the time, but what does an empowered, collaborative culture mean? People are trying to do these digital transformations, but they don't even understand what it should look like from the ground level. You can't make changes on the ground that are all going in the same direction without a grand vision. But a grand vision without understanding how that also affects people on the ground is useless. It has to come from both directions, and this where your collaborative framework has to come into play.

Viktor Farcic: But then, we have a third influence, which I see as an external one. Let's say I brought in this tool that's supposed to make me DevOps certified. Or likewise I brought in this consultant, and we're doing daily stand-ups. I get the impression that you go to conferences a lot, where everybody's trying to sell the nirvana these days.

Gregory Bledsoe: Of course, there's truth in that. There's a big market in telling people what they want to hear. The easiest way to sell something is tell them that you have a magic bullet that's going to solve all of their problems, and they'll eat it up saying: "Oh, yay! We're going to buy into this!" But that doesn't work because the person who's buying it didn't know what questions they needed to ask, and the person who's selling it, at that point, has already made the sale. But by then they've already got their foot in the door, and the more it fails, the more they get to charge. This incentive structure is fundamentally misaligned.

The market for telling people what they want to hear is too big, and there are too many people willing to sell into that market. We've got to change this from both ends. As consultants, if we want to really change the way this works and, as a result, maximize our value to the client, then we have to sell in a fundamentally different way. We have to go into the account and give them the hard truths right up front and get them used to hearing that from us rather than thinking: we'll just tell them what they want to hear. We'll promise them we can do anything, and then once we're in the door, we'll start trying to have the hard conversations with them. That simply doesn't work because, now, you'll just get subsumed into their culture, and you can't change their culture. You'll just get into the *yes* culture because they don't want to hear anything at that point. All they want to hear is yes, and you can't change it.

You got off on the wrong foot, and that's really hard to change. As consultants, we have to approach these client relationships differently. We have to be willing to tell them the hard truths right up front, and get them used to the fact that that's what they're going to get from us. But the thing is, after the initial shock, people really appreciate that honesty, and they understand that, now, they're attacking the right problems.

In DevOps, we work with three things: people, process, and tools—in that order. There's a reason for this order, because people drive the process. Once you understand what your process should be, you then have to find the tools that fill the gaps in your process and help you to both eliminate waste and reduce the wait time and friction. But the real problem is that it's too easy to buy a tool and then try to build a process around it and even force people to use it.

> *"The market for telling people what they want to hear is too big, and there are too many people willing to sell into that market. We've got to change this from both ends."*
>
> —*Gregory Bledsoe*

Viktor Farcic: But that's the thing. In my view, almost every tool is a result of somebody's process and culture, Kubernetes being a prime example. It's about different organizations that end up in a platform. One thing I don't understand is how people assume that something made in a completely different culture will work in their culture.

Gregory Bledsoe: You've just hit the nail on the head. The simple answer is that it won't. The first thing you have to understand is: What's the idea in the context of your culture, in the context of your organization's values, and in the context of your organization's specific business context? What's the process that you need? What's the idea for you to deliver value with the least wait time? Only when you've answered those questions do you go looking for the tools you need. You've got to ask the fundamental existential questions first: Why do we exist? What is the reason people are going to give us money? How do we pay off on that value as efficiently as possible? If you don't start with those questions, you can't get to the right answers.

Agile versus DevOps – is there any difference?

Viktor Farcic: But then if you ignore the implementation on conceptual grounds, is there any real difference between Agile and DevOps?

Gregory Bledsoe: Yes, there is. Accenture has recently bought SolutionsIQ, a consulting organization that specializes in building business agility. SolutionsIQ is really good at developing those deep and trusted relationships, where they're telling people the hard truths and helping them to incrementally move toward a less pathological and more empirical structure and delivery chain.

SolutionsIQ views DevOps as a delivery method for your Agile infrastructure and process, which is not wrong. But I view DevOps as encompassing Agile and extending it because DevOps took a lot of stuff from Agile in the first place. For example, the cross-functional collaborative team: we've extended that. We collapsed additional silos because we wanted the development in the business to work really well together in Agile. Then, with DevOps, at first, we wanted the development and the operations guys to work really well together. But then we said: "Well, why should we stop there?" By this point, you're now realizing that you've also got to bring in the monitoring and security guys, and before long, you realize you've also got to bring in the testers, and then pretty much everybody else. You've just got to extend the width of that collaboration and get everybody shifting left to solve all the problems as early as possible because, if it doesn't work that well, trying to bolt security on at the end doesn't work either. You've got to change that and shift it all left. That's the DevOps mentality, which embraces an extended Agile.

Agile and DevOps are the peanut butter and jelly in a Lean sandwich. They really go well together, and you can't be super-successful with one without the other, though this allusion may not work everywhere. In Germany, you could say, for example, it's like bratwurst and sauerkraut. The point is, Agile and DevOps complement and extend each other really well.

Interestingly, another problem I've noticed is that people who buy into a prescriptive Agile framework really get married to the cadence, the pace, and the experience. But with DevOps, you'll get to a point where you don't have to wait on the sprint to be able to deliver; you're able to deliver everything as soon as it's ready. When it's ready for production, it goes to production, and then you want to shorten the time it takes to get something ready for production. In my view, as you mature with DevOps and Agile, the sprint cycle can dissolve into continuous delivery. But you'll hit a wall if you're married to that prescriptive framework, and this is why I don't like them. You can use them as a guideline, but they're not scripture, and they're not holy. There's nothing that they teach you. All of the elements of Scrum and Kanban were made to teach principles, not to be the end-all and be-all mechanism.

Viktor Farcic: But they might be made to teach principles. I've not seen that in practice. I mean, people often say, "Oh, I'll do Agile." Well no, because out of those principles, we're not practicing this one.

> *"In my view, as you mature with DevOps and Agile, the sprint cycle can dissolve into continuous delivery. But you'll hit a wall if you're married to that prescriptive framework, and this is why I don't like them."*
>
> —*Gregory Bledsoe*

Gregory Bledsoe: That's right, and it's why when you're trying to do something new, a prescriptive framework can be helpful for a period of time. But it's also important to know when its value has declined to the point where the amount of waste and overhead it introduces has now outweighed the benefits. The issue is that it's a calculation that is difficult and different for every organization.

A prescriptive framework could get you away from the Waterfall culture, and to completely remove yourself mentally from Waterfall can be good, but you have to go beyond just those basic prescriptive elements. You have to adapt it to your organization, just like DevOps. But as we've said before, there's no one true way of DevOps. You have to adapt it to your organization. And that's the other big problem with DevOps implementations. People want to be told exactly what to do all of the time. They want to be in a world where someone else has to do all the thinking for them, but the answer is no. You have to get everybody in your organization thinking about these, and that's how you're going to get the best possible answers.

Viktor Farcic: But isn't that a vicious circle? You have a minority of people trying to change a majority of people that are entrenched into that old way of working. Then, in the case of the minority managing to change something, they've started doing the same thing because now, nobody moves from this new position.

Gregory Bledsoe: It can become a vicious circle. There are very important anthropological and sociological reasons why beliefs and habits stick, and we have what you can call the sameness or the consistency bias. The idea is that we want today and tomorrow to be the same as yesterday because we already understand the threats and opportunities of yesterday, and to have to continually refactor our own cognitive mechanisms to deal with new threats and new opportunities is hard. We're entering the age of exponential change, where every day will look more different than the day before, and until we can develop that systematic way of empirically validating your change—when you do that, then it's much less scary.

Take the cycle of innovation, and the original amount of time it took for innovation to spread and be built upon was a millennium. But then, it went to centuries and then decades, years, and now it's just months. Before long it'll be weeks, and then days before finally, innovation will be instantaneous and without pause. Why? Because we're entering an age of exponential change. We have to understand why it's hard for us to adapt, to change, and we have to understand that change can't be unanchored from our superstructures because we have these kinds of cultural and ideological superstructures that give us things such as values and ethics.

In the 20th century, we learned that when you try to change everything all at once, and when you try to detach from all of those superstructures, the results you get may not be that good. You just have to look at how, in the 20th century, 200 million people were killed by their own governments, who tried to detach from all of the superstructures of society. So, the key for us is that we have to not only learn how to manage this change but also how to embrace it.

Viktor Farcic: Is that something we can even stop?

Greg Bledsoe: The thing is we can't stop it. It's going to happen. What we need to do is to anchor it to something, and that anchor has to be our values. But the issue with this is that we have to understand what that looks like, and, for a lot of people, that means going all the way back to an Enlightenment philosophy. It's the reason why these conference talks, books, and podcasts are akin to a dark intellectual web tied together into forming new superstructures. These new superstructures that are going to guide us into the age of unprecedented exponential change are anchored to modernity and Enlightenment values, and we're returning to that, and we see that it really works. I feel like we're now entering the post-post-modernist age, and that the counter-counter-revolution is, as a result, beginning. But the key here is that DevOps is the tip of the spear of all of that.

I know that's kind of grandiose, but when you really start to get why all of this works, you'll see it works for the same reason that Western liberal democracy works. Empowering the individual and tying the success of the society to the success and freedom of the individual, their empowerment, and their sense of ownership over their own life is super-powerful. The standard of living in the world today is ridiculous, compared to what it was just a hundred years ago, and we're not really even celebrating that because we're too busy worrying about all of the things that are still bad. But if we can embrace this change and this new kind of post-post-modernism, then we can even accelerate that good change. If that's the case, then who knows where it can go?

DevOps in 2019 – success or failure?

Viktor Farcic: But would you say that DevOps in 2019 is a success story? Can I go to a company, and say: "Look, a lot of people are on board, and they saw success, and as a result, they're doing great. It's only you who's missing the train." Or, have we just seen the start of the transformation, and we're yet to see real adoption?

Gregory Bledsoe: In most cases, the adoption is superficial. It's trying to slap a process example on top of a pathological culture because cultures are built accidentally. Almost no one intentionally builds the culture they want, with a goal in mind. It's an accretion of reactions to events. That's how cultures normally accrue. To consciously deconstruct and reconstruct that is hard, which is a big part of what a true transformation is. There's a tiny minority of people who are intentionally trying to do that. That's got to be the next way that will unlock the winners from the losers because the market advantage you get from doing that is tremendous. You'll outpace your competitors. You have to because you're applying the maximum amount of brain power to every problem. That's one of the real secrets.

It may be that your executives are the smartest people in the room, or maybe not, but the smartest person in the room is not smarter than all of the other people in the room put together. When nobody wants to speak up because he or she knows that the smartest person in the room doesn't want to hear something, then you're locking out all of this problem-solving power. This is why markets work better than central planning because the smartest central planner in the world can't be smarter than every other person navigating the market.

Their collective intelligence is an emergent property. In many ways, it's like an ant colony. An ant colony is an emergent property, from every individual just doing very simple things based on his own instinct and their designated duties. He's following pheromone trails, and he's carrying food. But the ant colony as a whole is extremely efficient and intelligent in a similar way to how markets are. What we need to do is have our organizations turn into that. Because organizations that can successfully transform into that have to be more successful, it's a mathematical certainty.

Viktor Farcic: Does that mean the future lies in moving from pyramidal structures towards something flatter?

Gregory Bledsoe: Yes, because I believe we're going to move away from hierarchy to meritocracy in our organizations. The concept of holacracy is out there, and I do think people are experimenting with it. I don't know if holacracy is exactly what we're going to end up with, but we're going to end up with some kind of empowered constitutional organization where everyone is empowered to be the boss of his or her job. I think this is the ultimate expression, and that any organization can move toward this. I don't know if it's going to be official holacracy, something similar, or something very different. But the thing is, any leader within an organization can voluntarily stop using coercion and start using inspiration.

That's true leadership instead of management, and when you start doing that, you automatically start flattening out the hierarchy, and you automatically start building more meritocracy. So, it's possible that, when we start selecting leaders differently for different qualities, then this could happen without something official like holacracy. But it is going to be the difference between the organizations that live and the organizations that die.

Viktor Farcic: Exactly. Speaking of the future, what do you think is waiting for us? I'm not going to ask you to project ten years into the future because, as we talked about earlier, we don't even know what's going to happen in two years.

Predicting the future of DevOps

Gregory Bledsoe: Who knows? There are a few short and longer-term things that I really do think we can predict. I think the DevSecOps term is going to go away. People are going to realize that DevSecOps is really about maturing DevOps, where you didn't forget that security was a thing, and where you're shifting that left and including them in the design discussion. People will be able to ask questions like: "Well, this looks like an opportunity for a SQL injection. Have you thought about that?"

A pet peeve of mine is that SQL injection still exists because that question isn't asked in development. Developers are not incentivized to worry about security, and they're too far underwater to think about that in addition to just getting the feature out the door. That has to change, and that will radically alter security. DevSecOps is a good maturing DevOps, where you're shifting left. I think that term is going to be subsumed into DevOps. Right now, it's a term because people are discovering that we have to include security, we have to include compliance, and we have to include an audit because it's the only way we can adapt at scale.

Viktor Farcic: But what about the term DevOps? Do you think that the word will still have the same meaning in the future?

Gregory Bledsoe: I think the term DevOps will become synonymous with IT because everyone will at least understand that this is the way you do it now, and if you don't do it this way, you're doing it wrong. I think this is going to become understood, and that's still going to leave a stratification of results. Some people are going to do it much better than others, and those who can unlearn and relearn the fastest will gain a sustained competitive advantage. They'll be out in front of the pack, and that reason is why it's imperative that people embrace and adopt this now. The longer you wait, the worse your odds. It doesn't matter how deep the moat around your business is.

> *"DevOps will become synonymous with IT because everyone will at least understand that this is the way you do it now, and if you don't do it this way, you're doing it wrong."*
>
> —*Gregory Bledsoe*

Look at the big banks. They've got huge regulatory moats around their businesses, but it's not saving them. They're still getting chipped away, and the banks that can adapt are the ones that are going to be able to fend off the FinTechs. Look at the transportation or the hotel industry across the board. They thought having bought all of these properties was their hedge against the market, but their real competitor now doesn't even own any property, it's Airbnb. The cost to enter markets is lower than it's ever been, and it's only going to get lower.

For communication, it doesn't matter if you own the right of way to run cables through neighborhoods and nobody else has that and you think that's your moat because 5G is coming. 5G will change the game, and those services that you offer over physical wires and physical fiber optics are going to mean less than ever, and the barrier to entry will be lower than ever. Everyone is going to be disrupted, and it's just a matter of whether you're going to disrupt yourself, or whether an external competitor's going to disrupt you. The people who figure that out and understand they have to adapt to this exponential change will survive, and everyone else will die. That's the long-term prediction.

Viktor Farcic: But after you get disrupted, is there still time to survive?

Gregory Bledsoe: Yes, there is that window but it's shortening, and we don't actually know how short a window it is, which is why everyone has to get started now. The ones who are going to really put themselves in a position to be future-proof are the ones who are asking those existential questions, the ones who are bothering to think deeply about this. They're the ones who are going to be positioned to succeed.

You can't just start by saying "OK, we can't survive without DevOps, so let's put Jenkins everywhere; but then let's create a silo to manage." You've just exacerbated your fundamental problem. The people who know that's not the way you do this and that it's really Deming's 14 points, the most important of which is to turn everyone into an agent of transformation, are the ones who are going to succeed and be able to best navigate the age of exponential change.

Viktor Farcic: Absolutely true and especially when you mention Jenkins. I continuously visit companies, and no developers can ever touch it.

Gregory Bledsoe: It has to be that if you build it, you run it.

Viktor Farcic: Exactly. But it's difficult because it's a revolution. If there is a power struggle, you can't tell me if I build the entire vanity factory that would mean that I was running it yesterday.

Gregory Bledsoe: It's true. The power struggle is not just organizational, but ideological. It's scientific management or Taylorism versus Lean, that's what it is. The ones who embrace Lean and succeed at changing the minds of everybody in the organization, that's the trick right there.

Viktor Farcic: But how much more time do we need, because it's been a while since software started and we still think that it's a factory.

Gregory Bledsoe: Let me put it to you like this. Back in 2014, somebody figured out that 75 years ago, the average lifespan of a company on the Fortune 500 list was 75 years. Fast-forward to 2014, and it was down to 10 years. These companies were being replaced by new and more agile companies that were still trying to expand their markets.

That's another secret that I think people don't really understand, that the moment you stop trying to expand your markets and start trying to protect them, you're optimizing for protecting markets over expanding markets, and you've already started to die. There are smaller, nimbler companies with much less overhead and infrastructure waiting to feast upon your corpse before you're even done dying.

You're putting your leg in the piranha pool, and the piranhas are hungry. It's not the big fish that eat the little fish; it's the fast fish that eat the slow fish. We're going to see that the turnover among the Fortune 100 and the Fortune 500 companies is going to be huge. I think the average lifespan is going to go down to 5 years, to 3 years, and then you're going to see a huge turnover on these lists. So, how much time do we have? Well, the rest of your life. How long do you have to pull the emergency chute if your primary chute fails? The rest of your life.

Viktor Farcic: Exactly. I'm going to use that one; I love it. I really think your definition of the thinking behind DevOps is brilliant.

Gregory Bledsoe: Thank you! You can probably tell that I could talk about this literally all day, every day. The fascinating thing is that there's really no end to the discussion.

Viktor Farcic: Thank you again.

Gregory Bledsoe: Thank you.

18

Wian Vos

Solutions Architect
at Red Hat

Introducing Wian Vos

Wian Vos is an experienced DevOps/cloud consultant with a demonstrated history of working in the information technology and services industry. He is skilled in PaaS, Agile methodologies, DevOps, and cloud technologies. You can follow him on Twitter at @wianvos.

Viktor Farcic: Hi, Wian! Before we delve into our conversation about DevOps, could you tell us a little about yourself?

Wian Vos: I'm currently a solutions architect at Red Hat, one of the biggest open source companies in the world, based in Amsterdam. I've been doing DevOps since before it was called DevOps, and have been involved in infrastructure automation since 2005, and the containerization push since 2013. Over the course of my career, I've worked at ING Bank, Rabobank, and several other smaller government bureaus here in the Netherlands. More recently, I was a managing consultant for DevOps at CINQ ICT in Zaandam, and before that, I worked in Boston for two years at XebiaLabs.

Defining DevOps

Viktor Farcic: I want to start with the same question I've asked everyone else in this book: what is DevOps? Everybody has given me a different answer. Personally, I don't know why everyone defines it differently, but hopefully this will be something we touch upon in our discussion.

> *"DevOps has meant different things at different points in time."*
>
> —*Wian Vos*

Wian Vos: Actually, that's pretty much what I expected. I think DevOps has meant different things at different points in time. When the term was first coined, it was basically a push for a new way of working from the DevOps manifesto, which I thought, back in the day, made sense. But then DevOps got popular, and as with all things that get popular, the big vendors jumped on the bandwagon—my current employer, Red Hat, included—and turned it into a marketing term.

But what is DevOps to me? DevOps is a paradigm of how to run your IT business culture. If you look at the term in the purest sense of the word, it's a way to put development and operations in a same-team situation, all working toward the same business goal. I've been involved with DevOps for nine years now, and I've never been in one of those mythical teams, nor have I ever seen one of those mythical teams actually work. But what I have done is become associated with DevOps-like practices and DevOps tools. Through my experience, I've found that DevOps is basically all about culture and a way of working.

Viktor Farcic: So, if you've never seen DevOps working, and I must admit that I've seen it work rarely, if ever, is it because companies fail at it? Or is it because those companies have never actually even tried to incorporate DevOps in the way it should be incorporated?

Wian Vos: If you want to implement DevOps in a company, you face a couple of obstacles. To start with, there are the actual relationships between development and operations. Those aren't a big deal when you're dealing with a new start-up or companies that are implementing brand-new applications. Why? Because you can get a team together, and they can all do their thing.

But if you look at how traditional companies are basically organized, there's always been this traditional split between development and operations, and it's basically because each has a different vantage point. On the one hand, you have development striving for stability, while on the other, you have operations backed by the business striving for change. Getting those two together in a traditional company, and not in a start-up setting, is going to be hard.

Viktor Farcic: If that's the case, what are the biggest issues you think companies face when they want to enable DevOps in their organizations?

Wian Vos: I've always considered DevOps companies as ones that are invested in technology from the bottom up. It's not so much about creating one team, but more about teams listening to each other, and technology changes being decided from the bottom up, instead of handed down from the top.

You asked about the biggest problems companies face today. One of the biggest challenges I've seen with implementing actual DevOps is the moving headcount. Why? Because these teams—development and operations—have already battled each other for years, and now you have managers trying to put these people in one team. The old manager is then replaced by a new manager who has a different approach.

> *"I've always considered DevOps companies as ones that are invested in technology from the bottom up. It's not so much about creating one team, but more about teams listening to each other."*
>
> —*Wian Vos*

What are managers basically for, if not for people who have a headcount? Say I'm a manager who has 20 people and is going to let 10 people go. What am I now? Well, I'm half the manager I used to be. I know it sounds harsh and borderline disrespectful to the managers out there. From a DevOps perspective, I have encountered good managers. But it takes a very open, very peculiar company culture to actually make it work.

I think DevOps is a great catalyst for the enormous open source technological push that we've seen in the past 10 years. But in practice, it's horrible. Well, it's not horrible, it's just undoable.

What it means to be truly Agile... and the importance of Kubernetes

Viktor Farcic: Let me ask a follow-up question then. How many companies have you seen that are actually truly Agile?

Wian Vos: I've seen a lot of development teams that are truly Agile. I worked for Xebia for a long enough time to actually know what Agile is, where it was implemented, and what to look for.

But being truly Agile takes perseverance, which is pretty hard to find these days in the corporate world. It's not just doing two weeks in front of a board with a lot of sticky notes. It's much more than that; it's a mindset. It's not going into that hole of saying, "I want this feature now because I have money." It's more like saying, "Alright, let's plan this, put this on the backlog, and classify it."

I haven't seen many, if any, truly Agile companies, but I have seen companies trying to be Agile, and before that, companies trying to be good with Lean—which, in a certain sense, is good, because those companies try to incorporate Agile, and they try to incorporate Lean, which at the end of the day brings something positive to their company culture. But it doesn't necessarily make them Agile, Lean, or DevOps. If you're running an operations shop with ongoing business, Agile is the hardest thing to do.

Viktor Farcic: So, companies then don't change from a cultural perspective when they're above a certain size?

Wian Vos: That's not what I'm saying. What I'm trying to say is that the technology involved in DevOps is not the problem. The problem is the people, and when it comes to people, they're very hard to change, especially in a corporate culture. But, keep in mind, I have never worked at a start-up, ever. So, I don't have that start-up experience.

Viktor Farcic: I guess start-ups are a different ballgame because they're small and can, in theory, do whatever they want. They've haven't got any baggage to get rid of.

But that's the problem I have when I'm visiting companies and trying to explain to them the big picture of technologies. Let's take a microservice, for instance. They're the result, like any other technology or process, of a certain culture in a certain environment, and it ends up being a tool.

Wian Vos: Or a process, or a buzzword.

Viktor Farcic: But then if you don't actually take it all the way or if you just simply adopt the tool, then you're in a very bad place, just like the case with microservices. Can you have microservices without self-sufficient teams? Can you have self-sufficient teams without changing the culture?

At least in my experience, it fails miserably. But going back to tools, we've both worked for software vendors, and in my experience, I have the impression that absolutely every single software vendor in the world has now rebranded its tools as being DevOps. At conferences today, it's all DevOps. For me, all the tools that I've used for the last 10 years are DevOps.

Wian Vos: I don't want to say that's a problem per se, because, usually, the tools that get bought are like the DevOps magical bullets that don't exist. But labeling these tools with the term DevOps does help adoption by higher levels of management. If something is labeled DevOps, then you as an engineer or as a developer have a greater chance of working with it.

> " ...usually, the tools that get bought are like the DevOps magical bullets that don't exist."
>
> —Wian Vos

If you were to ask me the question, "Is it a bad thing that they basically took DevOps from us and ran with it?," my answer would be that I don't know. I certainly am opposed to the idea that if you just have enough cool, new, and open source tools, then you can call your company a DevOps company. That's something I'm really sick and tired of. I don't know if it's a bad thing or a good thing because it has brought us a lot of cool stuff to play with.

Viktor Farcic: Moving on, let's talk about Kubernetes. Is Kubernetes now the one to rule them all?

Wian Vos: For the next two years, it probably is. In the 10-year period before I became a Puppet engineer where I was doing all kinds of stuff at Puppet and XebiaLabs, and building Platform as a Service stuff, it was easy to call. Back in 2001, it was easy to say we're going to do WebSphere ND for the next three to four years, and probably a long time after that.

So, in the first decade of this century, it was easy to predict what you were going to do for the next five years, and where to invest, and where to specialize. But since 2009, and even 2010, I have no clue. First, it was Platform as a Service with provisioning. Then it was containerization, or even—and I don't know if you remember this—immutable infrastructure with Foundry, Heroku, and all that cool stuff.

Then came Docker, and that was like, *argh*! But let's not forget that the technology was there since the end of the 1990s. Docker just made it usable, and at the time, Docker was the coolest company around: everybody had heard of it, and everybody wanted to work with it. But all of a sudden, Kubernetes burst onto the scene, which is kind of funny because they're basically just as old as Docker, and now Kubernetes is anything and everything. And everybody is standardizing on it. And everybody does it. And everybody has to do it. And everybody wants to work with it. I think it's the most convincing technology I've seen in the last 10 years, just because we need to make sense of this public cloud, and Kubernetes fits into that brilliantly. We might get sick and tired of it in, like, three or four years, because it's a beast of its own. It's complex, and at times difficult. It's controlled by Google and us.

Viktor Farcic: What I find interesting about Kubernetes is that I don't recall the last time in my career that I actually saw a software, platform, application—or whatever you want to call it—adopted by absolutely every single software vendor in the world. Even traditional software vendors that tend to wait until everyone else adopts a new technology is behind Kubernetes, which I never would have guessed.

Wian Vos: In the 1970s, mainframes were pretty hot. But, in all honesty, the last time I think that happened was with Java application servers. So, I have to agree with you that it's a pretty big movement toward Kubernetes. Then again, most people don't really realize what Kubernetes actually is, because for the most part, if you hear people talk about Kubernetes, they're talking about container workload scheduling, which kind of covers the load.

But if you look at its real benefits and why it's winning, it's because it brings you a universal interface to any cloud out there. By implementing a Kubernetes cluster, you make deploying workloads almost transparent on AWS, Google Cloud Platform, Microsoft Azure, Electric Cloud, or any of those cloud port platforms, as long as you don't go for their offered on-prem container as a solution.

Looking at the cloud

Viktor Farcic: But then isn't that a threat to those same cloud vendors? If it's so transparent, then I can easily switch from one to another.

Wian Vos: I think that's a good situation for us as consumers. But it does make these vendors compete more for our business. For at least the last five to six years, if you talk to anybody who's somebody in IT, it's all about the cloud. In that time period, we had an unprecedented economic boom. So, I'm wondering what's going to happen once the economy start failing again: Will people have to cut costs again, and if so, then what happens? Are we going back to hardware?

Viktor Farcic: But is cloud computing more expensive than on-prem?

Wian Vos: Yes.

Viktor Farcic: I have a theory, and I might be wrong, that when you calculate the price per CPU, and if we include the tens of hundreds of people managing that infrastructure on-prem, I actually think it's not that much more expensive when you include the human factor.

Wian Vos: As long as your cloud infrastructure is small enough, you might be right. But if you look at cloud implementations on a large scale, if you're talking thousands and thousands of nodes spread across multiple clouds, they still need a lot of certified, and very expensive, people to run it. I can tell you that an AWS/Google Cloud certified person is a lot more expensive than somebody who has just shuffled around Cisco switches their entire life.

Viktor Farcic: That's very true.

Wian Vos: So, you could probably get two of them for the price of one cloud specialist.

Viktor Farcic: I once spoke with a person whose company was on-prem, and then they went to the cloud. Eventually, this company went back on-prem with the justification of "Oh, we learned finally, when we were in the cloud, how things should be, so we finally know what we need to do ourselves [on-prem]."

Wian Vos: I think that is a correct statement. Because, basically—and I'm only very experienced on AWS—if you look at how AWS works, it basically gives you all the same components as your own datacenter. What differs is that it also gives you, as an engineer or as a developer, the controls, which means you don't have to go into endless discussion with the network guys about this and that—this firewall setting, or that firewall setting—or put in a change request and go back and forth. No, you could just sit there, do it, change it—okay, done.

You still need to know what you're doing. It's not that Amazon has a magical network device that just spits out connections. It just doesn't work like that. So, from that perspective, I think it's good to take your infrastructure to AWS because it clarifies a lot of stuff you've been doing wrong. Do I think it's sustainable for everything? Probably not.

Viktor Farcic: But it's set certain expectations from your customer. If you are an infrastructure team and everybody else uses Azure, AWS, Google Cloud Platform, or whatever, and you're on-prem, then you need to kind of up your game, no?

Wian Vos: Yeah, and that's something we're going to see in the next three or four years. Companies are going to try to figure out, finally, how to do this hybrid thing of having the 60% production capacity that you always need, on-prem. You'll take your flexible capacity, which gives you the flexibility and the capability to take stuff to market quickly. I really think that that's the sweet spot we need.

Viktor Farcic: In hindsight, you might not be able to answer this question because you work for a company, but one thing I see a lot of today is confusion. Say we work for a company, and we finally made a decision to choose Kubernetes. We then have the problem of choosing one of the 57 different popular flavors and 500 less popular ones, which leaves us with the question of "Now what are we going to do?"

Wian Vos: I can only give you one piece of advice: choose ours—just kidding. That being said, I think Kubernetes is moving too quickly to choose DIY for production in an enterprise. I'm not saying that if you run a start-up you shouldn't choose DIY Kubernetes, because the feature push from Kubernetes is just awesome, and, truth be told, if I had had my way at my last gig, I would have done it DIY. But that's just hubris.

In reality, it's pretty arrogant for an enterprise to think that they can do their own DIY Kubernetes. The whole thing is a big project, and it's moving like nothing we've ever seen before.

> *"I think Kubernetes is moving too quickly to choose DIY for production in an enterprise."*
>
> —Wian Vos

Basically, Kubernetes almost has more commits than actual Linux Kernel in open source. As a result, I would definitely go for either a distribution, because a distribution solves a lot of the insecurities for you, or maybe a hosted service, where you get actual Kubernetes—not just a reserved namespace in somebody else's pool, but an actual Kubernetes service.

Viktor Farcic: You've mentioned the number of commits and things like that. To me, that's confusing, but it also presents the idea that Kubernetes needs to slow down for people to actually even grasp it. Because, right now, even choosing the Ingress network is a week's worth of work.

Wian Vos: It's funny that you'd mention that. I had a whole discussion around Kubernetes Ingress just this morning! But yes, I seriously agree. Just choosing your network plugins, edge routers, and stuff like that can easily result in you shooting yourself in the foot with some of the choices you've made.

Viktor Farcic: I think that's why whenever somebody tells me that I'm going to roll Kubernetes on my own, my question is simply, "Why?"

Wian Vos: Exactly! Why would you do that?

Viktor Farcic: You're not going to spend the same amount of time that somebody else has spent putting it all together, even when you speak with the people who've spent their whole lives with Kubernetes, such as Kelsey, for example, or Mike Powers. It's kind of like, "I don't know what to choose because, just this morning, a new thing came along."

Wian Vos: That's exactly what this is. It's a big beast. In fact, it's not unlike Linux was in the early 2000s. If you were to look at the number of actually viable distributions of Linux that there were around then, it was bizarre. There were so many different flavors, and things you could do, and that all boiled down to the big two or three things that are now Linux distributions. So, I think that Kubernetes is going to go the same way as Linux.

I think the current ecosystem is good, because it brings competition, and that brings change. But I think that Kubernetes is here to stay, simply because our data centers are getting more complex. I know I'm contradicting something I said earlier, but it's like the kernel for the data center, and it'll probably be around in the next decade or two. But there will be less of an ecosystem, with fewer choices.

The problem with enterprises

Spotify isn't doing its own DIY Kubernetes, and that's what got me thinking. Because, engineering-wise, Spotify is one of the most brilliant companies out there. If you see what they're doing and the stuff they're putting out there, and the slight number of outages they have, they must be doing something right. If companies like that are saying, "No, we are not going to do our DIY Kubernetes," then that should be a sign for everybody else to say, "Alright, if the smartest kid in the class is not going to do it, should I be doing this?"

Viktor Farcic: But isn't that one of the big problems with enterprises in general? The idea that somehow every enterprise thinks they're smarter than all the smart kids, that somehow they're different. It's something I hear all the time: "We're going to roll out on our own, the same ways we rolled out our own cloud 10 years ago and failed, the difference being that this time, it's going to be different!"

Wian Vos: Agreed. In my current role, I advise a lot of businesses on how to do DevOps and containerization. And yes, especially at the lower tech levels, there are a lot of people that did the provisioning thing, brought us all this change, and got the company in a different gear.

They're all thinking that this Kubernetes thing is going to be just like implementing Puppet or Jenkins. But you have to look at Kubernetes as if it's a different beast, or else it's going to jump up and bite you. I'm not trying to scare you and say that you shouldn't be trying it. Because, at the end of the day, it's fun to do, and it's a great experience. It builds a lot of understanding of how Kubernetes works, and, hopefully, in the end, you'll come to a conclusion that if you're smart, you're not going to want to do it yourself.

Viktor Farcic: Okay, so let's say that we've come to the conclusion that we're not going to do it ourselves. We're going to choose one of the existing platforms—then what? Do we put our old database in our Docker image and ship it in Kubernetes?

> *"The biggest problem in DevOps is always persistent data."*
>
> —*Wian Vos*

Wian Vos: Oh, man! That's just a nasty question. I figure you know that, firstly, the biggest problem in DevOps is always persistent data, which is stuff in a database, while the second thing is that traditional databases are not designed to play nice. A typical database in a large enterprise organization is just expensive, let alone the fact that it's a nightmare to manage. So, I would say that you should start by getting those out of your company.

Viktor Farcic: Okay, we agree on that one. But for me, what is motivating is that I have the impression that companies are completely unaware of how much work outside of Kubernetes they need to do in order for something to be successful there, even with their own applications.

Wian Vos: It's not just implementation, and it's not just building a Kubernetes cluster. It's day-two and day-three operations that are going to get you.

Viktor Farcic: That's very true.

Wian Vos: Again, it's not a given that you have to take everything you do to a Kubernetes platform. It's perfectly okay to run your databases outside of Kubernetes. Ask yourself this: do you really need that much agility on your database cluster? You might, but not everybody does. Then again, do you need Kubernetes? I don't know.

Viktor Farcic: But to me, that's a curious question, because I have to ask myself, in a few years' time, is Kubernetes even going to be a choice? Yes, we do have a choice not to be in Kubernetes. But if every other vendor is shipping new releases on Kubernetes, is it really even a choice?

Wian Vos: I think it should be, because if it's not a choice anymore, then innovation is dead, and if that was the case, we would have to come up with a whole new ecosystem for the operating system, which is never going to happen again. But there are interesting movements in the whole Kubernetes scene and in everything that's going on around it. For instance, we have received massive amounts of questions about running Kubernetes on bare metal, and I think that's going to be the next big thing for the next three months or so. Because why would you do virtualization on Kubernetes? I don't know—tell me, why do you want to run a kubelet on a virtual machine (VM) when you can just run it on basic bare metal?

Viktor Farcic: There is no good reason. But on the other hand, other people use VMs because they still don't know what they're doing.

Wian Vos: Yeah, that's very true.

Viktor Farcic: I see it more as an evolution, and once you really know what you're doing, then you'll get rid of the hypervisor as well—but not before.

Wian Vos: Maybe. I think one of the biggest problems is that we have a whole generation of IT people coming in that have never worked on anything else in a VM.

**The big
DevOps killer**

But if you look at Kubernetes and what you're doing with it, it really doesn't make any sense to have a hypervisor on that. Because to the Java Virtual Machine (JVM), which is basically a virtualization layer between an operating system and the application, you're running it in a container. The argument can be made that it's like a virtual separation. It's not virtualization, but you know what I mean. Then, to have another layer of virtualization under that results in you taking your stuff pretty far from that CPU and memory.

Viktor Farcic: That may be true, but then how about serverless? Is that the next thing?

Wian Vos: I think serverless is the big DevOps killer.

Viktor Farcic: In what sense?

Wian Vos: I think it's basically the same as we had at the end of the 1990s, and before that in the 1970s. You as a developer do not want to be bothered with stuff that operations are doing, and because of that, we've have had six to seven years where we all supposedly worked together. But now there's this new thing, which is actually an old thing, where you can just drop in your code, set a route, and there we go! Basically, it's abstracting away the work that operations are doing because there's still somebody who has to take care of that serverless system.

Viktor Farcic: There are servers then, after all.

Wian Vos: Yes, that's true. But remember, somebody needs to install and maintain it, because, of course, a serverless system will never go wrong—just like anything else will never go wrong within IT, right? I think it's the paradigm that ends DevOps.

And that's why I think serverless is the big DevOps killer.

Viktor Farcic: I'm talking now on a level of principles, not a specific implementation: what I'm confused about is how serverless is truly different from Kubernetes.

Wian Vos: It's not truly different; that's the thing. I do want to make the distinction between the serverless paradigm and actual serverless platforms. Kubernetes is just a big serverless enabler, and the serverless paradigm just says, "Alright, I'm a developer, I have the code, I drop it here, and I'm done." I think actual serverless platforms have been around since the time of Platform-as-a-Service stuff. If you had a well-implemented Platform-as-a-Service, that was a no-brainer for an application developer anyway.

I think there's one big paradigm that's come out from the shadow of DevOps that actually does work: Site Reliability Engineering (SRE). Having a great SRE team that gives you a platform that you as a developer can just use is awesome. But is that serverless? I don't know. In the SRE model, you still need an SRE engineer that comes to help you to integrate your code into the platform. Now, if you abstract away enough functionality from the developer, the developer doesn't need that engineer anymore. So, hey presto, a serverless platform—you don't need to worry about the server anymore. But don't forget that there are still servers there, and behind them is an SRE team that actually manages that stuff and innovates on it.

So, to you as a developer, that becomes serverless. What comes with that, though, is again the loss of interaction between developers and engineers, which is something I think will hinder innovation all over again, because nobody ever got better from not talking to one another.

Viktor Farcic: Exactly. I was confused when you said initially the death of DevOps. But yeah, now I agree.

Wian Vos: If nothing else, DevOps is communication between the application developers and the engineers who build the platform. I once wrote a blog post saying that, and got some really bad feedback on it. So, let me be clear. I'm not saying it's just that communication, but I do think it is a very important component.

The role of a DevOps engineer

Viktor Farcic: But if an important component of DevOps is communication between people skilled in development and people skilled in operations, then what the heck is the role of a DevOps engineer? When I look at job descriptions, I think that of the DevOps engineer tops any other profile at the moment.

Wian Vos: Basically, that's just to confuse recruitment.

Viktor Farcic: And the DevOps department as well!

Wian Vos: Imagine, for instance, you and I were going to start a company. We're going to need a DevOps team because we have a burning desire to put out this awesome application. Yet, in our position, we can hire five people. So, the question we have when we're putting together a DevOps team is both, "Who are we hiring?" and "What are we hiring for?"

Are we going to hire DevOps engineers? No. In that team, we want the best application developers, the best tester, and maybe a great infrastructure person and a frontend/backend developer. I want that DevOps team to be people with specific roles who fit together as a team.

Back when DevOps became a marketing term for software companies, recruitment also jumped on that bandwagon. Red Hat is building a DevOps team, so we now need a DevOps engineer, and recruitment says they're going to get you a DevOps engineer. But like you said, for a lot of people in the market, it's still a very attractive job proposition because it includes the word DevOps. In that person's mind, they're no longer doing engineering; they're now doing DevOps.

Viktor Farcic: I have to give credit to Agile in that sense. You never see an Agile engineer.

Wian Vos: No, but they do have Agile coaches, which is another way to say a manager who doesn't wear a tie. Though, to be fair, an Agile coach does have a different perspective on things. Namely, it's more coaching, and more enabling, instead of pushing and holding others accountable. If you look at Agile and project management, Agile is the carrot, and project management is the stick. They're different approaches, and I can tell you, the carrot always works better.

Viktor Farcic: So, your job is to visit companies and show them the light at the end of the tunnel, with the goal being to help them to improve. I'm wondering, what do you hate the most when you visit a company? What are the major obstacles to accomplishing whatever you're trying to accomplish?

Wian Vos: I think it's almost always people. The biggest problems I've ever had, and the stuff that has cost me the most time and energy, with implementing DevOps, Platform-as-a-Service stuff, new modern infrastructure, or new modern application enablers, is the fact that in many companies there's still this whole consortium of old architects. People who actually work with new technology and platforms and get the opportunity to run their applications on a new Platform as a Service, or serverless platform (or whatever you want to call it) come around quickly enough if they see benefits. While there are good architects out there, architects in a corporate setting are a different story, especially in government. In government, if you have a plan and it's a good plan, it's only a good plan if it was invented there.

For example, at one government bureau, we basically just built the new platform without architectural approval, and then tried to get that architectural approval four months into the project. Luckily, our sponsor was high enough up on the board of directors at this government company that they were able to push it through. If they hadn't, the whole platform would have been canceled by architecture—by architects just saying, "Yeah, but there's this little detail that we don't like," and stuff like that. It's very much like, "Alright, we didn't think of this, so this must be bad."

There was another government institution where I did the same thing. We had the CTO tell us, "Alright, I just want this built. I don't care how you do it. But do it to the best of your ability and inform the architects afterward, and just send them to me once you're done." It was very possible that we would implement a new feature and three months later an architect would just roll by and say, "You didn't tell me that this was implemented." Yeah, alright, but we implemented that feature three months ago and those platforms we built were pretty successful. I mean, if a developer came up to us saying, "Hey, could you change this or that?," we could do it in one or two releases that were, like, three weeks later. But if you have to go through that whole old-school enterprise architectural process, then you're lost; you're gone.

Viktor Farcic: Yeah. I have the same problem with planning.

Wian Vos: Though I have been called an architect on several occasions, by the way. For me, what separates a good architect from just any architect is the fact that you should never architect anything you can't build at least 80% of yourself.

Viktor Farcic: How many of these architects are actually implementing things? I mean, most architects I meet, their tools are Microsoft Office—they're writing Word documents—while a successful architect is the one who can write more than 200 pages.

Wian Vos: Last year, I was at CLOUDBUSTING, a mini-conference put together by Software Circus, which is this meet-up group we have here in the Netherlands. At the conference,

I heard a talk by a guy who had a great couple of examples of how architectural mishaps come to life when you let traditional IT architects into your company, because you can write a great architecture document, hand it to people that actually build things, and find that it's not going to work. Especially in today's software world, it's very arrogant to think that you can foresee everything upfront. Especially if you have never built it yourself—you don't know what works.

> *"My favorite architectural style is evolutionary architecture. We need provisioning, so let's take three tools, test them out for a week, and really give them a shakedown to see what works."*
>
> *—Wian Vos*

My favorite architectural style is evolutionary architecture. We need provisioning, so let's take three tools, test them out for a week, and really give them a shakedown to see what works. At the end of the week, you can be like, "Alright, this one works, but the other two don't. Therefore, we go and innovate on this. But how are we going to implement it? Let's try three or four different ways and just roll with it, and then choose the best one and innovate on that."

So, I really think that it's very important to have your architectural process not get in the way, and for you to have your architects in your team. If you're running an SRE team that's building a platform for a customer, make sure that the one with the architectural skills—but more so the architectural responsibility—is in that team and building it with you. Just like a lead engineer, who is authorized to make decisions with the rest of the team.

Viktor Farcic: Exactly. The only thing I would add is that they've also got to feel. I believe that nobody should be allowed to make any decision if he or she cannot feel the pain behind those decisions. Typically, architecture is just, "Here it is: a diagram to help you to implement it."

Wian Vos: True, but then again, that was initially what DevOps was all about. You take a part of your business responsibility, you give it to a team, and you build it and run it. So, if an application developer comes up with screwed-up code that doesn't behave, then it's not the operations person that gets called out of their bed at two o'clock in the morning, it's the actual applications person, and because of that, they're more motivated to build something that works.

Viktor Farcic: Brilliant. I don't want to take much more of your time, but do you have any closing comments?

Wian Vos: All I will say is this: there's no right or wrong answer in this whole DevOps discussion. It's more about the fact that I think DevOps has become more of a cultural boost, and I think it's very important to enable people who are actually using and building the platforms to choose the things that they know are right for the company. But also, they need to be allowed to share their knowledge within the company.

Celebrating your failures

I know it's mushy, but actually, one of the key points to know is to also celebrate your failures. If you fail to communicate that you failed and explore why and how you failed, you're missing out on a learning opportunity. As soon as you start celebrating your failures, people will feel less scared to fail. I also think that the most innovative engineer is an engineer who feels free to innovate.

Viktor Farcic: We just need to convince management not to fire people when they fail.

Wian Vos: Right! That's one of the most important mind-shifts that you, as a manager, need to make in DevOps.

Viktor Farcic: But isn't that kind of embracing the inevitable? Saying that you know that you're going to fail?

Wian Vos: True, but if you don't embrace failure, your team is going to cover it up for you, and they're not going to learn anything. Or if the person that failed might learn something, the rest won't learn anything. I think that's something that GitLab did maybe a year ago—admin 55—that whole thing.

Viktor Farcic: Exactly! I can't express how much respect I have for them after that. GitLab are my heroes, only because of how they handled the failure.

Wian Vos: They said, "Hey, we've royally screwed up. Here's how to have at it."

Viktor Farcic: Yeah, I remember. I was watching their video feed while they were fixing it as if it was a Latin American tele-novela. It was awesome.

Wian Vos: That was awesome, and I think that should be something most companies are willing to do. But right now, we're a long way away from that.

Viktor Farcic: Very long. At least when I visit companies, I don't feel that I am allowed to behave like that yet.

Wian Vos: Well, I must say, in Holland, it's getting better. As I've already said, I also worked in the US for two years, where it's a whole different ball game.

Viktor Farcic: I think this is a great place to stop. Thank you for your time. I really enjoyed this.

Wian Vos: No problem. Thank you very much.

Index

S

T

V

W

Pack⟨t⟩

www.ingramcontent.com/pod-product-compliance
Lightning Source LLC
Chambersburg PA
CBHW071230050326
40690CB00011B/2062